THE POLITICAL ECONOMY OF ASIAN TRANSITION FROM COMMUNISM

Transition and Development

Series Editor: Professor Ken Morita
Faculty of Economics, Hiroshima University, Japan

The Transition and Development series aims to provide high quality research books that examine transitional and developing societies in a broad sense – including countries that have made a decisive break with central planning as well as those in which governments are introducing elements of a market approach to promote development. Books examining countries moving in the opposite direction will also be included. Titles in the series will encompass a range of social science disciplines. As a whole the series will add up to a truly global academic endeavour to grapple with the questions transitional and developing economies pose.

Also in the series:

Economic Reforms and Capital Markets in Europe
Ken Morita
ISBN 0 7546 0884 0

Enhanced Transition Through Outward Internationalization
Outward FDI by Slovenian Firms
Andreja Jaklič and Marjan Svetličič
ISBN 0 7546 3134 6

Modeling Russia's Economy in Transition
Peter Wehrheim
ISBN 0 7546 3299 7

Foreign Direct Investment in Central and Eastern Europe
Edited by Svetla Trifonova Marinova and Marin Alexandrov Marinov
ISBN 0 7546 3026 9

Facilitating Transition by Internationalization
Outward Direct Investment from Central European Economies
Edited by Marjan Svetličič and Matija Rojec
ISBN 0 7546 3133 8

Emerging Market Economies
Globalization and Development
Edited by Grzegorz W. Kolodko
ISBN 0 7546 3706 9

The Political Economy of Asian Transition from Communism

SUJIAN GUO
San Francisco State University,
USA

Routledge
Taylor & Francis Group

LONDON AND NEW YORK

First published 2006 by Ashgate Publishing

Reissued 2018 by Routledge
2 Park Square, Milton Park, Abingdon, Oxon OX14 4RN
711 Third Avenue, New York, NY 10017, USA

Routledge is an imprint of the Taylor & Francis Group, an informa business

First issued in paperback 2018

A Library of Congress record exists under LC control number: 2006002756

Notice:
Product or corporate names may be trademarks or registered trademarks, and are used only for identification and explanation without intent to infringe.

Publisher's Note
The publisher has gone to great lengths to ensure the quality of this reprint but points out that some imperfections in the original copies may be apparent.

Disclaimer
The publisher has made every effort to trace copyright holders and welcomes correspondence from those they have been unable to contact.

ISBN 13: 978-0-815-39806-6 (hbk)
ISBN 13: 978-1-138-62114-5 (pbk)
ISBN 13: 978-1-351-14580-0 (ebk)

Contents

List of Figures

List of Tables

Acknowledgements

The author gratefully acknowledges the following publishers for permission to use or adapt the materials from my articles previously published: "Designing Market Socialism: Trustees of State Property," *Journal of Policy Reform*, vol. 8, no. 3, September 2005, pp. 207-228 and "Economic Transition in China and Vietnam: A Comparative Perspective," *Asian Profile*, vol. 32, no. 5, October 2004, pp. 393-410.

I also want to thank Andrew Josias and Gary Stradiotto for their research assistance. I also owe a large debt of gratitude to my wife, Yuan Yuan, and my son, Samuel Y. Guo, for their patience and support in writing this book. But, ultimate thanks and glories go to God.

Chapter 1

Introduction:
Patterns and Explanations

Asian communist countries demonstrated a different pattern of transition that was characterized by gradual, experimental, phased and partial reform as compared to the former communist countries in Russia and Eastern Europe that were illustrative of a "neoclassical" big bang or radical approach. The debate between shock-therapists and gradualists has dominated professional discussions on transitions from communism throughout the 1990s. On one hand, the proponents of the big bang approach argue for a quick and simultaneous introduction of all reforms. Works by authors in this category include David Lipton and Jeffrey Sachs, Anders Aslund, Andrew Berg and Jeffrey Sachs, Kevin Murphy et al., Jeffrey Sachs, Roman Frydman and Andrzej Rapaczynski, Wing Thye Woo, Jeffrey Sachs and Wing Thye Woo.[1] On the other hand, those who favor a more gradualist approach emphasize the sequencing of multi-stage reforms and the virtues of gradualism. Works by authors in that category include Richard Portes, Ronald McKinnon, Gerard Roland, Mathias Dewatripont and Gerard Roland, John McMillan and Barry Naughton, Peter Murrell, John Litwack and Yingyi Qian, Philippe Aghion and Oliver Jean Blanchard, and Shang-Jin Wei.[2] The ultimate intellectual difference between the two schools of thought lies in the extent to which each school accepts the validity of neoclassical economics in guiding the economic reforms and each school recognizes the role of political factors in economic policymaking. This difference in faith in neoclassical economics has influenced every debate in economic policy in the 20th century, and the debate between the two schools is unlikely to result in final agreement soon.[3]

The experience of the early 1990s was that big-bang approaches in Eastern Europe were painful, leading to unexpectedly large and persistent reductions in output growth after the radical departure and transition from state socialism, while gradualist approaches in Asian communist and post-communist states were surprisingly successful, leading to significant accelerations in output growth, except North Korea.[4] Nonetheless, the North Korean economy has revived in positive growth, particularly since it adopted more open and liberal economic policies since the late 1990s, even though it has been crippled by very unfavorable external conditions and constraints. To provide readers with a visual picture of the five communist and post-communist states in East and Southeast Asia, a map of their relative geographical locations and basic statistics of economic development are presented (see Map 1.1 and Table 1.1).

Map 1.1 China, North Korea, Vietnam, Laos, and Cambodia

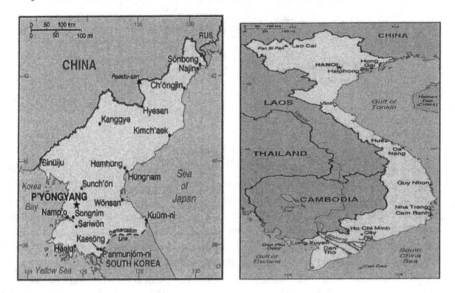

Table 1.1   Statistics of five communist/post-communist countries (2005)

	China	North Korea	Vietnam	Laos	Cambodia
Population	1.3 billion	22.9 million	83.5 million	6.2 million	13.6 million
Country Size	9.6 million sq km	120,540 sq km	329,560 sq km	236,800 sq km	181,040 sq km
Arable Land	15.4 %	20.76 %	19.97 %	3.8 %	20.96 %
GDP (p.p.p)	$ 7.262 trillion	$ 40 billion	$ 227.2 billion	$ 11.28 billion	$ 26.99 billion
GDP Per Capita (p.p.p)	$ 5,600	$ 1,700	$ 2,700	$ 1,900	$ 2,000
GDP Real Growth Rate	9.1 %	1 %	7.7 %	6 %	5.4 %
Industrial Growth Rate	17.1 %	N/A	16 %	-9.7 %	22 %
Exports (f.o.b)	$ 583.1 billion	$ 1.2 billion	$ 23.72 billion	$ 365 million	$ 2.3 billion
Imports (f.o.b)	$ 552.4 billion	$ 2.1 billion	$26.31 billion	$ 579 million	$ 3.1 billion
Military Spending (% GDP)	4.3 %	31.3 %	2.5 %	0.5 %	3 %

Source: CIA World Factbook; Asian Development Bank; World Bank.

However, both theoretical and empirical work "has not established the superiority of one course of reform over another... There are cases where fast and gradual reformers have succeeded and where they have failed."[5] Therefore, the debate remains controversial and inconclusive in the literature. To learn some valuable lessons about the choice of reform strategy from the different patterns of transition, it is useful to put the Asian transition in a broader comparative context in which transition has taken place across the two regions. China is often cited as the leading example of a successful gradualist approach to transition from communism. Some smaller Asian communist countries such as Vietnam, Laos, Cambodia, and North Korea have also adopted the similar gradualist approach. The key features of the Chinese model or the gradualist approach were an initial emphasis on agricultural reform and a gradual opening of the previously closed economy.[6] Asian communist states have by and large followed a similar strategy of transition, which resulted in a similar pattern of transition, which can be compared to the shock-therapist approach in Russia and Eastern Europe (see Table 1.2).

Table 1.2 Comparisons of gradualist and shock-therapist approaches

	Gradualist Approaches[7]	*Shock-therapist Approaches*[8]
Characteristics	An initial emphasis on agricultural reform and a gradual opening of the previously closed economy; Reforms were partial, incremental, and often experimental; caused no initial downturn and avoided declining incomes and high unemployment; made no use of large scale privatization; gradually reformed prices and trade control; maintained exchange controls; and adopted active state industrial policy while maintaining the party-state control	An all-out approach to replacing the traditional central planning economy with a market economy in a single burst of reforms; a rapid, all-out program including as many reforms as possible in the shortest possible time; caused initial economic downturn, declining incomes, and high unemployment; made use of mass privatization of SOEs through voucher or sale-out programs; rapidly lifting state control over the major factors of production and exchange while maintaining minimal macro-economic control
Outcomes	The result of such gradual or incremental changes is that these Asian countries continue to remain Leninist one-party states, embrace an eventual goal of communism, and move toward market socialism	The result of such rapid or radical changes is that Leninist one-party states and centrally planned command economy collapsed in Russia and East Europe and these countries move toward market capitalism

The central question is why these Asian countries adopted a gradualist approach to their transition that was different from their counterparts in Eastern Europe. Some explanations have been offered to address this question. Most of these explanations focused on exogenous economic and political conditions or different economic structures prior to reform in Asian countries that differed from those prevailing in Russia and Eastern Europe.[9]

- Unlike Eastern Europe that was more industrialized and overly specialized in heavy industry, Asian communist countries were predominantly agrarian societies with a huge surplus rural labor force ready to develop some new economic sector to support the old sector.
- The trade shocks due to the collapse of the Council for Mutual Economic Assistance (CMEA) were so enormous that trade within the former Soviet bloc was totally disrupted and a more radical approach to trade liberalization was imperative in these countries unlike in the early stages of Asian transition.
- The decline in the power of the Communist Party in most of Eastern Europe and the former Soviet Union was coupled with the weakening of centralized political control over the economy while the power of the Communist Party was strengthened as a result of economic growth and improvement of living standards in these Asian countries.

From this perspective, the pattern of transition was predetermined by the initial conditions or macroeconomic and structural differences between Eastern Europe and Asia and therefore no real lessons could be learned from the comparative experience of transition from communism. This explanation is well deduced from the structuralist approaches of transition theory.

Structuralist approaches place major emphasis on macro-level social conditions or socioeconomic and cultural prerequisites of transition, particularly the long-term influence of the level of economic development, industrialization, urbanization, education, social structures, political culture, the role of civil society, and other social conditions, because they assume that these macro-socioeconomic conditions can explain the causes, paths, and outcomes of transition.[10]

Structuralist approaches help us to understand why the old regime is challenged, threatened, or forced to reform, but can not tell us why and how the elites make the change in one way or another, in other words, why different countries take different approaches to transitions. Social and structural conditions may help to explain the dynamics of social change and transition, but they can hardly explain why different political actors make different choices, why their preferences change and policy choices shift from one to another, and why one choice prevails over another within the same social and structural context. Moreover, fundamentally flawed in these approaches is that the path of transition is predetermined by the initial conditions or macro-level economic and structural differences between Eastern Europe and Asia and therefore no lessons could be learned from comparative experiences. This is really deterministic. While initial conditions are important in determining and explaining *why* reforms are adopted, elite strategic policy choices best explain *how* reforms have been carried out, because it is elite strategic interactions and policy choices that have played a direct role in shaping the pattern of transition while structural factors an indirect one. Initial conditions, elite policy choices, and the pattern of transition should look like a set of antecedent causal relationships between z, x and y (see Figure 1.1).

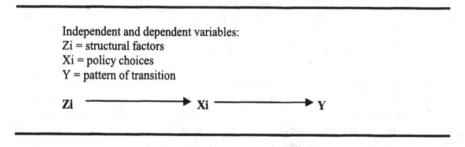

Independent and dependent variables:
Z_i = structural factors
X_i = policy choices
Y = pattern of transition

$$Z_i \longrightarrow X_i \longrightarrow Y$$

Figure 1.1 Causal relationship between Z, X, and Y

The initial conditions or antecedent causes of transition may differ significantly in different countries. However, these different pre-reform conditions or antecedent causes (such as predominantly agrarian societies, deepening economic recession or trade and financial difficulties) could prompt a common response or policy choice if the communist elite in the different countries shares a common belief in the efficacy of that response or policy choice, for example, the leadership's perception of the necessity for economic growth on one hand and the need for maintenance of communist power and preservation of party-state interests on the other. Just as individuals may take the same medicine to cure different physical problems, these countries may simultaneously choose similar reform policies to cope with different sets of political and economic problems. In this case, the specific antecedent causes (Z_1, Z_2, Z_3, Z_4, Z_5) in different countries prompt the leadership to act on a common set of policy choices, X_i, to produce a similar pattern of transition, Y (see Figure 1.2).

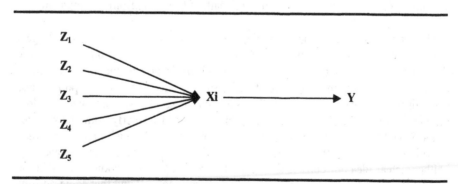

Figure 1.2 Explanation of the pattern of transition

In either case, the choice of similar reform policies, **X**, in coping with their economic and political problems (pre-reform conditions), produces a similar pattern of transition in these countries that is different from that of Eastern Europe. This analytical model of explanation is well deduced from the theoretical approach of strategic choice.

- Strategic choice approaches concentrate on the micro-level critical role of political elites and the interaction of their strategic choices, the splits within the old regime, the compromise or "negotiated agreements" between the "softliners" and "hardliners" on policy choices, and the process of transition.

- Strategic choice approaches emphasize the autonomy of elite strategic choices and political processes rather than the initial conditions and socioeconomic determinants of political and economic change, because elite calculations and preferences, strategic choices, and the interaction between the choices are viewed as decisive in determining paths and outcomes of transition though they do not deny the importance of economic factors.[11]

- Recent economics literature on the political economy of reform recognizes the critical role of political constraints, such as conflict of political ideologies, political resistance, political support, political acceptability and sustainability, asymmetric information, uncertainty regarding the outcome of reforms and the distribution of gains and losses from reform, in shaping reform strategies and affecting the choice of reform policy. Under these political constraints, it becomes sequentially optimal for the government to begin with partial reforms in some areas or sectors where possible and then extend to other areas or sectors, because gradualist reforms may be easier to get started, avoid excessive cost, especially for the government budget, allow trial and error and mid-course adjustment, reduce political resistance, help reformers gain incremental credibility, and create constituencies for further reforms.[12] The transition process in Asian countries of the last two decades have underscored the importance of the political economy of policy making rather than the initial conditions in understanding the path of transition from communism.

In Asian communist countries, the choice of reform policy has been largely constrained by the leadership' perception of the necessity for economic growth and the need for maintenance of the communist party's power and preservation of party-state interests, and therefore it has been the interplay between politics and economics or state and market that has led these Asian countries to adopt gradualist approaches to their reforms. Unlike most of formerly communist states in the Soviet bloc who were clear about their objectives of transition to democracy and market economy, the Chinese leaders and other Asian communist states had neither a clear idea nor consensus about where to go. What they knew was that the traditional centrally planned economy was not working well and that some reforms or policy changes were necessary to promote economic growth while maintaining the domestic political stability and the hard core of the political system. In China, the famous slogan is "groping for stone to cross river." China has experienced a lengthy process of readjusting reform objectives from "a planned economy with some market adjustment," to "a combination of plan and market," and now to "a socialist market economy."[13] In Vietnam and other Asian communist states, the intent of reform was to increase production, improve the living standard, and solve the pressing trade and fiscal problems. Reforms have been introduced piecemeal not only out of caution but also a desire to keep the process under control and maintain the balance between reform, growth and stability. Therefore, economically, these Asian communist countries continue to embrace some principles of socialism and espouse an eventual communism, and politically they remain determinedly Leninist party-states.[14]

In the real world, reforming an economy does not necessarily mean replacing an old system with a new system as many people believe. It could mean a developmental change within the general framework of the old system without fundamentally transforming the substance or foundation of the old system. In communist states, reform could mean the process of gradual transition toward some sort of improvement of the old system, from state socialism to market socialism, without creating a new economic system or a truly free market economy as it has been defined by economics theory. It seems that Asian communist countries have followed the logic of this developmental pattern and enjoyed the results of their reforms.

New economic sectors and agents are created, but limited within the political and legal framework defined by the communist party and its ideology, norms, policies, and political need, and many of them are also controlled by the party-state apparatus. These new economic sectors and agents might not be under the direct control of the government, but have to compete with predominant state-owned enterprises or party-state controlled agents. After more than two decades of economic reforms, commercial, labor, real estate, and stock markets have emerged and many other elements of a market economy have come into being in today's Asian communist and post-communist states. The state has sought new incentive systems or market mechanisms within the traditional sector, state-owned and collective owned, in order to allow its agents to respond more effectively to new competitors and adapt existing institutions to the new economic environment which permits more competition and more efficient markets.[15] The state has also allowed and encouraged new private sectors to emerge and develop, and these sectors have become an increasingly dynamic market force that compete with the traditional sector, state- and collective-owned enterprises for resources and markets. These sectors have even become dominant in some industries and agricultural sectors of the countries under study though the situation may vary from country to country.

How to characterize such reformed economies in East and Southeast Asia? They have obviously moved away from the command economy of state socialism, but the key issue is what direction and how far they have moved toward that direction. This study will compare the Asian transitions to examine and evaluate the nature and process of economic transition from state socialism[16] in the countries under study. This study will attempt to solve the following questions: What are the pre-transition models of state socialism in Asian? What are the causal variables that have contributed to reform efforts across these Asian countries? Why and how is this reform process different from what happened in Eastern European countries? How are reform policies proposed, adopted, and implemented? How is the reform process in these Asian countries similar to or different from one another? What is the goal of the economic reform? What is the nature of the economic reform? To what extent is the party-state playing a role in the economic reform? What are the trends, directions, and limits of the reform in these Asian countries? Has the economic reform transformed state socialism into market capitalism, state capitalism, or market socialism? With the collapse of communism and state socialism in Eastern Europe and the Soviet Union, is it only the capitalist economic model that remains? Is there another way that is neither capitalist nor state socialism? Or is there a third way for economic development? Can market socialism, a market-based form of socialism within the political context of one-party communist rule become a competitive and efficient economy like market capitalism? To provide a common basis for comparisons of these Asian countries and address these questions, the next chapter will define the pre-reform model of state socialism in these countries in order to establish reference points of departure in order to examine the major factors that have contributed to the choice of reform policies in these Asian countries, determine what has changed and what has not, in kind or in degree, and evaluate the nature of the economic reform and the direction of transition in these political economies.

Notes

[1]   David Lipton and Jeffrey Sachs, "Creating a Market Economy in Eastern Europe: The Case of Poland," *Brookings Papers on Economic Activities*, 1, (1990a), pp. 75-133; David Lipton and Jeffrey Sachs, "Privatization in East Europe: The Case of Poland," *Brookings Papers on Economic Activities*, 2, (1990b), pp. 293-341; Anders Aslund, "Principles of Privatization," in Laszlo Csaba, ed., *Systemic Change and Stabilization in Eastern Europe* (Dartmouth, UK: Aldershot, 1991), pp. 17-31; Andrew Berg and Jeffrey Sachs, "Structural Adjustment and International Trade in Eastern Europe: The Case of Poland," *Economic Policy*, April 1992, pp. 117-173; Kevin Murphy et al., "The Transition to a Market Economy: Pitfalls of Partial Reform," *Quarterly Journal of Economics*, vol. 107, no. 3, 1992, pp. 889-906; Jeffrey Sachs, *Poland's Jump to the Market Economy* (Cambridge, MA: MIT Press, 1993); Roman Frydman and Andrzej Rapaczynski, *Privatization in Eastern Europe: Is the State Withering Away?* (London: Central European University Press, 1994); Wing Thye Woo, "The Art of Reforming Centrally Planned Economies: Comparing China, Poland, and Russia," Journal of Comparative Economics, vol. 18, no. 3, 1994, pp. 276-308; Jeffrey Sachs and Wing Thye Woo, "Structural Factors in the Economic Reforms of China, Eastern Europe, and

the Former Soviet Union," *Economic Policy*, April, 1994, pp. 101-145; Anders Aslund, *How Russia Became a Market Economy* (Washington, DC: Brookings Institution, 1995).

[2] Richard Portes, "Introduction to Economic Transformation of Hungary and Poland," *European Economics*, March 1990, pp. 11-18; Richard Portes, "The Path of Reform in Central and Eastern Europe: An Introduction," *European Economics*, 1991, Special Issue No. 2, pp. 3-15; Ronald McKinnon, *The Order of Economic Liberalization* (Baltimore, MD: Johns Hopkins University, 1991); Gerard Roland, "Political Economy of Sequencing Tactics in the Transition Period," in Laszlo Csaba, ed., *Systemic Change and Stabilization in Eastern Europe* (Dartmouth, UK: Aldershot, 1991), pp. 47-64; Mathias Dewatripont and Gerard Roland, "Economic Reform and Dynamic Political Constraints," *Review of Economic Studies*, vol. 59, no. 4, 1992a, pp. 703-730; Mathias Dewatripont and Gerard Roland, "The Virtues of Gradualism and Legitimacy in the Transition to a Market Economy," *Economic Journal*, March 1992b, pp. 291-300; John McMillan and Barry Naughton, "How to Reform a Planned Economy: Lessons from China," *Oxford Review of Economic Policy*, vol. 8, no. 1, 1992, pp. 130-143; Peter Murrell, "Conservative Political Philosophy and the Strategy of Economic Transition," *East European Politics and Society*, vol. 6, no. 1, 1992, pp. 3-16; John Litwack and Yingyi Qian, "Economic Transition Strategies: Imperfect Fiscal Commitment Can Favor Unbalanced Investment," Mimeo, Stanford University, 1993; Philippe Aghion and Oliver Jean Blanchard, "On the Speed of Transition in Eastern Europe," Mimeo, MIT, 1993; Mathias Dewatripont and Gerard Roland, "The Design of Reform Packages under Uncertainty," *The American Economic Review*, vol. 85, no. 5, 1995, pp. 1207-1223; Shang-Jin Wei, "Gradualism versus Big Bang: Speed and Sustainability of Reforms," *Canadian Journal of Economics*, vol. 30, no. 4, 1997, pp. 1234-1247.

[3] Wing Thye Woo, "The Economics and Politics of Transition to an Open Market Economy: China," *Technical Papers*, no. 153, OECD Development Centre, October 1999, p. 58.

[4] John McMillan and Barry Naughton, eds., *Reforming Asian Socialism: The Growth of Market Institutions* (Ann Arbor, MI: The University of Michigan Press, 1996), p 5.

[5] Andrew Feltenstein and Saleh M. Nsouli, "Big Bang Versus Gradualism in Economic Reforms: An Intertemporal Analysis with an Application to China," *IMF Working Paper*, August 2001, p. 4.

[6] Richard Pomfret, *Asian Economies in Transition* (Cheltenham, UK: Edward Elgar, 1996), pp. 2-7.

[7] See footnote 2 in Jeffrey Sachs and Wing Thye Woo, "Structural Factors in the Economic Reforms of China, Eastern Europe, and the Former Soviet Union," *Economic Policy*, vol. 18, April 1994.

[8] World Bank, *From Plan to Market: World Development Report* (Washington, DC: World Bank, 1996), pp. 9-10; D. Lipton and J. Sachs, "Privatization in East Europe: The Case of Poland," *Brookings Papers on Economic Activities*, 2 (1990), pp. 293-341.

[9] Ronald I. McKinnon, *Gradual versus Rapid Liberalization in Socialist Countries* (San Francisco, CA: ICS Press, 1994), pp. 5-7; Jeffrey Sachs and Wing Thye Woo, "Structural Factors in the Economic Reforms of China, Eastern Europe, and the Former Soviet Union," *Economic Policy*, April 1994, pp. 101-145; Anders Aslund, *How Russia Became a Market Economy* (Washington, DC: Brookings Institution, 1995), p. 14.

[10] Seymour Martin Lipset, "Some Social Requisites of Democracy," *American Political Science Review*, 53, March 1959; Gabriel Almond and Sidney Verba, *The Civic Culture*

(Princeton: Princeton University Press, 1963); O'Donnell, *Modernization and Bureaucratic Authoritarianism: Studies in South American Politics* (Berkeley: Institute of International Studies, University of California, 1979); Robert Dahl, *Who Governs? Democracy and Power in an American City* (New Haven, CT: Yale University Press, 1961); Arend Lijphart, *The Politics of Accommodation: Pluralism and Democracy in the Netherlands* (Berkeley: University of California Press, 1968); Dankwart A. Rustow, "Transitions to Democracy: Toward a Dynamic Model," *Comparative Politics*, vol. 2, (April 1970), pp. 337-63; Dietrich Rueschemeyer et al., *Capitalist Development and Democracy* (Chicago: University of Chicago Press, 1992), pp. 12-39.

[11] Juan Linz and Alfred Stepan, eds., *The Breakdown of Democratic Regimes: Crisis, Breakdown and Reequilibration* (Baltimore: Johns Hopkins University Press, 1978); Guillermo O'Donnell, Philippe Schmitter, eds., *Transitions from Authoritarian Rule: Tentative Conclusions about Uncertain Democracies* (Baltimore: Johns Hopkins University Press, 1986); Giuseppe di Palma, *To Craft Democracies: An essay on Democratic Transitions* (Berkeley: University of California Press, 1990); Herbert Kitschelt, "Political Regime Change: Structure and Process-Driven Explanations?" *American Political Science Review*, vol. 86, no. 4 (December 1992), p. 1032.

[12] Raquel Fernandez and Dani Rodrik, "Resistance to Reform: Status Quo Bias in the Presence of Individual-Specific Uncertainty," *The American Economic Review*, vol. 81, no. 5, 1991, pp. 1146-1155; Mathias Dewatripont and Gerard Roland, "Economic Reform and Dynamic Political Constraints," *The Review of Economic Studies*, vol. 59, no. 4, 1992, pp. 703-730; Mathias Dewatripont and Gerard Roland, "The Design of Reform Packages under Uncertainty," *The American Economic Review*, vol. 85, no. 5, 1995, pp. 1207-1223; Martin Raiser, "Lessons for Whom, from Whom? The Transition from Socialism in China and Central Eastern Europe Compared," *Communist Economies and Economic Transformation*, vol. 7, no. 2, 1995, pp. 133-157; Dani Rodrik, "Understanding Economic Policy Reform," *Journal of Economic Literature*, vol. 34, no. 1, 1996, pp. 9-41; Marek Dabrowski, "Different Strategies of Transition to Market Economy: How Do They Work in Practice?" *World Bank, Policy Research Dept. Working Paper*, No. 1579, March 1996; Xinghai Fang, "Government Commitment and Gradualism," in John McMillan and Barry Naughton, eds., *Reforming Asian Socialism* (Ann Arbor, MI: The University of Michigan Press, 1996), pp. 337-352; Martha de Melo, et al., "Patterns of Transition from Plan to Market," *World Bank Economic Review*, vol. 10, no. 3, 1996, pp. 397-424; Martha de Melo, et al., "Circumstances and Choice: The Role of Initial Conditions and Polices in Transition Economies," *World Bank Mimeo*, 1997; Shang-Jin Wei, "Gradualism versus Big Bang: Speed and Sustainability of Reforms," *Canadian Journal of Economics*, vol. 30, no. 4, 1997, pp. 1234-1247; Jean-Jacques Laffont and Yingyi Qian, "The Dynamics of Reform and Development in China: A Political Economy Perspective," *European Economic Review*, vol. 43, no. 4-6, 1999, pp. 1105-1114.

[13] Fan Gang, "Incremental Changes and Dual-Track Transition: Understanding the Case of China," *Economic Policy*, vol. 19, December 1994.

[14] Edwin A. Winckler, ed., *Transition from Communism in China: Institutional and Comparative Analysis* (Boulder, CO: Lynne Rienner, 1999), pp. 45-46.

[15] John McMillan and Barry Naughton, 1996, p. 7

[16] Throughout this book, "state socialism" will be used interchangeably with "centrally planned command economy" which is based on the Soviet model established by Stalinism as the two terms capture the same substance of an economic model in modern history.

Chapter 2

Historical Background and Pre-Transition Models

The starting point for any study of the economic transition in communist states is the traditional centrally planned economy modeled on the Soviet economy. This chapter will trace the historical backgrounds of these developments in the establishment of centrally planned economy in Asia and define the pre-reform socialist models that constitute the points of departure from state socialism or centrally planned command economy across these countries, in order to define the beginning and the end of transition from state socialism and conduct a sensible assessment of political economic change across these countries.

Historical Backgrounds

CHINA

In 1949, the Chinese Communist Party defeated the KMT and had control over the country. One of the most important issues facing the CCP centered on what type of socialism the CCP would put in place. Although China attempted to develop its own peasant-based socialist economy, it could not repudiate Soviet ideological influence as China in fact depended upon the Soviet Union for logistics, technology, and infrastructure support. From 1953 to 1956, the CCP launched the socialist transformation movement to nationalize major industries and collectivize agriculture. This is the period of officially designated "Transition to Socialism" that corresponded to China's First Five-Year Plan, which was modeled on the Soviet economic planning system and characterized by efforts to achieve industrialization, collectivization of agriculture, and nationalization of industry, banking, trade, and shops. Private enterprise was virtually abolished. Major political developments included the centralization of party and government administration and the institutionalization of the party-state power.[1] The transition began as shown in Table 2.1

The Great Leap Forward (1957-1959) was another attempt by the Chinese communists to accomplish the economic and technical development of the country at a faster pace and with greater results – "to catch up with Britain and America within 15 years," which based on Mao's belief that it was achievable if domestic resources could be fully utilized, the peasantry and mass organizations could be fully mobilized, and the people could be ideologically aroused. To accomplish such an ambitious goal, the Great Leap Forward created new socio-economic and political organizations in the countryside – the People's Communes, which were placed under the control of local governments. Each commune was placed in control of all the means of production and operated as the sole accounting unit; it

Table 2.1   Transition of political and economic systems in China

Years	Political System	Power	Economic System
1949-1953	Leninist party-state in consultation with "democratic parties"	CCP under Mao	Consolidation of power and control over mainland; land reform; Korean war; and moderate social and economic policies.
1953-1956	Leninist party-state	CCP under Mao	Lower level collectivization; socialist transformation campaigns; First Five-Year Plan modeled on the Soviet command economy.
1957-1960	Leninist party-state	CCP under Mao	The Great Leap Forward; People's Communes; catch-up industrialization
1961-1965	Leninist party-state	CCP under Mao	Readjustment and recovery period; corrective measures and re-organization of communes; decentralization
1966-1976	Leninist party-state	CCP under Mao	Cultural Revolution; moral and political incentives
1978 -1989	Leninist party-state in consultation with "democratic parties"	CCP under Deng/elders	Economic reforms and open-door policy in experimental and gradualist manner; dual track price; increasing the role of market mechanisms while reducing government planning and direct control.
1989-1992	Leninist party-state in consultation with "democratic parties"	CCP under Deng/Jiang	Period of Readjustment
1992-2004	Leninist party-state in consultation with "democratic parties"	CCP under Jiang	Market socialism – "socialist market economy with the Chinese characteristics"
2004-present	Leninist party-state in consultation with "democratic parties"	CCP under Hu	Market socialism – "socialist market economy with the Chinese characteristics"

was subdivided into production brigades (concurrent with traditional villages) and then production teams. Each commune had administration, local security, militia organizations, small-scale local industry, schools, nurseries, communal kitchens, etc. Each commune was responsible for such major public projects as roads, irrigation works, reservoirs, and hydroelectric dams, which were seen as integral parts of the party's plan for an ideal new society. By the fall 1958, some 23,500 communes were incorporated from some 750,000 agricultural cooperatives, each averaging 5,000 households, or 22,000 people. By the early 1960s, an estimated 74,000 communes were established. The result was astonishing and disastrous largely due to unrealistic targets, hubris, corruption and poor accounting, and approximately 16 to 40 million Chinese died in a famine that was largely attributable to unrealistic and fanciful economic goals.[2] The disastrous effects of the Great Leap Forward provoked the leadership to re-think about the method of industrialization and the path of "transition to socialism" and adopt some more pragmatic economic policy and adjustment.

However, in the middle of 1960s, Mao Zedong believed that the creeping "capitalist" and anti-socialist tendencies were developing in this country and corrupting the cadres and masses. At the same time, there were internal disagreements between Mao and his colleagues who attempted to block Mao's effort to arrest the so-called "capitalist trend." Mao believed that restoring ideological purity and purging those who were not supportive of Mao's policies became necessary, and the only way to achieve these goals was to mobilize masses for the "class struggle" against those "capitalist roaders" ("those in power taking the capitalist road") within the party-state and remove them from the power. This major political movement was called the Cultural Revolution. During this period of time, Mao and his close allies (the "Gang of Four") adopted ultra-leftist economic policy based on utopian morality and political incentives and attacked those policies that promoted production and industrialization in more pragmatic ways as "capitalistic" and "revisionist." As a result, the economy was literally teetered on the brink of collapse at the end of the Cultural Revolution.[3]

The death of Mao and the demise of the "Gang of Four" ended the Cultural Revolution. Deng was reinstated, as were many reform-minded moderates who had been previously purged during the Great Leap Forward and the Cultural Revolution. Conversely, many left-wing ideologues, who came to power during the Cultural Revolution and endeavored to eliminate all modes of capitalism, were dismissed and rebuked for their actions. The new leaders concurrently distanced itself from Mao's economic policy and responded to economic crisis in pragmatic ways. This economic policy was established at the Third Plenum of the Eleventh National Party Congress Central Committee in 1978 – the "class struggle" was replaced by "the Four Modernizations."[4]

The eighties and nineties were characterized by economic reform as prescribed by the Four Modernizations doctrine. Economic liberalization began first in agriculture with the People's Communes replaced with the "household responsibility system" and farmers markets created to facilitate commercial exchange among farmers and between urban and rural areas. The CCP also adopted a cautious open-door policy to promote foreign trade and attract foreign investment by creating a special economic zone in the Southern city, Shenzhen, Guangdong Province, which was followed by four SEZs along the southeast coast, Shanghai, and some other coastal cities in later years. The transition is partial, gradualist, experimental, and phased in, with the party-state in control of the entire process. Plan and market are both considered as the methods of economic development and modernization regardless of capitalism or socialism. However, throughout the 1980s, the mainstream of economic thought in the CCP was to maintain the central planning system within which the market would play a supplemental role in the allocation of resources. The move away from this more traditional socialist doctrine was a more pragmatic policy of transition toward a market-based economy – "Socialist Market Economy" – a skillful compromise between reformers and conservatives in the 1990s. By the mid 1990s, the CCP finally confirmed that its long term objective of economic transition was the establishment of "a socialist market economy with the Chinese characteristics" while fully utilizing the world's free markets, capital, advanced science and technology to advance the Four Modernizations.[5]

With leadership devolving from Deng to Jiang to Hu, China remained steadfast in its economic transition from centrally planned economy to a market-oriented economy. Many elements of a market economy have come into being in the past two decades, and transformed the Chinese economy into a diverse structure of ownership with state, collective, personal, private, foreign, and joint-ventured enterprises and businesses coexisted in the economy – a mixed economy combining capitalist dynamics and socialist principles. Economic liberalization and marketization have made a significant progress and maintained a high economic growth rate for more than two decades. However, the political system with the communist party-state at the core has remained unchanged, and defined the political context and the parameters within which the economy can operate and move around. The new CCP leadership, Hu and Wen seem intent upon expanding China's economic liberalization even further along the same path to becoming a more advanced socialist market economy in the 21st century.

NORTH KOREA

After the North-South separation, North Korea established a centrally planned economy based on the Soviet model, which included two basic economic organizations by ownership: state owned enterprises and social cooperatives. The state owned the property rights and resource allocation was carried out through the state central planning. Prices, wages, and all factors of production were controlled and allocated by the central planners. The transition began as shown in Table 2.2.

However, North Korea modified the Soviet model into its own version of centrally planned economy based on the principles of *Juche* ideology or self-reliance. North Korea launched a series of campaigns to transform the industry and

Table 2.2   Transition of political and economic systems in DPRK

Years	Political System	Power	Economic System
1945-1946	Unconsolidated	Communist and Nationalist guerilla leaders	Unconsolidated
1946-60	Leninist communist party-state	Korean Worker's Party under Kim Il Sung	Soviet type centrally-planned economy
1960- 1979	Leninist communist party-state	Korean Worker's Party under Kim Il Sung	Maoist type mass campaigns and reform under Chongsan-ri method
1980-1994	Leninist communist party-state	Korean Worker's Party under Kim Il Sung	Limited liberalized central planning and open door policy, FETZs
1994-current	Leninist communist party-state	Korean Worker's Party under Kim Jong Il	Market socialism; price, wages, and foreign exchange reform

agriculture into a socialist economic system through "land reform," "nationalization of industry," "collectivization," and "Three-Year Plan" in the mid-1950s, which were largely identical with China in time. Through the Five-Year Plan of 1957-61 and the Seven-Year Plan of 1961-67, a centrally planned command economy was fully developed in North Korea. To indoctrinate people with Kim Il Sung's *Juche* ideas and transform the North Korean economy into "our style socialism," the North Korean leadership launched a series of mass campaigns, such as the "Flying Horse March" (*Ch'ollima Undong*), which was identical to the Chinese "Great Leap Forward" in 1958, and "Three-Revolution Team" movement, which was similar to but less radical than the "Cultural Revolution" in China. Although China and the Soviet Union were an influencing factor in shaping the formation of the North Korean economy, North Korea attempted to demonstrate its independence in building their own style socialism. North Korean economy grew rapidly during the postwar rehabilitation period and in the 1960, which was largely made possible by a large amount of aid form USSR, China, and CMEA, the socialist Eastern bloc.

In the late 1960s, North Korean leadership began to introduce some new economic measures called "*Chongsan-ri* Method," which was designed to correct several problems in collective farm management. The major measure was to give material incentives to collective farms for increased production. Other measures such as managerial responsibility, partial decentralization in the administration of local authority, etc. were also implemented. However, North Korean economic reform actually began in the 1980s when the country faced serious economic difficulties as a result of the rigid *Juche* ideology.

Beginning in the early 1980s, North Korea began to open up for foreign trade and foreign direct investment, in the hope that it would bring in advanced technology and boost up the declined economy. A Joint Venture Law was made in 1984 allowing foreign firms to join venture with the state companies. This partial opening to outside world was also encouraged by the positive results of the Chinese open-door policy. However, the reform policy produced limited results due to low credibility and unattractive terms of foreign investment laws.[6]

From the late 1980s onward, North Korea found itself in a serious situation that resulted from the break-up of the Soviet Union and the collapse of the Eastern Bloc. In 1990, Russia announced that it would no longer supply with subsidized oil, and all trade must be paid in cash – the previous bartering system, paying in Korean won and importing on credit was terminated.[7] As North Korea heavily relied on the Soviet Union and the Eastern bloc for trade, financial and technical assistance, North Korea suffered a trade shock equivalent to 40 percent of total imports in 1991, and by 1993, imports from Russia had fallen to less than a tenth of their earlier levels,[8] which triggered a most serious economic crisis in North Korean history.

In the wake of such dramatic shift on international politics, North Korea began to respond to its economic crisis by pursuing an open door policy more aggressively. In the 1990s, "Free Economic Trade Zones" (FETZs) were created with favorable investment environment (e.g. financial and tax reform, trade and foreign exchange rate reforms etc). Other partial reforms include shifting focus to production of light industry, partial decentralization of trade management, transforming collective farms into small work teams, allowing private plots in the backyard of farmers, and transforming industrial management system into a system based on associated enterprises.

However, North Korea remains under the shadow of *Juche* ideology. By the mid-1990s externals factors were compounded by a series of natural disasters. The crisis accelerated because of severe food shortages in the country, which resulted in an estimated 600,000 to 1 million people's death due to famine.[9] To promote economic recovery and growth, North Korea began to allow free farmers markets and private enterprises to develop since the late 1990s. North Korean leadership revised the Constitution in August 1998 to formally accept the concepts, such as "private property," "material incentives," and "cost, price and profit" in Article 24, 32 and 33 respectively.[10]

Since 2002, however, some more radical reform policies have been adopted, which has made some dramatic departures from the traditional command economy and significantly changed the economic system to a more market-oriented socialist economy. These reforms include:

- Expansion of FETZs – Sinuiju, Kaesong, Rasong, Nampo, Wonsan, etc.

- 2nd "*Ch'ollima* March" – liberalization of prices, wages, etc. On July 1, 2002, a new price system was introduced to allow the price level of goods to rise such that it reflected production costs and international prices. The official price of rice, for example, soared from 0.08 won per kilogram to 44 won, about 550-fold increase. The wages were also raised to reflect the increase in prices. Salaries of manufacturing workers, for example, also increased almost 18-fold from 110 won a month to 2,000 won a month.

- The government has taken measures to change its centralized production and allow factories to formulate their own independent production plans. The government has delegated administrative and managerial responsibilities from party officials to industrial and commercial managers. A multi-layered and partly decentralized economy has emerged.

- In 2002, the government also began to allow collective farms to pay rent for land with a portion of their harvest and began to buy grains or vegetables from the farmers at realistic prices (close to the farmers' market price).

- Laws are passed on stock and joint stock companies, local capital markets are developed, and some major state owned enterprises and assets in oil refining, mining, manufacturing, textiles, food processing are corporatized.[11]

All these new policies and changes have suggested that North Korea is no longer a centrally planned economy, but a market-oriented socialist economy. It has partially adopted some features of market economy. More liberal economic reform and controlled open door policy have started in this country.

VIETNAM

Like China and North Korea, Vietnam's economic development was greatly influenced and shaped by the Soviet Union. Beginning in the civil war with the South (1964–1973), communist North Vietnam received enormous aid from the Soviet Union and China, which helped spur a three-year economic rehabilitation program (1958–60) and a five-year plan (1961–66). These programs were aimed at promoting socialist transition and improving industrial and agricultural development. Soviet and Chinese aid helped boost electric power production, locate new mineral deposits, expand mining, and establish many new industries. Conversely, the South, supported by the United States, stagnated under an austere government, which focused less on economic development and more on political control.[12] The civil war ended with the communist victory and takeover of the entire country – a peace agreement was signed in 1973; the US withdrew in 1975; and a unified, communist regime took control over all of Vietnam in 1976.

Transition to socialism began to take place in the South. Table 2.3 summarizes Vietnam's economic transition in relation to governance.

Table 2.3   Transition of political and economic systems in Vietnam

Years	Political System	Power	Economic System
1945-1954	North – Democratic Republic of Vietnam	North – Vietnam Worker's Party	North – Soviet type central planning and war economy
	South – Under the French Protectorate	South – French Rule	South – Colonial economy
1954-1963	North – Democratic Republic of Vietnam	North – Communist Party of Vietnam	North – Soviet type central planning and war economy
	South – Republic of Vietnam	South – U.S. backed government under Ngo Dinh Diem	South – Capitalist market economy
1963-1975	North – Democratic Republic of Vietnam	North – Communist Party of Vietnam	North – Soviet type central planning and war economy
	South – Republic of Vietnam	South – Military Regime under President Thieu	South – Capitalist market economy
1976-1979	Socialist Republic of Vietnam	Vietnam Communist Party	Attempt to make a transition toward socialism in the south to create a unified Soviet type central planning
1979-1986	Socialist Republic of Vietnam	Vietnam Communist Party	Liberalization and introduction of market mechanism
1986-present	Socialist Republic of Vietnam	Vietnam Communist Party	Transition to "socialist-oriented market economy"

Vietnam began to introduce the Soviet type central planning and collectivization as early as in the late 1950s when the Viet Nam Lao Dong Party decided to collectivize agriculture and nationalize industry and trade in the northern part under its control. Identical to the Chinese model, cooperatives developed in three stages corresponding to the level of socialization and the form of ownership: mutual aid teams in which members retained private ownership of land and shared agricultural tools; lower-level production cooperatives in which the means of production were pooled but income was distributed according to labor and land rent; and high-level cooperatives in which all land and means of production were collectivized although members' private plots were allowed, and income was distributed according to work-points system. Brigades and production teams replaced peasant households as the basic work units. By 1975, before the unification, North Vietnam had 17,000 high-level cooperatives. During the same period of time, in the late 1950s and early 1960s, North Vietnam's Three Year Plan promoted the transformation of private enterprises into mixed public and private arrangements. By the end of 1959, 45 percent of private enterprises had been transformed into "state capitalism" and more private sectors were transformed in the later years.[13] The central planning agencies set targets and provided supplies for SOEs, and production and distribution of goods were conducted according to the planning. SOEs were managed by central "line ministries" or people's committees at local governments. In 1965, North Vietnam had 1,132 SOEs with 205 centrally run SOEs and 927 locally run SOEs, a total of 653,959 workers. By 1975, the number of SOEs had increased to 1,357 with 950,999 workers.[14]

After 1975, the Vietnamese Communist Party imposed the North Vietnamese model on the South, but faced resistance from southerners who boycotted collectivization, refused to harvest crops in time, and secretly killed livestock. Between 1976 and 1980, per capita food production decreased, per capita national income growth declined, and shortages of food and goods worsened.[15] Although Hanoi attempted to revitalize its economy through the Second Five-Year Plan (1976-1980), with unrealistic planned targets at 16-18 percent growth for industry, 8-10 percent growth for agriculture, and 13-14 percent growth for national income, the Vietnamese centrally planned economy failed to achieve those goals.[16] Furthermore, Vietnam's invasion of Cambodia in 1979 and subsequent boarder war with China weakened its economy further and deprived it of a consistent and reliable source of aide from China and other Western countries.

However, Vietnam implemented another major economic program, the Third Five-Year Plan (1981-1985). The Third Five-Year Plan centered on transitioning the South to communism while at the same time preserving some of its private sectors and entrepreneurial strengths. As early as 1979 at the Sixth Plenum of the Central Committee of the Fourth Party Congress, Hanoi acknowledged for the first time the efficacy and usefulness of market and entrepreneurship, and even allowed semi-autonomous small and light private businesses. Many of these ventures – typically small, peasant-based farming operations – were allowed to have wide latitude to operate independent of collectives or bureaucratic state institutions. The Sixth Plenum also endorsed the necessity of a muti-sectoral economy in Vietnam consisting of state, collective, joint state-private, private, and individual ownership. This became the starting point in Vietnam's implementation of economic liberalization. Beginning 1981, the VCP leadership issued Direction 100 CT/TU to make the output contract (*khoan san pham*) a national policy, which allowed peasants to sign contracts to farm collective land. Like China, each household fulfilled the contract by turning over the agreed amount of product to the cooperatives while retaining the surplus for consumption, sale on the market, or sale to the state at negotiated prices. Economic liberalization had a positive impact on the economy. Despite having devoted greater resources to the industrial sector (mainly heavy industry), agricultural output and light industry production were either sustained or expanded within the Third Five-Year Plan.[17]

In 1986, the Sixth Party Congress officially adopted a reform policy or *doi moi*, aimed at further opening the Vietnamese economy to the outside world and market forces. During the Fourth Five-Year Plan (1986-1990), as part of its effort to open up the economy to the international market and commitment to promote economic liberalization and production, Vietnam decreased import quotas and tariffs as a means to secure loans from the IMF, World Bank, and Asia Development Bank. At the same time, Hanoi continued to promote further economic reforms in agricultural contracts, land use rights, prices, SOEs, economic legislations, foreign investment law, streamlining of bureaucracy, and new markets.[18] The *doi moi* was a transition from a centrally planned economy to a market based socialist economy, but it has proceeded in a step-by-step or stop-and-go manner. Although progress was made, a comprehensive reform plan was lacking, and this has contributed to the lack of consensus on the direction and pace of economic reform. Tension remains between those who saw the state as having a major responsibility for ensuring social equity and controlling the economy and those who viewed the role of government as concentrating primarily on a broad economic policy framework and the provision of legal institutions and regulatory framework needed to promote market-based growth. By 1991, the Soviet Union had collapsed – depriving Hanoi of badly needed financial and technological assistance, which made further economic liberalization and opening up to the West a much needed policy choice for the Vietnamese leadership.[19] Vietnam is now an active member of both ASEAN and APEC, and has to carry out further reforms by virtue of its obligations to the two regional organizations.[20] Vietnam has made a significant progress in its economic liberalization and many elements of market economy have come into being. Though still anchored to socialist principles, the economy has become more market-oriented with a mixed ownership structure.

LAO PDR

In 1955, the Lao People's Party, later the Lao People's Revolutionary Party (LPRP), linked with the Pathet Lao resistance movement, was established under the leadership of Kaysone Phomvihan. The Lao PDR was proclaimed in 1975. Prince Souphanouvong was named president, but the real power lay with Kaysone Phomvihan, Secretary-General of the LPRP.[21]

The LPRP launched "accelerated socialization" and introduced a Soviet-style central planning economy, replacing the private sector with state enterprises and cooperatives; centralizing investment, production, trade, and pricing; and setting governmental regulations and restrictions on internal and foreign trade. In agriculture, accordingly, cooperatives were promoted as a base for future socialist transformation. During 1978 and 1979, more than 3,000 agricultural cooperatives were established although some private sector agriculture continued to exist.[22] The transition began as shown in Table 2.4.

Table 2.4   Transition of political and economic systems in Lao PDR

Years	Political System	Power	Economic System
Before 1953	Constitutional monarchy within French Union (Kingdom of Laos)	Held by the French (The King is only a symbol recognized by the French)	Colonial economy
1953-1959	Constitutional monarchy (Kingdom of Laos)	Held by King Sisavang Vong and Prince Souvanna Phouma as prime minister	Some measures of nationalization attempted
1959-1975	Constitutional monarchy (Kingdom of Laos)	Held by King Savang Vathanna; civil war, coalition government (1957-59, 1962, 1974) was attempted but ended in collapse	war economy
1975-1979	Communist party rule (Lao People's Democratic Republic)	Lao People's Revolutionary Party	Central planning; agricultural cooperatives
1979-1986	Communist party rule (Lao People's Democratic Republic)	Lao People's Revolutionary Party	Liberalization by introducing new economic policy
1986-present	Communist party rule (Lao People's Democratic Republic)	Lao People's Revolutionary Party	Transition to a market economy under the NEM

However, attempts to further collectivize agriculture encountered strong opposition and production stagnated. The LPRP took the first steps toward market oriented reform in 1979 by easing restrictions on private trade and encouraging joint ventures between the state and the private sector. The government reduced agricultural taxes and increased government procurement prices for most crops. However, it did not dismantle the central planning. More far-reaching reforms began in 1986 with the introduction of the New Economic Mechanism (NEM). The government abandoned the collectivization of agriculture, eased many restrictions on private sector activity, and gave state enterprises more decision making power. Enterprise reform and privatization with the leasing as the dominant form began in 1988 and accelerated until slowing down after 1993.[23]

The Sixth Party Congress in 1996 confirmed that economic reforms would continue, but that the state would retain overall control over the economy. In 1998 General Khamtai was elected president and appointed General Sisavat Keobounphan as prime minister. This strong alliance promised political stability and the continuation of economic reform, although the LPRP remained opposed to political reform along multiparty lines.[24]

Lao PDR remains a Leninist party state. The LPRP has around 65,000 members and is the country's only political party. It is governed by a central committee and headed by the nine-member Politburo. The military remains politically powerful: only two of the nine-member Politburo have no military background. The Politburo formulates policy making in virtually every aspect of public life. Organized opposition to the LPRP is weak. A number of small guerrilla groups exist, bandits launch occasional attacks, and a few dissident groups are based in the United States and Eastern Europe. The media are entirely state controlled. At present, the public participates in two elections, namely, those for the National Assembly and village heads. However, the party controls elections and determines the outcomes by pre-selecting the candidates. Most members of the government are members of the LPRP, and those who stand for election to the National Assembly must be approved by the party-controlled Lao Front for National Reconstruction, which comprises such organizations as trade unions, peasant associations, and religious and business groups, which is identical to the organizations in China. Moreover, a strong party structure whose organization parallels the government administrative structure significantly influences decision-making processes within the public administration. The Lao PDR is divided into 16 provinces, 112 districts, and more than 11,000 villages. Provinces, districts, and some villages are run by party committees.[25]

Lao PDR has adopted a "step-by-step" approach or a "gradualist path" in the transition process which shares much with other Asian transitional economies. The reason for Lao PDR to adopt such a gradualist approach is due to the party leadership's concern with maintaining power in the economic transition. The LPRP wants to maintain power and control, but also recognizes the need for economic reform. However, fostering market-oriented reforms and enhancing the private sector will lead to greater openness of the economy and society and undermine the party's power. Therefore, the Supreme People's Assembly adopted the constitution in 1991, which reiterated that a multiparty system would not be allowed. Thus, even though the constitution purports to guarantee freedom of speech and petition, the ruling party will not tolerate challenges to its exclusive exercise of power.[26]

The constitution emphasizes that the economy is market oriented and that all forms of economic ownership are permitted. Private property appears to be assured. However, Lending to state-owned firms is more common than lending to the nonstate sector, and the banking system is dominated by the state-owned banks. Recently, the government has made significant progress in privatizing SOEs and attracting FDI. However, private businesses face numerous constraints, including a lack of business skills and management capability; the weakness of the domestic financial sector, and hence the lack of credit; the excessive bureaucratic red tape, especially for exporters; the impediments to long-term private investment because of the time taken to approve FDI and the lack of guarantees in regard to extensions; the lack of a transparent system of property rights; the deficiencies in the legal and regulatory framework; and the insufficient infrastructure. Politically, as the private sector lacks an effective organization that represents its interests, it has only negligible influence on policy making. The role of the state in social and economic development continues to be essential in the transition process from the centrally planned economy to a market-oriented system.[27]

CAMBODIA

Since independence in 1953, Cambodia has experienced frequent, and unusually drastic, changes in its political and economic systems. Table 2.5 presents an outline of economic transition in relation to governance.

Table 2.5 Transition of political and economic systems in Cambodia

Years	Political system	Power	Economic system
Before 1953	Under the French	Held by the French	Colonial economy
1953-1970	Constitutional monarchy (Kingdom of Cambodia)	Held by Prince Norodom Sihanouk as prime minister	Market economy and then nationalization
1970-1975	Republic (The Khmer Republic)	Held by Lon Nol	War economy
1975-1979	Democratic Kampuchea	Khmer Rouge	Maoist agro-communism and central planning
1979-1989	The People's Republic of Kampuchea	Cambodian People's Party (Vietnamese backed)	Soviet-style central planning
1989-1993	The State of Cambodia	Cambodian People's Party (Vietnamese backed)	Liberalized central planning
1993-present	The Kingdom of Cambodia	Shared between CPP and FUNCINPEC*	Transition to a market economy

Note: *National United Front for an Independent, Neutral, Peaceful, and Cooperative Cambodia.

Before 1953, Cambodia had been a French colony for almost a century.[28] Under the first constitution, promulgated in 1947 under the French, Cambodia was governed by a monarchy with two parliaments elected by general elections: the

National Assembly and the Popular Assembly. All powers emanated from the King.[29]

After independence in 1953, under the leadership of Head of State Prince Norodom Sihanouk, Cambodia enjoyed economic prosperity and security comparable to its neighbors. In the late 1960s Prince Sihanouk became less influential and social cohesion began to erode.[30] Sihanouk was unable to appease the competing factions and was eventually toppled and deposed in a 1970 coup led by General Lon Nol.[31] In October 1970 the Khmer Republic came into being with General Lon Nol as president. Meanwhile Prince Sihanouk went to Beijing and mobilized forces to fight against the new republican government. The civil war spread all over the country.[32]

In April 1975 the Khmer Rouge captured Phnom Penh and established a new regime, Democratic Kampuchea, under the leadership of Pol Pot. This regime implemented a Maoist communist system entailing an extreme form of collectivism. All branches of government were unified under a single institution, the Party Central Committee.[33]

The massive agricultural mobilization, perhaps even larger in scope and more radical in nature than China's "Great Leap Forward," required the total evacuation of citizens from urban centers. Millions of Cambodians, especially from Phnom Pen, were forced to the countryside in order to develop an agriculture-centric communist economy.[34] The market and business activities were completely abolished, and there was no money or trade. No private ownership of any kind was allowed. Cambodia was cut off from the rest of the world except the PRC, the regime's main supporter.

The Pol Pot regime ended when Vietnamese troops and Cambodian resistance forces crossed into Cambodia and drove the Khmer Rouge from power in January 1979. Khmer Rouge forces withdrew from Phnom Penh, but continued to occupy areas along the Thai-Cambodian border. A new government, the People's Republic of Kampuchea (PRK), was established backed by Vietnamese troops, receiving major assistance from the former Soviet Union. The PRK regime was controlled by the communist party, Kampuchean (or Khmer) People's Revolutionary Party (KPRP), which evolved into today's Cambodian People's Party (CPP).

Politically, on October 23, 1991, the four main political factions signed the Peace Accords in Paris. This laid the groundwork for general elections in 1993 monitored by the United Nations Transitional Authority in Cambodia (UNTAC) and for the development of a liberal, multiparty system and a market economy. Following post election turmoil and intensive negotiations, the three major political parties – the National United Front for an Independent, Neutral, Peaceful, and Cooperative Cambodia (FUNCINPEC), the CPP, and the Buddhist Liberal Democratic Party – formed a coalition government. This political compromise resulted in an uneasy arrangement of two co-prime ministers as well as co-ministers of the interior and defense. Serious political tension emerged within the CPP-FUNCINPEC coalition government in 1997 leading to fighting among the armed forces in Phnom Penh. In late 1997 agreement was reached to hold Cambodia's second national election in 1998. Thirty-nine political parties ran, and three parties – the CPP, FUNCINPEC, and the Sam Rainsy Party – gained seats in the National Assembly. A new CPP-FUNCINPEC coalition government was formed in November 1998 and dominated by the CPP. The intertwining of the CPP and the state gave the CPP and Prime Minister Hun Sen a great advantage to restrict opposition parties' activities in rural areas, use coercive mechanism to co-opt and coerce voters, control local authorities (communes), and cultivate patronage politics throughout the country to support the CPP's continued domination. This political pattern, under "hybrid regime," dominated by the CPP, remains unchanged until today.[35]

Economically, after taking over the power, the KPRP sought a gradual transition from radical communism to moderate socialism or modified Soviet model, which combined a planned economy with markets, restored the banking system and national currency, abolished forced labor, introduced an eight-hour workday, inaugurated pay based on work performed, and tolerated and accepted the private entrepreneurship. The KPRP affirmed that the economy would have three main parts: the state economy, the collective economy and the family economy. Within the family economy, limited degrees of private ownership and entrepreneurship were permitted, which aided in the economy's recovery from war and eventually became legitimized as a fourth component. By 1985, the private sector became a vibrant and legal sector.[36] However, the overall goal of post-war recovery was to guide the economy toward socialization through state appropriation of all land and reorganization of agriculture into "solidarity groups" and collective farming.

The KPRP wrought further liberalization with the First Five-Year Plan (1986-1990), and sought re-building of agricultural and transportation infrastructures, creation of new industries and markets (lumber, rubber, fishing), enhancement of electricity, distribution of goods, increase in exports, and political and economic rapprochement with its Mekong neighbors (Laos and Vietnam) as well as other socialist nations.[37]

Cambodia actually embarked on the transition to a market economy in 1989, seeking external assistance from the West after the former Soviet Union collapsed. The new regime permitted limited private ownership of property and private enterprises, opened up the economy to international trade, and encouraged foreign and private investment in Cambodia. However, the private sector developed slowly, and the privatization of state owned enterprises began through long term leases to the private sector.[38]

Cambodia's transition to a market economy has accelerated since 1993. From 1993 through 1996 the economy grew at around 6 percent per year, led primarily by the service and industry sectors, and the inflow of foreign private investment and development assistance expanded rapidly. One of the most pressing governance issues is resolving dispute concerning access and tenure to land, forest, and fisheries resources. The lack of a clear legal framework and weak institutional capability to enforce existing laws are major obstacles to private sector development. Cambodia has by and large followed a transition path similar to

Vietnam and China – has gradually phased in market reforms and wider transparency.

Pre-Transition Socialist Models

Although not all these Asian countries necessarily qualify as "a command economy" as compared to their counterparts in Eastern Europe, the party-state in these countries played a similar predominant role in the national economy, major industries, foreign trade, finance, capital, and communication. The party-state set the goals, plans and policy agendas of the national economy, defined the basic parameters for all economic activities, controlled the major industries, supplies, products, prices, land and other major factors of production, initiated reforms if necessary and established the limits of reform. The Chinese called their old system "the highly centralized planned economy," the Vietnamese "the bureaucratic, centralized state-subsidy system, the Laotian "the centralized bureaucratic-management mechanism," and the Hun Sen regime in Cambodia "the Socialist production model." On the whole, their former model was in nature "state socialism" in the tradition of the Soviet model, which shares a number of notable characteristics, such as the party-state domination in policy making, central planning, state ownership, underdeveloped factor markets and commercial exchange, depressed mass consumption, vertical information flow system, and lack of material incentives.

CHINA

In China, the socialist transformation of urban industry and rural agriculture was roughly completed in the late 1950s. The initial success of the Chinese socialist transformation led Mao to believe that China's transition to communism could be accomplished earlier than he had expected. He initiated a more radical transformation in all aspects of society by using moral and political campaigns to transform China into a pure communist society during the Cultural Revolution between 1966 and 1976. The period between 1949 and 1978 was characterized by the attempt by the CCP to establish a new socialist planned economy based on a complete public ownership including collective and state sectors, wiping out virtually all private forms of ownership. The result of this transformation is the establishment of a Soviet-type "centrally planned command economy" in China, although the Chinese economy might differ from the Soviet economy in certain degree. It had the following characteristics:

- The Soviet-style state socialism. State owned and controlled the major means of production and exchange and therefore virtually all factors of production. State was the primary actor that set values attached to goods and services. State determined who would receive what products at what levels. State dominated, owned, planned, controlled, and regulated all major economic activities. The party-state, through its Central Planning Commission, set the goals, plans, policy agenda of the national economy, prices, wages, and output quotas, and allocated supplies and products according to national plans. The party-state initiated reforms if necessary and established the limits of reform.

- The highly centralized bureaucratic state. The power was centralized in the hands of communist party organs, the central planning agencies, and industrial ministries. Taxes and profits were accumulated by the central government and reallocated as budgetary grants to the local governments and as investment grants to enterprises throughout the country. Industrial branch ministries oversaw all economic activity and had national industrial monopolies.

- A collectivized agricultural sector. The Chinese agricultural structure was divided into three levels: communes, brigades, and production teams. Each subordinate unit received allocations of inputs and investment funding or subsidies, and in return was obliged to deliver to its superior unit a specified quantity of produce or procurement quotas set by centralized planning. All the means of production, including the land, machinery, draft animals, industrial facilities, were collectively owned. Annual and seasonal plans at production-team level determined resource use and production patterns for the entire unit, which then assigned labor, in large groups, on large plots of land. Incomes of all team members, largely in material quantities, were distributed proportionally based upon their work points accumulated annually.

- The policy of economic self-reliance. All foreign trade and business were monopolized and administered by the Ministry of Foreign Trade through specialized state trading corporations. Protected from the threat of both domestic and international competition, industrial enterprises and industrial ministries had little incentive to reduce their costs, raise productivity, or improve the quality of their products.[39]

NORTH KOREA

In North Korea, the Soviet model of economic system was adopted by the "socialist transformation" of the economy accomplished by 1962 when private ownership of the means of production, land, and industrial enterprises were replaced by two basic forms of ownership: state and cooperative ownership. The entire economy was placed under the centrally planned economic administration, which decided on production, prices, wages, and other factors of production. The emphasis was directed to self-reliance and heavy industries. North Korean agriculture was transformed at two stages: land reform in 1946 in which private owned land was confiscated and redistributed to landless farmers without compensation to land owners and collectivization in the mid-1950s in which small-scale, household agricultural economy was transformed into collective farming. The socialist transformation can be divided into four stages, each having specific tasks. The first period from 1945 to 1962 was characterized by the Stalinist model of socialism involving the coercive expropriation of the means of production, land reform, the socialist transformation, and the *Ch'ollima Undong* (the Flying Horse movement) based upon Kim Il Jung's *Juche* ideology, which was designed to indoctrinate people with socialist ideas and re-create socialist new men striving to realize the ideals Kim Il Jung envisioned. The second period ran from 1962 to 1983 during which North Korea adopted more Chinese methods of socialist construction using moral and political incentives and brainwashing of the masses in accordance with the party ideology. The third period was from 1984 to 1989 during which the economic policy was reassessed under the influence of the economic reforms in China and the Soviet Union and began to stress international trade and foreign investment through special trade zones and joint ventures. In 1990 the country entered the fourth period of its economic policy that incorporated more market elements into the economy when North Korea found itself in a serious situation that resulted from the collapse of communism in former Soviet Union and Eastern Europe.[40] The North Korean economy was one of the world's most highly centralized and planned, even by pre-1990 communist standards. It had the following characteristics:

- All industrial firms were either state-owned or cooperatives, the former contributing more than 90 percent of total industrial output in the 1960s.

- Collectives are the predominant forms of ownership and organization in agriculture while the remaining rural enterprises were organized as state farms. Small garden plots, fruit trees, the raising of poultry, pigs, bees, and the like were limited for personal consumption. Surplus farm products from these "backyard plots" were allowed to sell at the peasant market, which only constituted less than 1 percent of total retail transactions.

- In commerce almost all retail network was under state and cooperative ownership and nearly all goods were distributed through either state or cooperative stores. Prices for goods and services were controlled by the state.

- North Korea adopted an inward-looking development strategy or "self-reliance" policy (Kim Il Sung's *Juche* ideology), demonstrated in policies on domestic industrial development, foreign trade, foreign capital, imported technology, and other forms of international economic exchange. Priority was assigned to establishing a self-sufficient industrial base while consumer goods were produced primarily to satisfy domestic need. Since North Korea was one of CMEA members, its foreign trade and economic activities were primarily oriented toward these countries in accordance with the general directive binding on all Soviet-bloc's socialist countries.

- Machine building or heavy industry was regarded as the key to industrialization. Most economic resources were devoted to the production of heavy machinery, metals, and minerals.

- As in other Soviet-type or command economies, all major economic decisions concerning production, output targets, allocation of resources, prices, redistribution of national income, investment, etc. were made through the central planning blueprinted by the State Planning Committee. The party-state and its agencies largely determined what to produce and who got what. State control also extended to foreign trade, banking, transportation, communication, and all other sectors of the economy.[41]

VIETNAM

In Vietnam, after the communist victory in 1975, the Vietnamese Communist Party (VCP) played the leading role in establishing the foundations and principles of socialist transformation, deciding on strategies for economic development, setting growth targets, and launching socioeconomic transformations and reforms. Planning is a key characteristic of a centralized command economy. The VCP set the goal of unifying the economic system of the entire country under communism and taking the country through a period of transition to socialism in three stages. The first would conclude with the second Five-Year Plan in 1980; the second would integrate the South into the "line of socialist revolution" and "line of building a socialist economy" which would involve "socialist industrialization" through five successive five-year plans till 2005; and the third would extend till 2010 and would "perfect" the transition to socialism.[42] To achieve the goal of socialist transformation, the party launched a series of programs of nationalization and collectivization and transformed the economy into Soviet-type state socialism characterized by the predominant state ownership, five-year plans, and collective agriculture. At the time of unification in 1976, the northern part of Vietnam had many characteristics of a centrally planned economy, although it was not an Eastern European-type state socialism in which nearly everything belonged to the state sector and all prices were set by the state. The northern part of Vietnam had the following characteristics from which the departure was made under *doi moi*:

- Enterprises were run by either the state, local government, or cooperatives, and agriculture (except for household plots) was collectivized. More than 96 percent of peasant households were classified as members of "high-level cooperatives" by 1975, which was essentially modeled on the Chinese "socialist transformation," and central control over planting decisions and farm work was accomplished.

- Management of the economy was based on comprehensive central planning, tailored by industrial ministries and provincial planning agencies, and all planning was made in material balances.

- All key prices, wages, money, interest, and exchange rates were controlled by the state, with the market playing only a marginal role in decisions about resource allocation. There were barely any capital, labor, and other factor markets.

- Large subsidies in the budget went to state enterprises, which enjoyed a so-called "soft-budge constraint" (i.e., any losses would be covered by the state budget).

- All foreign trade was monopolized and administered by the Ministry of Foreign Trade through specialized state trading companies. The country joined the Soviet-bloc's Council for Mutual Economic Assistance (CMEA) and coordinated its five-year development and trade plans closely with those of the Soviet Union and other CMEA member states. Planning agencies set trade goals on the basis of the overall planning targets and quotas required by bilateral trade agreements with various CMEA members.

- Official foreign exchange rates were of accounting significance only, with administered prices bearing hardly any relation to world market prices. The government officially detached the domestic market from the world market, the capital goods market from the consumer goods market, and the national market from the sub-national markets.

- In the South, initial emphasis was on economic restoration rather than transition to socialism, but in 1976, private enterprises were pressured to enter into joint ventures with the state firms, and in early 1977, agricultural collectivization (proceeded by compulsory quota sales) was carried out to hasten economic integration with the North. The government also attempted to nationalize banks and major industries in the South to bring the financial and industrial sectors under state control and communize the commercial, market-oriented Southern economy. By that time, the whole country had entered a new stage – "transition to socialism" in which, according to Party Secretary Le Duan, "the whole country fulfills a single strategic task of carrying out socialist revolution."[43]

LAO PDR

In Laos, some similar programs of nationalization and agricultural collectivization were launched in 1976 under the Lao People's Revolutionary Party (LPRP), which was essentially Leninist, modeled on the old Indochina Communist Party, supported by so-called "mass organizations" of the transmission belt for the party, such as the Federation of Lao Women, the People's Revolutionary Youth, and the Lao Federation of Trade Union. The LPRP government began to introduce a three-year plan in 1978 with the goal of bringing Laos onto the CMEA's five-year planning cycle in 1981-85.[44] Despite the lesser extent to which a centrally planned economy on the Soviet model was created, due to the least developed economy in the world, the Laotian economy shared some characteristics of state socialism in many ways.

- Banking, transport, communication, forestry, and all larger industrial enterprises were nationalized and owned by the state. Larger factories that were directly run by the Ministry of Industry, Handicrafts and Forestry account for 80 percent of Laos' industrial production. Factories processing agricultural crops, including rice mills, were under control of the Ministry of Agriculture. Smaller workshops and small-scale manufacturing and handicraft enterprises in private hands engaged primarily in the production of commercial goods.

- Attempts were made to collectivize agriculture though opposition from peasants forced the government temporarily to curtail the program and to proceed more carefully thereafter, following the Chinese model from lower-level mutual aid teams to higher-level cooperatives. More than 3,000 cooperatives were established by the end of 1985, comprising 61.5 percent of all peasant families farming 58 percent of all cultivated land.

- State long-term economic goals and polices were implemented through five-year plans modeled on Soviet-type state socialism. SOEs have no managerial autonomy. Prices, salaries, investment, reinvestment, financing, and output targets were all determined by central or provincial authorities in accordance with the central planning. A single financial institution – the State Bank – conducted all banking activities. State finances became burdened with heavy subsidies to state enterprises. The state distribution system provided basic goods to the population either in the form of coupons to be used in state stores or at low and stable prices.

- All foreign trade was monopolized and administered by the State Trading Company or conducted by provincial governments, state enterprises and the army. Private companies that attempted to engage in foreign trade had to be granted a license and limited to dealing with certain products. Trade within provinces and inter-provincial trade were predominated by the state trade network and the local people's collective network.[45]

CAMBODIA

In Cambodia, a total collectivization of agriculture and a complete nationalization of the economy were rapidly carried out under the Khmer Rouge regime (Democratic Kampuchea) from 1975 to 1979. Radical socialist transformation was forcefully instituted and private ownership was totally abolished. Money, markets, even barter trade were abolished, and a command economy was fully instituted with centrally-directed production and distribution.[46] During the 1980s, the Cambodian economy experienced a modified Soviet-type "planned economy with markets" under the Heng Samrin regime (the People's Republic of Kampuchea) installed by Vietnam. Despite the changes from the DK regime to the PRK regime, the current regime, in many ways, including all of the members of the present leadership with revolutionary background, had its ultimate origins in the same revolutionary victory of 1975 as did the rival Pol Pot DK group.[47] At least until 1989, the PRK economy still had the following characteristics of Soviet-type state socialism:

- There were three major types of economic organizations, state, cooperative, and family. Under the state ownership came all industry, finance, transport, communication, foreign trade, and some large-scale agriculture, especially industrial crops. The family economy included most retail marketing, individual artisan, handicraft, repair workshops, some agriculture, and much commodity import trade. The cooperative sector included a significant portion of agriculture and certain urban enterprises such as restaurants.[48] However, "after the 5th Party Congress in 1985 a fourth, private sector, began to emerge, and in 1989 a fifth sector comprising state-private joint ventures."[49]

- In agriculture, 97 percent of the rural population was organized into 100,000 "solidarity groups" (*krom sammakis*) of fifteen families each who would cooperatively produce and share in the rewards. These groups received land that was to be cultivated collectively while being allowed to have a small private plot for each household.[50]

- The Kampuchean People's Revolutionary Party (KPRP), led by Heng Samrin, set Cambodia's economic development policies and defined Cambodia's new socialist direction and the role of the state in economic affairs. A system of central planning, with physical production targets and administrative controls, was created. All major economic decisions concerning production targets for each economic sector, allocation of resources, prices, redistribution of national income, investment, etc. were made by the government. As in other Soviet-type state socialist economies, five-year plans were devised to implement party's economic goals and policies which coordinated with those of the state planning commissions of Vietnam and Laos.[51]

- All foreign trade was controlled and administered by the Ministry of Local and Foreign Trade. The state trading agency, the Kampuchean Export and Import Corporations, was responsible for exports, imports, and foreign aid. The National Trade Commission was created to be in charge of both internal and external economic coordination. The KPRP, like its predecessors, Sihanouk and Pol Pot, urged the Cambodians to pursue the economic policy of self-reliance and develop the economy "in the spirit of mainly relying on one's own forces" while stressing economic and technological cooperation with Vietnam, the Soviet Union, and countries of East Europe.[52]

Conclusion

All the Asian countries under study adopted the Soviet model of central planning, collectivized agriculture, and state ownership in initial phases of their socialist transformation after the communist party took over power. While some degree of variations may exist, we can conceptualize many commonalities these countries shared in their economic systems from which a transition was made since the late 1970s.

1. Similar historical and cultural traditions of authoritarianism that was antagonistic to democracy and market;
2. Similar party-state political apparatus with highly centralized, monistic, dictatorial, paternalistic leadership and power structure;
3. Similar ideological commitment and philosophical absolutism, which served as a means of controlling and mobilizing the population and legitimizing the political and socioeconomic policies and arrangements;
4. Similar centralized and planned economy, based upon the socialist mode of production, exchange, and distribution, sharing much in common with respect to their ownership of the means of production, economic institutions, decision-making, and allocation of resources, and therefore suffering from common systemic failings and problems; and
5 Similar pattern of economic transition, with their reforms characterized by regime-led, gradual, partial, experimental, and phased transition.

However, new developments have been taking place in these countries since the late 1970s, particularly through the 1980s and 1990s, which has marked a new stage in the economic development and transformed the centrally planned command economy into some kind of market-oriented or based economy. All market reforms in these countries carried different name tags, such as *doi moi* in Vietnam, NEM in Lao PDR, and "socialist market economy" in China, and all initially started with agricultural reform, trade liberalization, controlled opening of the previously closed economy, and then expanded to the areas of prices, finance, taxation, ownership, and legal systems. However, what factors or situations forced or propelled the leadership of the communist party in these countries to implement the market reforms that were aimed at transformation of the socialist planned economy they had sought to establish in their communist movements and revolutions? Economic failure has been identified as the major cause for the reform and economic transition. But, what caused the economic failure? What other factors must also be considered to understand this phenomenal development in these communist and post-communist states? This will become the major task of the next chapter. The answer to this question would help us further understand the choice of reform strategy and policy in different countries between a Big Bang strategy (for which Poland, the Soviet Union, and many Eastern European countries are the model) and a gradualist approach (which is typified by the most successful case of China).

Notes

[1] The People's Republic of China: "The Transition to Socialism, 1953-1957." http://www-chaos.umd.edu/history/prc.html#transition

[2] The University of Chicago Chronicle: "China's Great Leap Forward." March 14, 1996 Vol. 15, No. 13. http://chronicle.uchicago.edu/960314/china.shtml

[3] China Online; Discovering China. "The Middle Kingdom." http://chineseculture.about.com/gi/dynamic/offsite.htm?site=http%3A%2F%2Flibrary.thinkquest.org%2F26469%2Fcultural-revolution%2F

[4] The People's Republic of China IV: "China and the Four Modernizations, 1979-1982." http://www-chaos.umd.edu/history/prc4.html#postmao

[5] People's Republic of China: "Reforms, 1980-1988." http://www-chaos.umd.edu/history/prc5.html

[6] Doowon Lee, "North Korean Economic Reform: Past Efforts and Future Prospects," in John McMillan and Barry Naughton, eds., *Reforming Asian Socialism* (Ann Arbor: The University of Michigan Press, 1996).

[7] Alexander Zhebin, "Russia and North Korea: An Emerging, Uneasy Partnership," *Asian Survey*, vol. 35, no. 8, 1995, pp. 726-739.

[8] Rhee Sang-Woo, "North Korea in 1990" Lonesome Struggle to Keep Chuch'e," *Asian Survey*, vol. 31, no. 1, 1991, pp. 71-78.

[9] Marcus Noland, "Famine and Reform in North Korea," *Working Paper*, Institute for International Economics (July 2003), p.1.

[10] Brief accounts of NK socialist transformation after revolution and establishment of centrally planned economy http://www.cx.unibe.ch/oefre/law/icl/kn__indx.html

[11] James Brooke, "Quietly, North Korea Opens Markets" http://www.fortunecity.com/meltingpot/champion/65/pyongyang_watch.htm; Victor D. Cha, "North Korea's Economic Reforms and Security Intentions," Testimony before US Senate Committee on Foreign Relations, http://foreign.senate.gov/testimony/2004/ChaTestimony040302.pdf

[12] Infoplease, Vietnam. "Two Vietnams." http://www.infoplease.com/ce6/world/A0861793.html

[13] Malanie Beresford, *National Unification and Economic Development in Vietnam* (London: Macmillan, 1989), Chapter 8; Andrew Vickerman, *The Fate of the Peasantry: Premature Transition to Socialism in the Democratic Republic of Vietnam* (New Haven: Yale Southeast Asian Studies Monograph Series 24, 1986).

[14] Adam Fforde and Stefan de Vylder, *From Plan to Market: The Economic Transition in Vietnam* (Boulder: Westview Press, 1996); Thanh Son, "45 nam xay dung va phat trine nen cong nghiep Viet Nam" (45 Years of Vietnamese Industrial Development), in Vien Kinh Te Hoc, *45 nam kinh te Viet Nam 1945-1990* (45 Years of Vietnamese Economy, 1945-1990) (Hanoi: Khoa Hoc Xa Hoi, 1990), pp. 72 and 76.

[15] Tri Vo Nhan, "Party Politics and Economic Performance: the Second and Third Five-Year Plans Examined," in David Marr and Christine P. White, eds., *Postwar Vietnam: Dilemmas in Socialist Development* (Ithaca: Southeast Asia Program, Cornell University, 1988), pp. 80-81.

[16] The Library of Congress, Country Studies (Vietnam). "The Second Five-Year Plan." http://lcweb2.loc.gov/cgi-bin/query/r?frd/cstdy:@field(DOCID+vn0071

[17] The Library of Congress, Country Studies (Vietnam). "The Third Five-Year Plan." http://lcweb2.loc.gov/cgi-bin/query/r?frd/cstdy:@field(DOCID+vn0072

[18] The Library of Congress, Country Studies (Vietnam). "The Fourth Five-Year Plan." http://lcweb2.loc.gov/cgi-bin/query/r?frd/cstdy:@field(DOCID+vn0073

[19] Thayer Watkins. San Jose State University Economics Department. "Vietnam's Doi Moi Program." http://www2.sjsu.edu/faculty/watkins/vietnam.htm

[20] ASEAN. "ASEAN Free trade Area." http://www.aseansec.org/viewpdf.asp?file=/pdf/afta.pdf

[21] Clay G. Wescott, ed., *Key Governance Issues in Cambodia, Lao PDR, Thailand, and Viet Nam* (Manila, Philippines: Asian Development Bank, 2001), Chapter 3, http://www.adb.org/Documents/Books/Key_Governance_Issues/

[22] Yves Bourdet, "Rural Reforms and Agricultural Productivity in Laos," *Journal of Developing Areas*, no. 29, January 1995, p. 165.

[23] Clay G. Wescott, 2001.

[24] Ibid.

[25] Ibid.

[26] Ibid.

[27] Ibid.

[28] David P. Chandler, *A History of Cambodia* (Boulder, Colorado: Westview Press, 1993).

[29] Raoul M. Jennar, *The Cambodian Constitutions: 1953-1993* (Bangkok: White Lotus, 1995).

[30] David P. Chandler, *The Tragedy of Cambodian History* (New Haven: Yale University Press, 1991).

[31] Library of Congress. Country Report, Cambodia. "The Cambodian Left; The March 1970 Coup d'Etat; and the Fall of Phnom Pen." http://lcweb2.loc.gov/frd/cs/khtoc.html

[32] David P. Chandler, 1991.

[33] Ibid.

[34] Library of Congress. "Society under the Angkar." http://lcweb2.loc.gov/cgi-bin/query/r?frd/cstdy:@field(DOCID+kh0038

[35] Kheang Un, "Patronage Politics and Hybrid Democracy: Political Change in Cambodia, 1993-2003," *Asian Perspective*, vol. 29, no. 2, 2005, pp. 203-230.

[36] Exploitz. Cambodia: New Economic Policy and System." http://www.exploitz.com/ Cambodia-New-Economic-Policy-And-System-cg.php

[37] Exploitz. "Cambodia -- First Plan, 1986-1990." http://www.exploitz.com/Cambodia-First-Plan-198690-cg.php

[38] Lay Prohas, "Transition from centrally planned economy to a market economy in Cambodia," in Mathews G. Chunakara, ed., *Indochina: From Socialism to Market Economy* (Hong Kong, China: Indochina Concerns Conference, 1996).

[39] Susan L. Shirk, "The Politics of Industrial Reform," in Elizabeth J. Perry and Christine Wong, *The Political Economy of Reform in Post-Mao China* (Cambridge, MA: Harvard University Press, 1985), pp. 197-198.

[40] Marina Ye Trigubenko, "Economic Characteristics and Prospect for Development," in Han S. Park, ed., *North Korea: Ideology, Politics, and Economy* (Englewood Cliffs, NJ: Prentice Hall, 1996), pp. 143-144.

[41] Andrea Matles Savada, *North Korea: A Country Study* (Washington, DC: U.S. Department of the Army, 1993), pp. 107-110, 127.

[42] Ronald J. Cima, *Vietnam: A Country Study* (Washington, DC: U.S. Department of the Army, 1987), pp. 149-150.

[43] Börje Ljunggren, "Market Economies under Communist Regimes: Reform in Vietnam, Laos, and Cambodia," in Börje Ljunggren, ed., *The Challenge of Reform in Indochina* (Cambridge, MA: Harvard University Press, 1993), pp. 58-59.

[44] Richard Pomfret, *Asian Economics in Transition* (Cheltenham, UK: Edward Elgar, 1996), pp. 67-68.

[45] Martin Stuart-Fox, *Laos: Politics, Economics, and Society* (Boulder, CO: Lynne Rienner, 1986), pp. 97-129; Ichiro Otani and Chi Do Pham, "The Lao People's Democratic Republic: Systemic Transformation and Adjustment" *Occasional Paper 137*, International Monetary Fund, May 1996, pp. 9, 11, 24, 27, and 43.

[46] Michael Vickery, "Notes on the Political Economy of the People's Republic of Kampuchea (PRK)" *Journal of Contemporary Asia*, vol. 20, no. 4, 1990, p. 439.

[47] Michael Vickery, *Kampuchea: Politics, Economics, and Society* (Boulder, CO: Lynne Rienner, 1986), pp. 25-27.

[48] Ibid., pp. 128-129.

[49] Michael Vickery, 1990, p. 442.

[50] Russell Ross, *Cambodia: A Country Study* (Washington, DC: U.S. Department of the Army, 1990), p. 160.

[51] Ibid., pp. 156, 158.

[52] Ibid., pp. 159, 168.

Chapter 3

Explaining Asian Transition from Communism

This chapter attempts to identify causal variables that contributed to reform efforts across these Asian countries and explain why these governments launched the reforms and made their transitions from centrally planned to market-based or market-oriented economies. Countries differ, and so do the reforms in different countries. "Nonetheless, there are commonalities across reform experiences and thus a basis for comparison and reflection about general causes and dynamics."[1] China, North Korea, Vietnam, Laos, and Cambodia are communist states that had close ties with the Soviet Union at their early stages of communist development and followed the Soviet model of agricultural collectivization, priority of heavy industry, state ownership, central planning, and state monopoly of foreign trade, although Laos and Cambodia never fulfilled state socialism to the same extent as other Asian communist states did in their political and economic transformation. Therefore, they all faced some similar pre-reform structural problems and economic difficulties, which accounted for the dynamics of social changes and transition or, in other words, the socioeconomic and structural problems were the main factors that contributed to the reform efforts in these countries since the early 1980s.

Common Causes

The purpose of this chapter is to provide an adequate causal explanation for such a phenomenal historical experience: why the Asian communist states adopted economic reforms and made their transitions from the centrally planned economy to market-oriented or market-based economy. Different theoretical approaches to transition have provided various analytical frameworks for a comparative study of transition across regions and nations, and suggested a large number of explanatory variables for the transition in different countries under different circumstances. However, most of scholars tend to focus on one-dimensional or single-level variable in rich detail, and the choice of focus often reflects individual scholars' judgment of which level of analysis is likely to be most fruitful and can contribute to a good understanding of the causes, patterns and outcomes of transition. While single-cause explanations can illustrate different aspects of transition, generate questions and hypotheses, and yield some partial explanations, they do not provide an adequate causal explanation for the question of why the transition occurred in these countries and in particular times, because, rather than any single force or variable, a joint effect of multiple causal forces propelled the transition to occur in these countries. As Gabriel A. Almond and Laura Roselle suggest, in their overview of the literature in communism studies in the last several decades, no single theoretical model under examination captures the whole of the political reality, and "the multi-model theoretical approach gives us a more secure understanding of political patterns and potentialities."[2] The idea of causal depth is well explained by Richard Miller in his book *Fact and Method*,[3] and the same idea of causal depth can also be applied in this study. We can argue that it is a combination of systemic, economic, ideological, political, and international factors that contributed to economic reforms in communist states. Asian transition from communism may be usefully viewed as a sub-category of a more generic phenomenon of transition from communism in the late 1990s.[4]

- Systemic/economic crisis. Former centrally planned economic system impeded productivity. The state maintained a tight control over the economy through the targets of state planning and the method of administrative command, rejecting the role of market forces in the economy. Enterprises had no autonomy and workers had no incentive and creativity. The lack of capital, technology, management skills, inefficiency and incentive problems, soft budget constraints, bottlenecks and shortages, all were observed in any socialist economy. Economic necessity was the mother of reformist invention. At the root of the economic troubles was their crisis of the central planning system and nonproductive economies. Economic conditions and performances were getting worse, and most of these countries had experienced hard economic times without effective, feasible solutions. The old systems lacked the capacity to revitalize their economies and improve their economic performances.

- Ideology crisis. As the communist countries fell far behind the Western capitalism in terms of economic productivity, social well-being, and quality of life, as well as so many systemic or structural problems could not be resolved, more and more general population and political elite became disillusioned with the once-utopian ideology of communism.

- Political factors. Reformists within the system became stronger and they sought a way out of the crisis and wanted to try different alternatives to traditional model of state socialism. Market became a most viable alternative they chose.

- Changing of the guard in leadership. The generational and educational factors are formative factors shaping the characteristics of the new leadership. Most of them are technocrats and better educated than old revolutionaries, and they are more reform-oriented and open-minded political leaders.

- Learning experience. The economic transition is also shaped by the multi-faceted socialist reform experience, such as lessons from the Lenin's NEP, the pre-Gorbachev Soviet reform after Stalin, Gorbachev's "Glasnost and Perestroika," the broader international reform experience of all parts of the communist world, including Imre Nagy's Hungarian "Goulash Market Socialism" and Alexander Dubcek's Prague Spring's "Socialism with a Human Face." Given the similarity of structures from which they began and the common nature of many of the problems with which they tried to deal, these Asian countries learned to adopt successful measures and avoid failures.[5]

- International factors/external influence. External shocks in the late 1980s and the early 1990s, such as the collapse of communism in the Soviet bloc, the cutback in aid from the former Soviet Union, decreased trade between these countries and the former socialist countries, and the resulting foreign exchange shortage delivered a critical blow to the already faltering economy.

Country Variations

Country variations can be observed from the experience of five countries in East and Southeast Asia under study. Domestic factors may play a larger role in large countries while external influences may play a more important role in small countries. However, it is a combination of multiple factors that contributed to country variations in economic transition from state socialism. Figure 3.1 outlines the main line of causality, from Block 1 to Block 5. The economic transition begins with Block 1: systemic crisis, economic crisis, and external changes and impact. The Soviet influence was one of the major factors that determined how the socialist model was adopted in a country. Therefore, the Soviet changes and impact also played a significant role in Asian transition from state socialism. However, it played a more important role in smaller countries than in a big country such as China. Block 1 causes Block 2: the realization among the leadership that the system of traditional centrally planned economy or classical socialism was failing led to attempts to incorporate market mechanisms to make socialism efficient and productive – which marks the end of classical socialism and the beginning of market socialism. Block 1 and Block 2 together cause Block 3: the leadership perception of crisis situation and their strategic choices of reform policy determined the sequencing of reforms in different areas, beginning from the agricultural area. Block 4 contains the major areas of reforms: agricultural reform, price reform, opening up policy, financial reform, enterprise reform, sharing holding reform, which were employed by these countries to achieve their reform policy goals. As the leadership perceived the necessity of balancing the economic reform and the political stability, the reform became a partial, gradual, experimental, and phased-in process, which also varied from country to country in its scope, content, and pace. Block 5 contains a list of transition outcomes, such as individual household farming, market oriented economy, integration into the world economy, development of factor markets, emergence of private and non-state sectors, and economic growth, which corresponded to each of the reform policies and measures. The outcomes have transformed these communist countries into a kind of market-based or market-oriented, hybrid economy. Country variations from prototype occur because the prototype does not preclude variations due to specific circumstances and historical contexts in different countries. For example, China's transition was significantly different from the former Soviet Union because of their different levels development. Cambodia and Lao PDR were profoundly affected by the county's proximity to Vietnam. North Korea's reform was different from other Asian states because it was knocked in and constrained by its external relationships with the outside world. In what follows, we will examine the country variations in the causes of reform and transition from the centrally planned economy to market socialism (China, North Korea, Vietnam, Laos) or market economy (Cambodia).

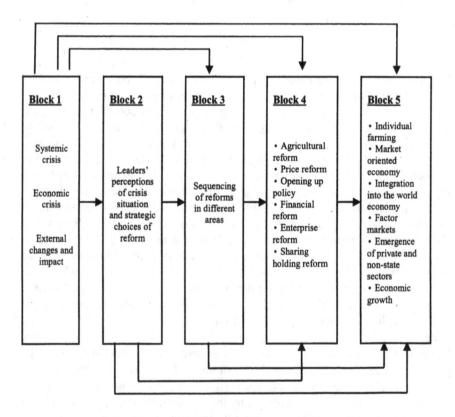

Figure 3.1   Causality of economic transition in East and Southeast Asia

CHINA

The Chinese reform was a direct result of severe national trauma of the Cultural Revolution that demolished the administrative structures of the party and the government, plunged the country into a big turmoil for 10 years, with 30 percent of party officials and 75 percent of the top economic officials purged, more than 700,000 people persecuted, of which about 35,000 died. The "leftist" economic policy was guided by the principles of common ownership, mass mobilization, moral incentive, centralization, and self-sufficiency, which resulted in disastrous consequences in the agriculture and industry. Many of top party-state officials began to question the utility of the principles at the early stage of socialism and believed that more pragmatic methods should be adopted in economic policy making. It was in this pragmatic context that Deng Xiaoping uttered his famous "cats" theory in support of economic reform. Part of their reform strategy was to permit family farming without privatization of land, use of material incentive, selected decentralization, and a limited open-up of the economy to the world market.[6]

The economic reform was also driven by another major concern of the top leadership – how to restore the popular trust in the CCP leadership after the traumatic consequences of the Cultural Revolution. There was a general agreement among the CCP leaders on the necessity of economic reform which would allow the CCP to deliver the promised goods and raise people's living standards through the "Four Modernizations." However, the communist leaders disagreed on the method, content, sequence, and scope, because many of the Chinese leaders, planners, officials, and economists believed that the central planning system had not reached its limits due to the disruptions of the Cultural Revolution and that economic performance and people's living standards could be improved by simply improving the planning system, introducing material incentives to individuals and local governments, allowing certain markets to play certain roles, and increasing agricultural investment, etc.[7] The different visions of reform led to continuous debates and conflicts within the regime over the different choices of reform policy in post-Mao China throughout the 1980s and 1990s, which will be further studied in the next chapter.

In the late 1970s and the early 1980s, many party and state leaders began to be aware of the systemic flaws in the Soviet model of centrally planned economy and sought a way to reform it. In China, former highly centralized plan system impeded productivity. The state maintained a tight control over the economy through the targets of state planning and the method of administrative command, rejecting the role of market forces in the economy. Since private enterprises were virtually wiped out and replaced by various forms of state and collective ownership, the Chinese enterprises were almost all under the party-state control or influence. Enterprises had no autonomy and workers had no incentive and creativity. Egalitarianism existed in the state distribution system with everyone "eating from the same big pot" – creating an "iron rice bowl."

Although the pre-reform leadership had tried to resolve the problem by granting the local government more power of economic decision making, the simple measure of decentralization had failed to bring out any substantial changes in the economic structure and operation mechanism. As Chinese economists described, the Chinese economy had moved in a vicious circle – it was lifeless when controlled, but disorder occurred when it as decontrolled, triggering another round of control and decontrol, and so on.[8]

In agriculture, although the commune system and collective farming achieved most of the main goals for which it was established, such as development of rural infrastructure and irrigation systems, creation of a rural management system that served political and social needs, creation of rural industries that fostered economic support systems, they failed to improve agricultural productivity and output, either in quantity, quality or variety because of the absence of economic incentives for individuals and collectives and the inefficiencies of the rural economic management as was common in the industrial area.[9]

China's market reform and economic liberalization can be considered as a response to the failure of its previous economic and social programs of the Great Leap Forward and the Cultural Revolution. However, as was the case in Vietnam, Laos, Cambodia and any other communist states, the origins and policy choices of the Chinese reform were also determined by the elite politics, – a change in the ruling elite would become necessary for the change in the economic policy. As the economic reform of the 1980s coincided with a period of leadership succession, the succession contest provided a compelling cause for Deng Xiaoping who used innovation in economic policy to discredit Hua Guofeng and obtain support from different groups of the party-state elite.[10] After Mao's death and the demise of the Gang of Four, Deng Xiaoping and his allies who had been marginalized for many years slowly obtained and secured the power. Deng Xiaoping allied with the conservative reformers and the older generation of party leaders, such as Ye Jianying, Chen Yun, Li Xiannian, in his effort to defeat Hua Guofeng and augmented his support and power base for the reform programs he advocated. This enabled Deng Xiaoping and reformers to promulgate the wide-ranging and significant market reform program. Understanding the futility and repercussions of both the Great Leap Forward and the Cultural Revolution, the Third Plenum of the Eleventh National Party Congress Central Committee in 1978 decided that the party's central focus must shift from the "class struggle" to economic development and "Four Modernizations," and the party must adopt pragmatic economic policy and advanced technology to promote economic growth and modernizations. Reform and opening up of the economy became the necessary conditions for achieving the party's new policy goals.[11] The transition of power to younger, better educated, more reform-minded leaders and technocrats has continued uninterruptedly for more than two decades. Such a transition also ensures the continuity of market reform policy pioneered by Deng Xiaoping and other earlier communist reformers.

NORTH KOREA

In North Korea, inherent structural problems, such as the imbalance between heavy and light industry, the lack of capital and technology, inefficiency and incentive problems, soft budget constraints, bottlenecks and shortages, which were observed in any socialist economy, produced unbalanced growth in the 1970s and began a period of stagnant growth in the 1980s.

Furthermore, external shocks in the late 1980s and the early 1990s, such as the collapse of communism in the Soviet bloc, the cutback in aid from the former Soviet Union and China, decreased trade between North Korea and the former socialist countries, and the resulting foreign exchange shortage delivered a critical blow to the already faltering economy. This led North Korean leaders to start thinking about lessons, practical implications, and possible solutions in response to the new challenges. Its neighboring socialist state, China, has provided a successful example of gradual and controlled reform under the communist rule although North Korean leaders have tried to learn from China cautiously.

The goal of building a "powerful and prosperous nation" (*kangsong taeguk*) also requires economic reform to achieve modernization of the economy and the military. To solve the above problems and achieve the national goal, the North Korea government prescribed partial reform and open-door policy in the mid-1980s, which were more or less equivalent to the Chinese and Vietnamese model.[12] As Pyongyang recognized that it had been unable to promulgate successfully its goal of self reliability and sustainability, particularly after the collapse of the Soviet Union in 1991, Pyongyang began to seek wider economic liberalization and open-door policy. Significantly, Pyongyang has largely abolished the ration system, promoted the selling of products in markets by state enterprises, increased prices and wages, allowed wider currency flotation, phased out subsidies to state-owned firms, and tolerated and even encouraged greater degrees of private ownership and entrepreneurship (especially among farmers).[13]

The phenomenon of North Korean economic liberalization cannot be fully understood and analyzed without acknowledging the influence of Beijing and Moscow. Their economic transitions have exposed North Korea to policy alternatives and, in particular, China's economic reform and open-door policy have provided a successful example for North Korea and encouraged it to make a necessary change.[14] As China's economic transition has benefited from Hong Kong, North Korean new economic changes could not be realized without the continued support of Seoul. North Korea has achieved notable rapprochement with South Korea under the "Sunshine Policy," which has established closer economic and diplomatic ties between the two Koreas. The program has established wider economic links in the form of a free economic and trade zone at Kaeson for South Korean enterprises, in addition to the northeastern port cities of Unggi, Ch'ngjin and Najin.[15] Foreign capital has entered North Korea and operated not only in the free economic and trade zones but also in Pyongyang.[16] Taken together, these developments have been instrumental in helping to avert famine, fostering wider liberalization, and increasing standards of living.

VIETNAM

As in other socialist countries, economic necessity was the mother of reformist invention in Vietnam. The economic crisis of 1979 was caused internally by the overhasty socialist transformation of the South that depressed industrial, commercial and agricultural outputs, the declining productivity of the Northern economy, and externally by the sharp cutoff of all Chinese aid and trade and the American embargo for the Vietnamese invasion in Cambodia.[17] In 1988-89, the termination of CMEA assistance and the withdrawal of support by the Soviet Union were external forces that pushed the VCP to adopt more liberal economic policy and open up its economy to the world economy.[18]

The starting point of economic reform was in September 1979 when the Sixth Plenum of the Central Committee of the Fourth Party's Congress mapped out urgent measures to address the crisis that had arisen from programs of socialist transformation and construction based on subjectivism, wishful thinking, and inadequate economic premises.[19] The Party Central Committee decided to make a tactical retreat by making some adjustments to the plan, relaxing some controls on private production, suspending the socialization campaigns in the South, launching a price reform, experimenting output contracts (*khoan san pham*) in agriculture, and allowing some degree of autonomy in decision making in industrial enterprises.[20]

However, the great push for further reforms came when reformists took over some key posts at the Sixth Party Congress in 1986 and these individual leaders urged the party to be committed to *doi moi* and responded to the crises in more pragmatic ways.[21] The general characteristics of Vietnamese reform are similar to China: transition from centrally planned economy to a market-oriented economy under state direction and guided by socialist principles. Following a conservative retrenchment between 1982 and 1985, the VCP adopted *doi moi* in 1986 to expand the role of market and private sector, decentralize management authority, and open up the economy to the outside world.

One immediate response to the trade shock after the collapse of the Soviet Union was to turn to the West for foreign capital and markets. Hanoi, like Beijing, Pyongyang, and Vientiane, took a graduate approach to the open-door policy in order to maintain its control over the economy and the stability of socialist regimes. However, Hanoi had to decrease import quotas and tariffs as a means to attract foreign investment, secure loans from the IMF, World Bank and Asia Development Bank, and obtain AFTA (ASEAN Free Trade Area) membership and WTO accession.[22]

Vietnam's economic transition was also in many ways a byproduct of the international geopolitics of the eighties and early nineties, too. The transition from command to market economy was part of a more generic phenomenon of transition from communism in the late 1990s that swept through Moscow and Beijing. Hanoi's adoption of *doi moi* was in many ways encouraged by the successful reforms of Deng Xiaoping and was in particular a response to the collapse of the Soviet Union, which deprived Hanoi of badly needed financial and technological assistance. During the 1980s, the Soviet Union was Vietnam's largest trading partner and major aid donor – about $1 billion per year, reaching 57 percent of GDP in 1989. CMEA supplies of key inputs, especially refined petroleum and fertilizers, ceased in 1991. After the collapse of communism in the Soviet Union and Eastern Europe, Vietnam could no longer rely on the Eastern block for economic and financial support.[23] Increasingly isolated and on its own, Vietnam had few tenable options with which to choose from though the choice meant a risky course for the VCP leadership.

LAO PDR

In 1986, the Lao PDR Government launched its "New Economic Mechanism," with the aim of moving away from a centrally planned economy towards an open market – "to develop an integrated market economy open to international trade."[24] Since then, there has been steady progress towards economic reform. In Laos, there are a number of reasons for reform: small-scale subsistence farming, failed collectivization that reduced agricultural production, influence of China's and Vietnam's reform, the collapse of the Soviet Union, the influence from international aide agencies such as IMF, World Bank, and Asian Development Bank.

The promulgation of state-centric, command-style economy had proved in many ways difficult for Vientiane by the mid-1980s because most of its population was agrarian and the economy was based on small-scale subsistence farming.[25] Furthermore, the Laotian population was highly illiterate, unskilled, and widely diffused across a large and often inhospitable countryside. As the party leadership recognized at the Party Congress in 1985, at which market-oriented reform (NEM) was adopted, the idea of establishing a centrally planned economy in a country with virtually no communication infrastructure for a population scattered in small valleys had proved unrealizable. Moreover, the inefficiency of SOEs required constant state subsidies which drained the state of financial resources and generated a huge deficit. Agricultural collectivization failed due to peasant resistance forced by the party officials and decreased rice production created food shortage and peasant discontent. Therefore, the first decision the party made was to decentralize administrative and economic management which would allow the local governments and enterprises freedom and autonomy in the form of self-management and self-reliance. The party leadership also concluded that decentralization was not enough for the economy to move beyond subsistence activities, and Laos had to adopt capitalist market methods and free trade to promote economic development while maintaining the party's political control and the end goal of communism.[26] This meant that Vientiane wanted to tailor its reforms in a slow, cautious and appropriate manner that would foster growth and development (e.g. new markets, industrialization, literacy and skills, infrastructure, transportation, de facto entrepreneurship) without having to face the obstacles and consequences of meteoric change.[27] In other words, Vientiane wanted to make sure that the promotion of market, economic liberalization, and open-door policy must not pose a threat to the LPDP.

Like Hanoi and Pyongyang, Vientiane's decision to liberalize was also influenced to a large degree by the successful gradual reforms in China and the collapse of the Soviet Union which deprived Vientiane of much needed trade and assistance, which further exacerbated Laos' economic malaise and compelled it to make major policy changes from a centrally planned economy to a market-based economy.[28] Although the Soviet Union did not fall and the Council for Mutual Economic Assistance was not disbanded in the 1980s, Soviet aid to Vietnam was cut and by domino effect, Vietnamese aid to Laos also reduced. After 1991, the collapse of communism in the socialist block delivered a critical blow to the already faltering economy. Because of its dependence on the socialist block for financial support, the Laotian economy began to experience financial difficulties and drawbacks of being internationally isolated. Desperately in need of foreign aid, Laos began to turn to Thailand and the West to fill the void left by the socialist block. On the other hand, the warmer relations between China and Laos, such as the forgiving of Laotian debt by China, increased two-way trade and assistance, and encouraging results of China's economic reform and policy, became a contributing factor for Laos' economic liberalization. The influence of Vietnamese reform, *doi moi*, also contributed heavily to Vientiane's decision to reform. The influence of Vietnam played a most important role in Laos' political, economic, and military development and transition. Vietnamese troops were directly involved in the operation in the Laotian government's crackdown on the Hmong rebellion in the northern province of Xiang Khouang. Vietnam's economic ties with Laos were also important to the Laotian government, particularly Vietnamese investment in such strategic sectors as construction, transport infrastructure, forestry, and agro-processing; joint-venture agreements in the banking sector; financial and auditing assistance; and the outflow of Vietnamese workers to Laos. Politically, both countries maintained their traditional, political and ideological solidarity. Laotian officials were routinely sent to the Ho Chi Minh National Politics Institute in Hanoi for training.[29] Therefore, Vietnamese reform policy, *doi moi*, heavily influenced the Laotian government's decision to reform and adopt the MEN.

Meanwhile, international organizations, particularly international aid agencies, such as the IMF, World Bank and Asia Development Bank, entered into bipartite aid agreements with Vientiane, hoping to induce greater liberalization through assistance and reform programs. Such foreign aid and programs had proved no threat to the communist government in China and Vietnam, but much needed resources for the Laotian economic development. To secure more foreign aid, Vientiane implemented wider economic reforms, reduced tariffs and quotas, and adopted more open-door policy beyond its initial liberalization.

CAMBODIA

Several causes of economic reform in Cambodia can be identified from the literature: the devastation caused by Pol Pot which led to failed collectivization amongst other atrocities, a Soviet pull-back of resources as well as an influence from Moscow and Vietnam for economic reform, and a demise of communist ideology in Cambodia. All are connected causally to one another that led to all events following the years of Pol Pot.

First, Pol Pot, his legacy and rule, was the essential catalyst for the subsequent economic reform in Cambodia. Cambodia, like neighbors Vietnam and Laos, was wracked by civil war, famine and economic implosion, and a desperately-chaotic situation that the nation was longing for peace and a better future. The country had poor infrastructure, low economic output, poorly performing factories, relied heavily on foreign aid, and was critically lack of technology, infrastructure, and formal institutions due to the paranoid genocide of Pol Pot.[30] Pol Pot had a radical goal in his economic plan, which was quite reminiscent of Maoist Great Leap Forward, which put Cambodia in a utopian experiment with primitive communism based on a self-reliant and agricultural production.[31] The result was disastrous. One demographic study of Cambodia concludes that Cambodia's population – perhaps 7.4 million in 1975 – may have fallen to an estimated 5.8 million by the time the Vietnamese toppled the DK government. Although the study does not attempt to speculate on the number of deaths from starvation alone, the figures can only lead one to conclude that the political, economic, and social system of Democratic Kampuchea was, in reality, an absolute disaster for the people of Cambodia.[32] Pol Pot's plan utterly failed leaving Cambodians little choice but to take a new economic direction. Therefore, it is the war and chaos of the seventies that would in many ways foster the economic liberalization of the eighties and nineties. Cambodians' yearning for better lives gave the Vietnam-backed KPRP a strong mandate to navigate a course of liberalization, re-build economic infrastructures, and implement new reforms to shift from radical communism to moderate socialism. This would entail the re-establishment of a planned economy with markets; the restoration of the banking system and national currency; abolition of forced labor; introduction of an eight-hour workday; and the inauguration of pay based on work performed.[33] In agriculture, attempts to re-collectivize took place between 1982 and 1987, particularly through introduction of *krom samaki* (solidarity groups), which reflected the KPRP's commitment to communist ideology. However, as the decade of the 1980s drew to a close, private sector and family economic activities were encouraged in response to the failures of collectivization, and more economic liberalization was introduced in Cambodia.[34]

Second, the transition was also due to external influence or learning from the reforms in the former Soviet Union and NICs in Asia. The KPRP government relied heavily on foreign subsidies from the Soviet Union and Vietnam. CMEA aid to Cambodia amounted to 80 percent of the government's budget. When CMEA ended aid to Cambodia in 1991, a new economic policy was urgently required.[35] As Gorbachev's perestroika became more dominant in Moscow, the Cambodians who were studying in Moscow were exposed to the novelty of perestroika. The mandate to reform was also confirmed and supported by Vietnam where the VCP adopted *doi moi* policy. Therefore, the similar reforms happened among the

Mekong neighbors (Vietnam, Laos, and Cambodia) was no coincidence.[36] This is "state isomorphism."[37] Vietnam had indeed achieved a regional sphere of influence with Laos and Cambodia, and used it to impart its reform plans, *doi moi*, upon Phnom Pen. Almost at the same time, the large infusion of aid from Moscow began to dry up as the Soviets pulled back from their interests abroad to focus on their own ailing economic situation. Taken together, this learning effect and concurrent Soviet aid withdrawal created both the desperate need for a new economic policy and the increased reliance on other external sources of aid and capital in order to recover from its collapsed economy, thus spurring on liberalization in Cambodia. Therefore the second reason for economic reform can be seen as an external factor helping to usher in a new epoch of economic change.[38]

A third factor for economic reform was an ideological factor. Communism lost its luster for Cambodians, and the party leadership became apathetic and lost interest in promoting communist dogma. Party-state cadres were allowed to supplement their salaries with earnings from private business transactions. Marketing one's skills for profit privately filled this gap. In agriculture, "collectivity within solidarity groups started to dissolve under pressures from the widespread revival of private enterprise," and the local and central governments began to acknowledge the failure of collectivization.[39] As socialist policies became increasingly unpopular, it was in the regime's interest to allow for economic marketization. As the cadres accumulated more wealth while leaving most of Cambodians in poverty, it became evident to Cambodians that egalitarian socialism was an illusion. As a result of the continued failure of the socialist system to produce at even subsistence level, the ideological underpinnings of the Cambodian economy and social system began to collapse.[40] "Cambodia...is a case in which nationalism, populism, and peasantism really won out over communism,"[41] a case where the aforementioned forces were more salient than socialist ideology. However, the major economic transition did not take place until 1993 when free elections monitored by UNTAC brought a new coalition government to power, which introduced another round of economic reforms and officially promoted the transition to a market economy. Since then, the rebuilding and reform of the Cambodian economy has proceeded under the framework and guidance of the IMF and also aided by the donor community of the international society.[42]

Conclusion

To solve those problems and difficulties, leaders of these communist states recognized the need for change and reform. However, unlike most of formerly communist states in the Soviet bloc who were clear about their objectives of transition to democracy and market economy, the Chinese leaders and other Asian communist states had neither a clear idea nor consensus about where to go and how to go. What they knew was that the traditional centrally planned economy was not working well and that some reforms or policy changes were necessary to promote economic growth, improve people's living standards, and therefore to strengthen the legitimacy of their leadership.

Different policy choices and sequencing of reform were not determined by the "initial conditions" of these countries, but primarily determined by the interplay between politics and economics, the outcome of the intra-party power struggle between reformers and conservatives, the understanding of the relationship between state plan and market mechanism, and the leadership's concerns about the consequences of reform that might threaten the power of communist leadership and political stability of the regime. This will become the central task of the next chapter, which will attempt to address the following questions: Why is the Asian transition process different from what happened in Eastern European countries? How was the reform policy proposed, adopted, and implemented in these Asian countries? How were the sequencing of reform and thus the pattern of transition determined?

Note

[1] James Riedel and William S. Turley, "The Politics and Economics of Transition to an Open Market Economy in Viet Nam," *Technical Papers*, no. 152, OECD Development Centre, 1999, p. 42.

[2] Gabriel A. Almond and Laura Roselle, "Model Fitting in Communism Studies," in Frederic J. Fleron, Jr. and Erik P. Hoffmann, eds., *Post-Communist Studies and Political Science: Methodology and Empirical Theory in Sovietology* (Boulder, CO: Westview Press, 1993), pp. 62-63

[3] Richard W. Miller, *Fact and Method: Explanation, Explanation, Confirmation and Reality in the Natural and the Social Sciences*, (Princeton, NJ: Princeton University Press, 1988).

[4] Howard J. Wiarda, *Introduction to Comparative Politics* (Wadsworth, 2000), pp.124-128; Graeme Gill, *The Collapse of a Single-Party System: The Disintegration of the Communist Party of the Soviet Union* Cambridge University Press, 1995); Russell Bova, "Political Dynamics of the Post-Communist Transition: A Comparative Perspective," in Frederic J. Fleron and Erick P. Hoffmann, eds., *Post-Communist Studies & Political Science* (Westview Press, Boulder, 1993), pp. 239-263.

[5] Christopher Marsh, "Learning from Your Comrade's Mistakes: the Impact of the Soviet Past on China's Future," *Communist and Post-Communist Studies*, vol. 36, 2003, pp. 259-272.

[6] Wing Thye Woo, "The Economics and Politics of Transition to an Open Market Economy: China," *Technical Papers*, no. 153, OECD Development Centre, October 1999, pp. 17-26.

[7] Susan L. Shirk, *The Political Logic of Economic Reform in China* (Berkeley, CA: University of California Press, 1993), pp. 23 and 34.

[8] Gao Shangquan, *China's Economic Reform* (New York: St. Martin Press, 1996), p. 2.

[9] World Bank Country Study, *China: Reform and the Role of the Plan in the 1990s* (Washington, DC: World Bank, 1992), p. 35.

[10] Susan L. Shirk, pp. 36-37.

[11]   The People's Republic of China IV: "China and the Four Modernizations, 1979-1982." http://www-(CONT.) chaos.umd.edu/history/prc4.html#postmao

[12]   Doowon Lee, "North Korean Economic Reform: Past Efforts and Future Prospects," in John McMillan and Barry Naughton, eds., *Reforming Asian Socialism: The Growth of Market Institutions* (Ann Arbor, MI: The University of Michigan Press, 1996), pp. 332-333.

[13]   North Korean Country Report, "Outlook for 2003-2004, Policy and Economic Trends," Economist Intelligence Unit, http://store.eiu.com/index.asp?layout=show_sample& product_id=50000205&country_id=KP

[14]   Ibid.

[15]   Country Study and Guide: North Korea, "Developmental Strategy," http://reference.allrefer.com/country-guide-study/north-korea/north-korea64.html

[16]   BBC News World Edition, "Foreign Investors Brave North Korea," http://news.bbc.co.uk/2/hi/business/3558283.stm

[17]   William S. Turley and Mark Selden, eds., *Reinventing Vietnamese Socialism: Doi Moi in Comparative Perspective* (Boulder, CO: Westview, 1993), p. 23.

[18]   James Riedel and William S. Turley, p. 8.

[19]   Le Duc Thuy, "Economic *Doi Moi* in Vietnam: Content, Achievements, and Prospects," in William S. Turley and Mark Selden, p. 97.

[20]   James Riedel and William S. Turley, p. 15.

[21]   Ibid., p. 42.

[22]   ASEAN, http://www.aseansec.org/viewpdf.asp?file=/pdf/afta.pdf; WTO, "Accessions, Vietnam." http://www.wto.org/english/thewto_e/acc_e/a1_vietnam_e.htm

[23]   Richard Pomfret, *Asian Economies in Transition: Reforming Centrally Planned Economies* (Cheltenham, UK: Edward Elgar, 1996), p. 62.

[24]   Yves Bourdet, "Laos in 1995: Reform Policy, Out of Breadth?" *Asian Survey*, vol. 36, no. 1, 1996, p. 89.

[25]   Exploitz Country Report: Laos, "Rural-Urban Distribution," http://exploitz.com/Laos-Ruralurban-Distribution-cg.php

[26]   Bernard Funck, "Laos: Decentralization and Economic Control," in Borje Ljunggren, ed., *The Challenge of Reform in Indochina* (Cambridge, MA: Harvard University Press, 1993), pp. 129-130.

[27]   Laos Country Brief, "Economic Overview," Australian Department of Foreign Affairs and Trade, http://www.dfat.gov.au/geo/laos/laos_brief.html

[28]   Laos Country Report, "The political scene: The president visits China amid warming bilateral ties," Economist Intelligence Unit, http://store.eiu.com/index.asp?layout =show_sample&product_id=50000205&country_id=LA

[29]   Yves Bourdet, "Laos in 2000: The Economics of Political Immobilism," *Asian Survey*, vol. 41, no. 1, 2001, pp. 164-170.

[30]   Russell R. Ross, ed., *Cambodia: A Country Study* (Washingon, D.C.: U.S. Government Printing Office, 1990), 142.

[31]   Kimmo Kiljunen, *Kampuchea: Decade of the Genocide* (London: Zed Books Ltd., 1984), pp. 14-17; David P. Chandler, *Brother Number One: A political Biography of Pol Pot* (Boulder, CO: Westview Press, 1999), pp. 3 and 13.

[32]   Karl D. Jackson, *Cambodia 1975-1978* (Princeton: Princeton University Press, 1989), p. 150.

33 "Cambodia: New Economic Policy and System," http://www.exploitz.com/Cambodia-New-Economic-Policy-And-System-cg.php

34 Caroline Hughes, *The Political Economy of Cambodia's Transition, 1991-2001* (London and New York: RoutledgeCurzon, 2003), p. 28.

35 Ibid., p. 31.

36 "Cambodia – First Plan, 1986-1990," http://www.exploitz.com/Cambodia-First-Plan-198690-cg.php

37 Ioannis Kyvelidis, "State Isomorphism in the Post-Socialist Transition," *European Integration online Papers* (EIoP), vol. 4, no. 2, February 2000, http://olymp.wu-wien.ac.at/eiop/pdf/2000-002.pdf

38 Evan Gottesman, *Cambodia After the Khmer Rouge: Inside the Politics of Nation Building* (New Haven: Yale University Press, 2003), p. 272.

39 Shaun Williams, "Where Has All the Land Gone? Land Rights and Access in Cambodia, Volume 1," *Cambodia Land Study Project*, Oxfam, Phnom Penh, May 1999, pp. 2-3.

40 Evan Gottesman, pp. 280, 283.

41 Michael Vickery, *Cambodia: 1975-1982* (Boston: South End Press, 1984), p. 290.

42 Mario de Zamaroczy and Sopanha Sa, "Macroeconomic Adjustment in a Highly Dollarized Economy: The Case of Cambodia," International Monetary Fund, May 2002, http://www.imf.org/external/pubs/ft/wp/2002/wp0292.pdf; International Monetary Fund, "IMF Concludes 2002 Article IV Consultation with Cambodia," February 28, 2003, http://www.imf.org/external/np/sec/pn/2003/pn0321.htm

Chapter 4

Strategic Choices and Sequencing of Reform

In Chapter 3, we attempted to identify causal variables that contributed to reform efforts across these Asian communist countries and explain why these governments launched the reforms and made their transitions from centrally planned to market-based or market-oriented economies. This chapter will focus on the strategic choice resulted from the interplay between state and market and explore the significance of the sequencing of political and economic transitions and the interplay between politics and economy in determining variations in transition outcome. Through comparison, this chapter also attempts to draw some real lessons about how the sequencing of political and economic transitions influences. the prospects for democracy and economic restructuring, though the choice of the sequencing model varies across these Asian countries.

In reform practice, the leadership in any transitional economies will face many different choices concerning their reform paths and strategies in a given context or under circumstances directly encountered, given, and transmitted from the past. What key variables have shaped their strategic choices, pace, content, direction of reform and therefore the pattern of Asian transition from state socialism? Many empirical studies on the communist transitional economies have suggested that the strategic choices largely reflect different views among leaders on what would be politically and economically feasible.[1] Unlike their counterparts in the Soviet Union and Eastern Europe, the communist elite in Asian countries were short of a comprehensive plan or consensus on the pace, content and direction of economic reform and, therefore, reforms largely proceeded in a step-by-step or stop-and-go manner. Partial reform without a long-term goal and a comprehensive plan was the key feature of these Asian countries in their transitions from state socialism. Reforms are considered partial if economic reforms are introduced without significant political reform or economic reforms are carried out in an incremental dual-track fashion without complete abandonment of the old economic system. The transition process in all Asian countries has demonstrated such a partial, phased, and gradualist pattern in contrast to the comprehensive, shock-therapist, and radical approach of formerly communist countries in Russia and Eastern Europe. In Asian economic transitions, the reform often started where possible and the reform pace and direction have been shaped by a decade long disagreement, debate, and balance between reformers and conservatives along the three main dimensions – in other words, the strategic choice was largely determined by the following key variables (Figure 4.1):

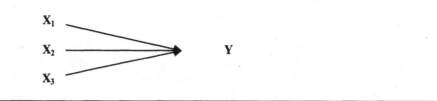

X_1 = The relationship between moderate and radical reformers
X_2 = The relationship between reform and stability
X_3 = The relationship between socialist principles and market reform practices
Y = Patterns of transition

Figure 4.1 Causal relationship between independent and dependent variables

Although strategic choice could be constrained by many other variables, this study will focus on the three most important key variables. In what follows, we will examine Asian economic transitions along these three empirical dimensions and explain why these countries have adopted a gradualist approach in economic transition.

The Power Relationship Between Moderate and Radical Reformers

There has been no consensus among communist leaders about the content, scope, pace or extent of reforms. In the broadest terms, the leaders of Asian communist countries fall into two groups – more conservative leaders or moderate reformers, on the one hand, and more liberal leaders or radical reformers, on the other. The reform strategic debate and the tensions between them usually determine the choice of reform policy and, ultimately, the path of transition.

CHINA

In China, after the purges of Mao's followers and, particularly, the fall of Hua Guofeng's "whatever" factions, the reformers took control over the entire party-state apparatus in the early 1980s. They were led by a group of veteran party leaders who had been the principal victims of the Cultural Revolution. But the differences between the moderate and radical wings of the reform movement became evident in the late 1970s. As Harry Harding, an influential China scholar, points out, "the tensions between these two groups should not be characterized as a struggle between those who favor reform and those who oppose it."[2] They all agreed on the necessity of reforms that could improve the economic performance of the Chinese socialist economic system, promote China's economic modernization, and raise standards of living for the Chinese people. However, they disagreed on the content, scope and pace or extent of reforms. More conservative leaders or moderate reformers, such as Chen Yun and Peng Zhen, are cautious and skeptical about dramatic departures from the planned economy and party-state political system that were the legacy of the Soviet model that China had imitated under Mao or the Maoist style of political economy. More liberal leaders or radical reformers, such as Hu Yaobang and Zhao Ziyang, entertain bolder reform measures that would make a radical departure from the traditional political economy of state socialism and launch China in the direction of a market economy.[3] Deng Xiaoping often played a role of balancer between the two groups, resulting in a dual-track, phased, and gradualist pattern of transition. Harry Harding provides the best picture of the division between these two groups.

First, the moderate reformers proposed making the market an important supplementary mechanism for the allocation of resources and the determination of prices, with the operation of the market restricted to agricultural goods and inessential economic sectors, industries or areas, launching China in the direction of a planned commodity economy. Chen Yun, the chief spokesman for moderate reform, treated the Chinese economy like a bird in a cage and likened the economy to a bird and the plan to a cage: "If the cage is too small, the bird will die; but if there is no cage at all, the bird will fly away, unrestrained." In contrast, the radical reformers favored a central role for the market in the economy, with the development of markets for almost all factors of production, including capital, labor, and industrial machinery, launching China in the direction of a market economy.

Second, the moderate reformers favored a slow, gradual, and experimental approach to reforms, with lengthy periods of readjustment during which the imbalances generated by reform could be repaired. They wished to maintain stringent administrative control over certain important aspects of the economy, especially investment and foreign exchange, and feared that a rapid relaxation of controls over the economy would create severe disequilibrium in the management of the Chinese economy. The radical reformers, in contrast, favored a more rapid and comprehensive structural reform to quickly remove the inefficiencies and rigidities of the traditional economic system. They were willing to take risks for the sake of economic efficiency, even if the result was a temporary disequilibrium in the economy. This debate was especially severe when the party was drafting a proposal for the reform of the urban economy in 1984. At that time, Chen Yun suggested structural reform over a period of thirty years, while Hu Yaobang insisted on completing the process in three to five years. Whenever reform created serious imbalances, the moderate reformers would want to slow the process and take administrative measures to correct it.

Third, the moderate reformers insisted on maintaining the basic principles of socialism prescribed by Marx, Lenin, and Stalin (the planned economy, public ownership of the means of production, and distribution according to labor), therefore preserving administrative guidance from the planning agencies, limiting the development of private and other non-public sectors, and controlling the exchange of land and labor on the marketplace. The radical reformers, in contrast, tended to provide a much less restrictive definition of socialism than their moderate counterparts, excluding the planned economy from the list of principles of socialism and recasting the principle of public ownership more flexibly, so as to allow for the existence of a diversified ownership structure while maintaining the dominant position of public ownership.[4]

The tensions between these two groups and the interaction of their reform strategies caused the alternation of periods of advance and periods of retreat since China's reforms, because compromises between these groups must be reached before major policy changes could occur. The constant political bargaining and occasional shifts in political alignments among the supporters of different factions gave China's economic reforms incremental nature, and the appearance of "two steps forward and one step backward."[5] The cyclical pattern was reinforced by Deng Xiaoping who, in an effort to balance between these two groups, supported both the periods of advance and retrenchment proposed by both radical and moderate groups.[6] "The fact that he also actively accommodated the concerns of the conservatives would put him close, if not sometimes in, the middle of the central plan-market spectrum throughout the 1978-90 period."[7] Whenever reforms generated problems such as inflation, inequality, runaway investment, reckless expenditure, or the outbreak of a dissident movement, the moderate reformers would blame their radical colleagues, tried to limit the extent of reform and economic liberalization, and called for a slowdown in the pace of reform, a tightening of administrative control over the economy, a remedial measure to restore equilibrium, a crackdown against dissidence and crime, and a periodic campaign against unorthodox ideas in economics, politics, literature and art. The radical reformers would be forced to defend reforms against critics, find an appropriate theoretical interpretation for their reform measures, and make a concession to the retrenchment launched by the moderate reformers, which actually reinforced the cyclical character of the Chinese reform. Almost all major party documents and policies reflected a compromise between the two groups on policy making.[8]

For example, the Central Party Committee decision on urban economic reform in 1984 reflected a compromise between the two groups on the relationship between plan and market, which continue to reassert planning as a basic characteristic of a socialist economy while calling for a reduction of mandatory planning. A dual-price system was introduced to achieve the balance between plan and market. "The partial liberalization and partial decentralization character of the 1984 enterprise was to the liking of both the conservative and the liberal reformers."[9] The reforms in the areas of state enterprises, financial industries, monetary policy, foreign trade, and so forth have also been incremental and experimental. Reforms would begin with some experimentation practices before they are more widely adopted over time. The open-door policy is characterized by a gradual opening up to the world, from the establishment of four "special economic zones" (SEZs) in Guangdong and Fujian in 1979, through the designation of fourteen coastal cities as open cities for foreign investment in 1984 and the development strategy of "great international cycle" (*guoji da xunhuan*) for coastal areas in 1988, to the opening up of inland western areas in 1997. It took about two decades to expand the same open-door policy to all regions of the country. Such a gradualist approach was actually a compromise resulting from the continuous debate between the two groups on the nature and speed of socialist reform; it was a policy designed to confine foreign influence to officially designated areas while the open door policy could be maintained and its benefits could be expanded gradually.

As a result, the Chinese reformers, in general, have implemented reforms in stages, beginning with the easier and less controversial reforms and proceeding with more complex and less popular reforms after the success of the initial reforms has created enough political support and momentum to the further reform. The entire process of China's economic transition has been incremental and experimental in nature. Reform programs have been adopted and implemented in selected pilot sectors, areas, cities, or enterprises before being undertaken on a wider basis. Those that succeeded would be adopted on a wider basis while those that failed would be abandoned or modified.[10]

That is how reform and opening in China has expanded gradually: an initial step of reform begins in rural areas before spreading to urban areas; it starts the opening policy with establishing SEZs, which is followed by a gradual expansion to the coastal regions, before spreading the same economic policies to the inland Western regions; it starts with the village and township economies, individual household economies, private economies and joint-ventured economies before undertaking major reforms in the state-owned economic sector, particularly corporatization of SOEs through shareholding reform; it starts with microeconomic reform based on expanding the autonomous powers of enterprise management and production through profit retention and responsibility contracting systems before launching macroeconomic reforms, including price, planning, finance, banking, and so forth.[11] "Herein lies the primary reasons for the slow, gradual, incremental and evolutionary nature of China's economic reform: the existence of two competing economic programs. As in most situations of this kind in other countries of the world, the resulting economic policies drew upon both programs."[12] Therefore, the entire process of reform and opening has been shaped and determined by the tensions between moderate and radical reformers and the interaction of their reform strategies.

NORTH KOREA

In North Korea, the incremental or gradual nature of reform is also evident since the early 1980s and also attributable to the differences between hardliners (hawkish group) and pro-reform softliners (technocrats, such as Kang Song-San, Kim Dal-

Hyun, Li Gun Mo, Yon Hyung Muk) within the Korean Workers' Party (KWP) over how far and how fast reform should proceed. The hardliners have tried to set limits on the extent of reform and reduce the speed of reform while softliners have attempted to win acceptance of reform ideas and implement reforms.

During the early and mid-1980s, a series of debates took place in policy-making circle over whether or not to adopt the open door policy and economic reform. The conservatives insisted on the policy of self-reliance and the "Three Revolutions" (ideological, cultural, and technological) while the reformers emphasized the necessity of scientific knowledge and modern technology to overhaul its industries built with the Soviet assistance following the Korean War and the useful experiences of China and the Soviet Union in economic reform and open-door policy in promoting economic and technological modernization. It seemed that Kim Jong Il took a middle ground position in the debate by putting a greater emphasis or priority on the necessity of science and technology for carrying out the technological revolution while continuing to maintain the *Juche* ideology (independence in politics, self-reliance in economics, and self-defense in national security). This middle-ground approach was supported by Kim Il Sung who recognized the obsolescence of North Korean industries and facilities built with the Soviet assistance following the Korean War and the urgent need of technological transformation of the North Korean economy.[13] Although this middle-ground approach is slow in pace and limited in scope, when compared to other socialist countries, North Korea has started a gradual opening and partial market reform since the 1980s.

For the North Korean economy, 1984 was the year that partial reform and open-door policy started. In August 1984, the "August Third People's Consumer Goods Production Movement" was announced and carried on the front page of *Rodong Sinmun*, Workers' Party Daily, which allowed direct sales and production of some consumer goods outside the central planning – bypassing centralized quotas, procurement, and pricing. This was followed by the revision of the "Provision on the Independent Accounting System in State Enterprises" in December that was to give SOEs more autonomy and financial accountability for their profits and losses. The amended 1998 constitution actually introduced market elements in its economic system by emphasizing the importance of cost, price, and profit in the state sector and allowing partial private ownership of farm land and individual business. As Article 24 stipulates, the state shall protect private property and guarantee its legal inheritance. This is the first time North Korea has recognized and allowed private property rights to its citizens. In the rural area, each peasant household is allowed to cultivate 50 *pyong* (165 square meters) private plot of land to grow vegetables and cash crops from which they may use themselves or sell to others. Farmers' markets were opened for exchange of these agricultural goods and gradually expanded in size and scope, with a recent trend toward specialization in marketed commodities in different regions. Due to accumulating capital from profits in marketplaces, many individuals or groups of people have started business by raising funds among themselves. Since early 1996, the working group (*Boon-Jo-Je*) in the collective farms has been reduced to 7 to 8 persons composed by families or relatives, allowed to dispense freely with whatever exceeds the production target. This may ultimately become a stepping stone for further reform. The purpose of this reform is similar to that of the household contract system in China, which was aimed at increasing agricultural production. International trade and inter-Korean trade were also encouraged and international tourism as a new industry was opened up for joint investment projects. The Joint Venture Law enacted in September 1984 served as an open door measure to attract foreign investments. To provide banking services for the foreign and joint-ventured companies, the Korean Nakwon Finance Joint Venture Company and the Korean Joint Venture Bank were founded in 1987 and 1989, respectively, which conducted all international banking operations on market principles with interest rates on loans and deposits determined accordance with the rates on the international money markets, which was autonomous from the rest of the economy which operated on socialist principles and central planning. In 1992, three new laws related to foreign investment, aiming at attracting foreign capital and technology, were enacted to provide more favorable conditions for foreign investors: the Law on Foreigners' Investment, the Law on Contractual Joint Venture, and the Law on Foreign Enterprises. These laws applied to those foreign or joint-ventured enterprises operated within the "Free Economic and Trade Zone (FETZ)" of the Rajin-Sonbong area near Tumen River in the Northeast of the country. North Korea has started a gradual opening from one area to new special zones in multiple areas such as Kyaesung, Wonsan-Tongchon, and Pyongyang-Nampo. The FETZ was experimental in nature and very similar to China's SEZ although North Korean leaders repeatedly declared that the country pursued "our own style of socialism."[14] The Law on Leasing of Land also allows leasing of land for up to 50 years which can be renewed, resold, transferred, and inherited. More liberal foreign investment legislation has been adopted to facilitate the effort to attract foreign investment. No less than 47 new laws and regulations on foreign investment were enacted between 1992 and 2000.[15] The new legislation also included laws on special economic zones, copyrights, arbitration, foreign trade, and etc. In 2002, major economic reforms include the lifting of price controls, devaluation of the currency, and etc. On July 1, 2002, a new price system was introduced to allow the price level of goods to rise such that it reflected production costs and international prices. The official price of rice, for example, soared from 0.08 won per kilogram to 44 won, about 550 times the old price. Obviously, such increases in prices were actually introduced by the state policy, not as a result of market forces. The wages were also raised to reflect the increase in prices. Salaries of manufacturing workers, for example, also increased almost 18 times from 110 won a month to 2,000 won a month. The government also devalued the North Korean currency against the US dollar by roughly 68 times from a rate of 2.15 won per dollar to 150 won per dollar.[16] The rationing system shrank with the food rationing system retained for families without wage earners. State employees were now required to pay their rent and utilities. The government also loosened some restrictions on foreign ownership in joint ventured businesses and enterprises, allowing foreign investors to take more than 50% stake in joint ventures.[17] The government took measures to change its centralized production that had originally required detailed planning to a decentralized system that allowed factories to formulate their own independent production plans although the central government continued to have an overall central planning system in place. "North Korean authorities now control only the largest and most important enterprises, while instructing all others to fend for themselves under the slogan of 'self-reliance."[18] In 2002, the government also began to allow collective farms to pay rent for land with a portion of their harvest and began to buy grains or vegetables from the farmers at realistic prices (close to the farmers' market price). The farmer's market is now simply called "market," allowing all kinds of goods to be traded there. "The majority of the North Korean people now depend on farmers' markets and other market transactions for much of their necessities."[19]

All these new policies suggest that North Korea has partially adopted some features of market economy, and its economic reform and open door policy have started since the 1980s.[20] Kim Jong-Il himself attempted to justify his new economic reform policy by saying that "things are not what they used to be in the 1960s. So no one should follow the way people used to do things in the past... We should make constant efforts to renew the landscape to replace the one which was formed in the past and to meet the requirements of a new era."[21] As a North Korean official, Ch'oe Hong-kyu, a bureau /director in the State Planning Commission, explained clearly, "Kim Jong-Il stresses that all the outdated and dogmatic 'Soviet-type' patterns and customs should be renounced in the fields of economic planning, finance, and labor management... Foreign trade should be conducted in accordance with the mechanism and principles of capitalism."[22]

The key features of these reform measures were a combination of state planning and commodity-market relations through the introduction of costs, prices, profits, and material incentives in the state-owned enterprises, the revitalization of commodity exchange in the rural area, and the establishment of a special economic sector as an open-door window to attract foreign capital and new technology. What has emerged in North Korea is "dual structure" or "hybrid system" combining state and market roles or market and socialist principles in reform practice. As repeatedly stated in a DPRK official newspaper *People's Korea*, "we should manage and operate the economy in such a way as to ensure the maximum profitability while firmly adhering to the socialist principles."[23] Such reform efforts are comparable to those measures introduced in other Asian socialist economies such as China in the early and mid-1980s. However, the North Korean reform and open-door policy did not achieve a significant progress due to both external and domestic constraints.

Externally, the open-door policy was constrained by the U.S. containment that prohibited economic exchanges with North Korea on the basis of the Trading With the Enemy Act and the resolution of the nuclear issue that prevented economic cooperation between North Korea and Western countries. The prospect for the improvement in North Korea's foreign relations was further clouded by the issue of North Korea's resumed nuclear program. The credibility of the North Korean government is still questionable to foreign investors, particularly from the Western world. "External world has strong skeptical views on whether North Korean internal environment can guarantee business activity sufficiently and whether there is profitability in doing business with North Korea, let alone the credibility issue of North Korea."[24]

Internally, poor infrastructure, geographic location of FETZs, tedious procedures, and administrative interference with enterprise management, etc, have all limited the improvement of domestic investment environment. Although decentralization has been implemented and state subsidies have been discontinued for most of SOEs, the basic economic system has not changed, and the managers have not been given the power in employment and personnel appointment. Their economic behavior has not changed as compared to that prior to policy changes. As the money losing SOEs are not allowed for bankruptcy, state subsidies actually continue to exist through state bank loans or government budgets. The lack of incentives – both individuals and enterprises – has continued to constrain the improvement of productivity. The government continues to require the foreign-owned enterprises to pay wages in hard currency, and this policy is not attractive to foreign investors. Moreover, reform and opening policies were constrained by the leadership's fear of regime instability or collapse as occurred in the Eastern European former communist countries and the existence of influential conservative hardliners within the party and the military. The fear among the North Korean leaders was real in regards to the open-door policy because the North Korean people may be disturbed when they found out that they were far worse off than South Koreans and it would be such a shock that it would put the communist regime in danger.[25]

The reform and opening policy has been also constrained by the *Juche* ideology and the conflict between hardliners and softliners. During the 1980s, especially in the mid-1980s, a series of debates took place in Pyongyang policy-making circles over whether or not to adopt the open door policy and economic reform. The conservative hardliners seemed to argue that the country should continue to carry out the *Juche* ideology and its policy of self-reliance and persevere in the Three Revolutions (the ideological, cultural, and technological revolutions) without outside help, while the pro-reform softliners argued that North Korea should learn more about the Chinese and the Soviet experiences with economic reform and should also open its door to the outside world. The younger Kim placed himself in the middle of the debate between the conservative hardliners and the pro-reform softliners by putting a great deal of emphasis on the development of science and technology for the technological revolution but advocating at the same time that the education of the younger generation in his father's *Juche* ideology should be maintained. Kim Il Sung also recognized that North Korea needed more advanced technology, capital investment, and long-term credit if the country was able to re-equip the outdated industrial plants. Therefore, the outcome of the 1984-86 policy debates was a compromise in the sense that North Korea was to open its door selectively to meet the need for technical transformation while maintaining *Chajusong* (independence) in carrying out the Three Revolutions. As a result of the policy debates, the chairman of the state planning was replaced in February 1986 and Premier Kang Sung-San was replaced by Li Gun Mo who was a Soviet-trained technocrat and considered a leading member of the group of reformers. Because of illness, however, Li was replaced in December 1988 by Yon Hyung Muk, another Soviet-trained technocrat, a close follower of Kim Jong Il and a reformer.[26]

However, in the aftermath of the Chinese Tiananmen Square incident and the collapse of communism in the former Soviet Union and Eastern Europe, the power relationship between conservative hardliners and pro-reform softliners was skewed to the former, backed by the paramount leader Kim Il Sung and the elderly revolutionary leaders, who believed that the North's economic difficulties could be resolved through non-market measures within the existing socialist economy framework.[27] The disagreement and tension between conservatives and reformers in the KWP have continued to shape the policies of reform and opening in North Korea in the post-Kim Il Sung era. Given the nature of political regime, opening and reform ultimately rest with Kim Jong Il's choice of policy. However, his choice is constrained by intraparty politics and strategic preferences among different departments. Military-first politics under Kim Jong Il is a reflection of military interests and its predominant position in the power structure. The military has shown a rapid ascension in the power hierarchy since the death of Kim Il Sung in 1994. The most powerful institution is now the National Defense Commission (NDC), in which six members are from the military of the ten most powerful leaders. The military has played a more important role in shaping the policy making under the Kim Jong Il regime and has taken a hardline policy at almost all fronts. However, despite opposition from the military, technocrats drawn mostly from the state council and lower strata of the party organizations can also influence the pace and direction of opening and reform, because Kim Jong Il has to reply on them in order to overcome economic stagnation and promote his idea of building a *kangsong taekuk* (literally, "a strong and prosperous great power"). Increased role of technocrats in economic opening and reform and increased power of the military in the power structure would lead to an inevitable conflict of interests between the two groups. The balance of power between the two is likely to shape Kim Jong Il's choices of new opening and reform policy.[28]

VIETNAM

Similar approaches have also been adopted in Vietnam, beginning with the easier reforms first, where the benefits would outweigh the costs. The incremental or gradual nature of reform is also attributed to the differences between hardliners and softliners within the party or the power relationship of the two groups. In Vietnam, the leadership system after Ho Chi Minh has been a system of competing factions held together by the principle of collective leadership. This factionalism is reflected in the division between hardliners and moderates, pro-Beijing and pro-Moscow groups, and southerners and northerners.[29] In general, the conservative members of the VCP leadership belong to a broad coalition of party ideologues, leaders and members of the party work, mass organization, and political organizations in the security and military sectors, and SOE managers who are strong believers in socialist orthodoxy with a strong preference for a "socialist-based market economy" in accordance with socialist ideas and practices. They are worried about the corrosive impact of the market economy and the development of private sectors on the VCP leadership and the socialist direction of reform. The reformist factions belong to a coalition of technocrats, leaders in the government sector, senior party members, military commands that developed commercial interests in the economic reform, and citizens advocating change, who are more interested in the efficient functioning of the system than the survival of ideology with a strong preference for a comprehensive market reform and opening of the economy to the world market. They want Vietnam to change and develop more rapidly to "catch up" with neighboring states and join the global market to enhance its long-term development prospects.[30]

Policy debate about the nature of socioeconomic development in Vietnam began during the economic difficulties of 1979-80. The traditional Stalinist model was criticized, but not without opposition from conservative hardliners, and new policies in the early 1980s still reflected a desire to preserve the basic institutions of the traditional Stalinist model. Policy debates are reflected in the open party documents and publications.[31] Nguyen Duy Trinh took a conservative position, arguing against "the tendency that said that all sectors, especially the individual and capitalist, should be allowed to expand" and maintaining that "the scope for relying on markets should be limited by the need to subordinate them to the plan – the basic reason for failure is the slow pace of change in methods of planning and management structure."[32] Nguyen Lam took a more radically pro-market position, arguing against "planning everything," favoring the use of markets and multiple planning levels and stressing the need to pay attention to the material interests of peasants, regions, and so on.[33] As a result, the reform policy in the first half of the 1980s, in general, was a compromise between the two groups in a sense that the private sector and free markets should play a role subordinate to the state plan and subsidized supply would continue as part of the state central management, with resources allocated directly into high-priority areas.[34]

However, at the Sixth Party Congress in December 1986, the policy debate began to favor reformers as Nguyen Van Linh was restored to the VCP's politburo and identified the state's central economic management as a key factor inhibiting both economic growth and micro-level reforms. Those early policies were rejected, starting with far greater formal decentralization through the slogan of "commercialization" (*thuong mai hoa*) of the state economy, allowing markets to play a more important role in the allocation of resources and encouraging nonpublic sectors to exist and develop in production and services. However, such a shift away from long-accepted orthodoxy created opposition from conservatives led by To Huu, who prevented implementation of the plenum resolution, and this again slowed the pace of transition.[35] As a matter of fact, "the program of *doi moi* approved by the Sixth Congress was hardly radical or bold. Many delegates remained wedded to ideological orthodoxy, as indicated by sharp debates over whether private enterprises should be allowed to hire up to 10 or 30 workers and whether capitalist economy should be allowed to 'return' to the north."[36] The party resolution continued to emphasize the effort to develop and strengthen the public sector in the economy. In the early 1990s, the state was still the dominant owner of the means of production within industry. The nonstate share of industrial production was estimated at 23 percent, while that of retail business and trade had increased from 30 to 70 percent during the last years of the 1980s. In banking, mining, communications, and many other sectors state ownership dominated completely. Furthermore, the state sector was increasing its share both of GDP and industrial output. Thus, the economic transition was only a process of commercialization or liberalization of the state sector, with state units acting with greater autonomy according to commercial or market criteria, with privatization playing a marginal role.[37]

In the 1990s, particularly during the 1997 Asian financial crisis, the internal conflict between conservatives and reformers intensified. Conservatives blamed the crisis on capitalism and believed that Vietnam's lack of economic integration was a blessing. Reformers blamed the crisis on "crony" capitalism, imperfect markets, and too much government intervention. Since the Eighth Party Congress in 1996, the Politburo has been deadlocked and unable to implement any bold reforms to stimulate the economy, because it is divided along factional and ideological lines and unable to come to an agreement on the direction of the reform program. Reformers believe that economic growth is contingent upon exploiting Vietnam's comparative advantage, joining the global market, courting foreign investment, and engaging in international trade, while conservatives see these as ways that the First World will continue to exploit Vietnam and keep it poor and underdeveloped.[38] Debates, attacks and counter-attacks, and compromises between the two major groups continued after the Eighth Party Congress, and these factions could cut across formal organizational and sectoral lines.[39]

The tensions between these two groups have not only determined the policy choice of economic reforms but also the sequence of economic and political reforms. However, such tensions should not be characterized as a struggle between those who favor reform and those who oppose it. Disagreement is over the pace and scope of the reforms, between those who push for more radical or speedy reforms and those who favor gradual and steady reforms. For example, in the area of ownership reform, the ideological contention within the party is no longer whether a private sector should be allowed but whether such a sector would be allowed to develop larger than the state sector, and how much freedom of expression can be allowed in the area of political reform. However, the power balance has by and large been skewed in favor of the conservatives allied with the military and security groupings that dominate in the decision-making process, particularly in the area of political reform. The reformers, on the other hand, have been given the prerogative to play a more pronounced role in economic reforms as long as regime security and stability are not threatened and fundamental principles and policy lines are not breached.[40] A protracted, stop-go cycle in the Vietnamese reform was largely caused by shifts in the balance of power between reformers and conservatives and choices made by decision makers who had their different perceptions, ideological concerns, personal interests, and considerations of regime survival.[41]

The entire process of reform and opening has been shaped and determined by the tensions and power relationship between moderate and radical reformers and the interaction of their reform strategies. Faced with powerful resistance for the conservatives, the reformists have been careful in their approach to reform and find ways to compromise when pushing for reforms. The lack of agreement between the conservatives and the reformists over the direction, extent, pace, and depth of reforms has made the party indecisive over many pressing structural problems faced by the country. The result is a gradual, partial, and piecemeal response to those problems and challenges.[42] According to editors of the *Wall Street Journal* and the *Far Eastern Economic Review* in Hanoi who interviewed Phan Van Khai, Vietnam's prime minister, he explained to the editors why Vietnam must take a gradualist approach to his country's price reform: "reductions have been made several times toward a single-price system, but our country has recently emerged from war and a centrally planned economy. Therefore we have to take it step by step. Otherwise, if we go too fast, it would lead to a collapse."[43]

LAO PDR

In Laos, the Fourth Party Congress in 1986 launched the reform program called the New Economic Mechanism (NEM). Changes in economic policy in Laos have also been associated with shifts in the balance of power within the Lao People's Revolutionary Party (LPRP) – between the reformers and the conservatives – which have favored a more gradual approach to reforms. After the collapse of communism in East Europe, debate and criticism became more overt in response to events in the late 1980s and the early 1990s. A group of younger, better educated party cadres who had close contact with technocrats and intellectuals seized upon debate over the constitution in 1990 as a means of criticizing the party and its aging leaders and pushing for more radical reforms. However, the hard-line conservatives within the party, backed by the army, purged the outspoken reformers from the party and reinforced the dominance of the party. Any attempt to push for contested election and multiparty system like those in East Europe was considered as a counter-revolutionary act and a serious threat to the leadership of the LPRP. The new economic policy and SOEs reform, through marketization and open-door policy, were modeled on the experience of China and Vietnam and controlled by the party leadership.[44]

During the 1990s, the role of the army, the Lao People's Army, has been growing steadily in political life. At the Fifth Party Congress in March 1991, the army gained three positions out of nine on the Politburo. Five yeas later, at the Sixth Party Congress in March 1996, the number jumped to seven, of which six were generals and one a former colonel. From the point of view of elite strategic choice of reform policy, although the Congress reaffirmed its commitment to reform policy, the most striking result was the change in the balance of power between "reformers by conviction and "reformers by necessity." The position of the former group was weakened as their most known advocate, Khamphoui Keoboualapha, was removed from the Politburo and more positions were occupied by the military elite and party elite in favor of a slower reform path.[45]

At the Seventh Party Congress in March 2001, the old guard maintained its grip on power with eight of the nine-member Politburo staying on although two more seats were added to the Politburo, expanding its membership from 9 to 11, to make the top leadership look younger. Two of the three newcomers were educated in Vietnam and the former Soviet Union, and the third was the military chief of staff. The government was also reshuffled in late March to reflect the change in the party leadership and the close interweaving between the LPRP and the state in Laos. In the political report to the Seventh Party Congress, the LPRP continued to appeal to socialism and Marxist-Leninist principles, with no significant breakthrough in political and economic reforms.[46]

CAMBODIA

Cambodia has experienced different forms of leadership and ideology even after the end of Pol Pot's regime. In Cambodia after Pol Pot, most of the CPP and government officials supported the restoration of Stalinist central planning in the industrial and service sectors, and the introduction of small cooperatives and household production. Their economic policy was largely influenced by the VCP.

The CPP superceding the Pol Pot regime had its origins in the same CPK, formed in 1951, but took a less radical and more pragmatic perspective on revolutionary ideology. The post-Pol Pot regime in Phnom Penh was initially known as the Kampuchean National United Front for National Salvation (KNUFNS), which later became the Kampuchean People's Revolutionary Party (KPRP), which was later renamed as the Cambodian People's Party (CPP). Political organization reflected Leninist practice in terms of party structure and the relationship between the party and the state. By 1989, although the country's name had changed from the People's Republic of Kampuchea to the State of Cambodia, its political, bureaucratic and administrative structures reflected a communist legacy and model with an interweaving of political organizations and government departments: "(i) the former interventionist role of the state, (ii) persistent centralism, and (iii) the absence of a clear delineation between the public administration, as an instrument of the executive branch, and the other institutions of the state".[47] Opposition parties are voted into office, but the CPP still retains the dominance and control of decision-making both at the national level and in the local communes, as it has for the past decade.[48]

Although the political organization remains Leninist, the CPP took a pragmatic approach to the economic policy. The radical social engineering experiment under Pol Pot regime and the civil war left the country devoid of most of the human capital and physical infrastructure necessary for post-Pol Pot economic reconstruction and development. Cambodia desperately need aid from Western capital and multi-lateral lending institutions as its economic reconstruction cannot be supported by the Soviet, Cuban, Indian and Vietnamese aid. These factors forced the People's Revolutionary Party of Kampuchea to react with pragmatism rather than ideological dogma in their management of the economy. Thus, as Roberts notes, when we consider the issues of transition from 'Communism' to 'post-Communism', we must also bear in mind the nature of the orders involved, and add to this milieu the overarching characteristics of traditional political authority, such as absolutism, elitism and patronage and clientelism."[49] "Three core characteristics of the transition from 'Communism' to 'post-Communism' seem clear. First, there has been a dual transition in political and economic terms, and there has been a continued jockeying to attain or maintain a specific balance of power between the two main parties as the single party state pluralized under external pressures. Secondly, Cambodian politicians have been trying to resolve the problem of power distribution in an expanded polity but with a reduced jobs base that has left elected representatives from Opposition parties without access to positions of wealth- and status-creating power. Thirdly, levels of economic aid from multiple independent and international sources have increased dramatically since Cambodia's international isolation effectively finished with the signing of a peace agreement that lay at the heart of this stage of Cambodia's political transition."[50]

Today, in the Cambodian system, combining remaining patterns of communist principles of organization with traditional hierarchies of power, elite politics, power struggle among three dominant political parties and within the dominant party CCP, and their strategic interactions continue to determine the direction and pace of transition and transformation. In 1993, the power-sharing arrangements resulted in parallel structures of authority and administration headed by the two "co-premiers:" Hun Sen of the CPP and Prince Norodom Ranariddh of FUNCINPEC. This parallel structure was duplicated throughout the government where each ministry was divided equally between the CPP and FUNCINPEC. They remained factions – with their own media, bureaucratic and bodyguard units – though the CPP retained a monopoly over the courts, the local authorities, and security apparatus. As each party pursued strategies to strengthen their power bases, the conflict and tension between the parties have shaped reform policy and transition. At the heart of the tensions between the parties was the CPP's domination in the coalition government and its refusal to integrate FUNCINPEC supporters into the administration at the sub-national level. In July 1997, fighting erupted between the parties resulted in a new coalition government led by the CPP and with FUNCINPEC as a junior partner. The increasing dominance of the CCP in the government has become more evident after the 2002 local election, and it has begun to enjoy more room for maneuver to push through reforms. [51] The competition between the main political parties combined with the need to balance political power between them has allowed King Sihanouk to play a role of "power balancer" in the power struggle that has pressed FUNCINPEC to opt to stay in power and work with the CPP. This continued pattern has continued to shape all aspects of the domestic politics.[52]

However, the CPP itself is divided: Chea Sim (CPP President), Sar Kheng (CPP Minister of Interior), and former party president Heng Samrin belong to one faction. Hun Sen and his supporters belong to the other. However, Hun Sen has emerged as the undisputed leader despite the apparent schism. Chea Sim was said to fear Hun Sen as he feared a tiger. Sar Kheng could not do anything against Chief of the National Police Hok Lundy (one of Hun Sen's reliable allies) despite the fact that the latter was under his authority.[53] The balance of power between these factions has interacted to shape the policy initiative, implementation, and direction of economic transition.

The Relationship Between Reform and Stability

At the cognitive level, how the party leadership perceives the need of political control and stability matters in the interplay between politics and economics. To Asian communist leaders, the fall of the Soviet Union and Eastern European communism confirmed the fundamental need of political control to maintain political stability and the necessity of economic reform to improve economic performance. Therefore, the policy choice and sequence of reform are greatly influenced by the leadership's concerns about the consequences of reform that might threaten the power of communist leadership and political stability of the regime.

CHINA

In China, although economic reforms have promoted economic growth and increased the living standards of the Chinese people, the post-Mao leaders have recognized the "faith crisis," legitimacy, polarization, unemployment in SOEs, corruption, and social security as major problems threatening political stability and the existing political order. A series of political events – the spontaneous "contest" for deputies of local peoples' congresses at Beijing universities in the early 1980s, the student and dissident movements in the early and mid-1980s, the nationwide pro-democracy student movement in 1989, and the collapse of communist regimes in the Soviet Union and Eastern Europe – have reinforced the post-Mao leadership's belief that political control is needed to maintain political stability and that economic reform should be cautious enough to help keep stability, not jeopardize it. Deng Xiaoping noted repeatedly that, what really counted was development, but without stability, there would be no economic development. Therefore, stability is considered the prerequisite for reform and development. Change should be gradual and within the current political structure. This line of thought has dominated China's economic reform and development since 1978 and continued to define the parameters of reform and development since Jiang Zemin – not too radical and not too liberal.

For the reformists, reform would bring about socioeconomic development and prosperity, which in turn would enhance regime legitimacy and political stability. For the conservatives, reforms should be conducive to the stability and prosperity of the country rather than causing social disturbances. In particular, Deng Xiaoping emphasized the "Four Cardinal Principles" as a fundamental prerequisite to the socialist reforms and the Four Modernizations. These Four Cardinal Principles define the direction, scope, content and limit of the post-Mao reforms.

Deng's "Four Cardinal Principles" are by no means considered by the post-Mao regime as rituals, but as defining the core elements of the system, and any attempt to weaken these principles has never been tolerated. During the 1980s, the top reformist leaders, such as Hu Yaobang and Zhao Ziyang, proposed and attempted to open up more political space or create "more relaxed political environment," such as allowing more toleration of debate on political reforms, more press freedom, and more lifting of political taboos within the party policy line. Their limited liberal reform efforts had the unintended effect of ideological decay and increasing student and dissident activities. These reformist leaders and their political allies were removed from office and politically persecuted, and those steps toward a more "relaxed" political environment were quickly reversed after the suppression in 1989. In the years since, no political leaders have had the courage to challenge Deng's doctrine. Economic liberalization was emerging with more political rigidity, more austere control over any liberalizing tendencies both within and outside the regime, and more a conservative backlash in political life. China's leaders have shown little tolerance for challenges to the party leadership and maintained a tough stance against public protests and independent social organizations. This intolerance locks the CCP regime in a constant struggle to hold back a rising tide of self-organizing and independent social and economic organizations that have extremely limited legal space for their political maneuver. Since the 1989 student dissident movement, no political dissident movements have been able to inspire similar widespread public sympathy and support.[54]

The post-Mao leadership has pursued a pattern of economic modernization with no attempt to fundamentally transform the Chinese communist political system. Political reforms were regarded as a means of facilitating economic reforms, and served the purpose of strengthening and improving the Party leadership. Party leadership claimed that successful and further economic reform required "social stability and unity," and should be carried out only under party leadership. Thus any tendency towards political liberalization and democratization was seen as a threat to such leadership and stability. The focus of reform has been placed in the economic area.

The emergence of the neo-left and the neo-right in the 1990s is the reaction to the political and social consequences of market reforms. Ironically, the two currents share something in common politically – both support the strengthening of the party rule and central power and oppose the effort of democratic reforms in China although they may disagree in the speed, scope, and content of economic reforms. The differences between them "have evolved naturally and logically from the official ideological stances staked out in the early years of the reform program."[55] Since the middle of 1990s, China's economic reform picked up speed, abandoned many key elements of state socialism, and embraced many methods commonly used in a capitalist market economy, steering China toward a more open and market-oriented economy. However, the conservatives have continued to attack Deng's economic policies. In 1995, a leading CCP leftist study group circulated among the party leadership the first of several "10,000 character" manifestos in the late 1990s, criticizing market reform practice and viewing income gaps, corruption and unemployment as straying away from the socialist road. It was reported that it struck a sympathetic chord among some high-level leaders and certain sectors or institutions. The conservatives are primarily located in the state planning, military, propaganda organs, political education at universities, social science academies, the mass media, party schools, and the western and central regions. Their influence began to increase in the late 1990s, stressing stability, collectivist values, equity, planning, and state regulation of the market. They also advocated policies that would roll back, slow down, or redirect market reforms on the socialist road. The conservatives slowly regained their ability to influence higher leadership because their comeback coincided with the Asian financial crisis, the bombing of the Chinese embassy in Belgrade, and the WTO concessions. It was also because the moderate reformers in the top leadership, such as Jiang Zemin, Zhu Rongji, and Li Ruihuan, were deeply concerned with stability, seeking to strengthen party leadership and maintain political stability. The tensions and conflicts between different ideological tendencies and forces have continued to affect the CCP top leadership.[56]

In the late 1990s, following a ten-year freeze on discussions concerning political reform, neo-authoritarianism and liberal intellectuals began to discuss political reform. Neo-authoritarians emerged as the "new right" that emphasized elitist rule, a strong central government, a market economy, and nationalism. The crux of this school of thought lies in the belief that China's market reform and development of market economy can only be guaranteed by a "benevolent elite power" which has the capacity of enforcing "orderly change from above" and reduce "transactional political costs" in China's transition to the market economy. The neo-authoritarianism has been widely shared by many intellectuals, and come along with the revival of "national studies" (*guo xue*) on China's traditional values and culture as a reaction against the currents of radicalism and westernization in the process of China's market reform and modernization. This revival is labeled as "neo-conservatism,"[57] which can also be categorized as the "new right." Radical liberals, such as economist Cao Siyuan, attempted to counter attack the new right and emphasized the importance of political participation, democratic reform, separation of powers, checks and balances, and Western ideas and values in the process of China's reform, opening, development and modernization. However, it seems that the neo-authoritarianism had the most influence on the party leadership,[58] as both the new left and the new right shared the same concerns about the serious consequences of economic and social transition and modernization, supported the strengthening of central power and authority, and provided theoretical weapons and justification for the top leadership of the CCP to strengthen central power and political legitimacy in maintaining the party-state system, enhance the CCP "ruling capacity" (*zhizheng nengli*), and claim the total representation of the requirements of China's advanced productive forces, the orientation of China's advanced culture, and the fundamental interests of the Chinese people – "Three Represents" (*sangedaibiao*). What the "Three Represents" emphasized is not political pluralism but the central power, the party's role and guidance over political, ideological, cultural, social, and economic direction in China. In 2000, China's Academy for Social Sciences conducted a survey of middle ranking party-state officials attending the Central Party School. The survey found that "political reform" meant little more than streamlining the bureaucracy. Corruption, unemployment, and unrest had become their major concerns.[59] This suggests that stability remains a predominant concern of the party-state leadership. Stability has overridden reform and development no matter who becomes the top leader, from Deng Xiaoping to Jiang Zemin to Hu Jintao. Premised on the fundamental need for political stability, the CCP's reform policy has limited the content, scope, pace, and direction of reform, an extended no further than a greater role for the market mechanism, less emphasis on egalitarianism and utopianism, pursuit of proportionate and balanced growth, decentralization of economic decision-making, and closer integration of China into the world economy.[60]

NORTH KOREA

North Korea's reform and opening policies were constrained by the leadership's fear of regime instability or collapse as occurred in the Eastern European former communist countries. At the same time the leadership of North Korea has taken the reform and open door policy in order to get some "fresh air" – capital and technology – from the West, it also has taken counter-measures and launched "self-reliance" campaigns, based on the so-called "mosquito-net theory," to prevent the harmful capitalist culture and alien ideology from coming into its country.[61] The reform policies and programs have been made to respond to domestic economic crisis and many changes in the socialist bloc, but it has been made in the context of the ideology of *Juche* and the party-state system. The continuity of the *Juche* ideology and the party-state system has prevented any dramatic change that might destabilize the regime. The reform is to improve and strengthen the system, rather than to replace it. This priority defines the direction, content, scope, sequence, and nature of the economic transition.

In the aftermath of the Tiananmen Square incident in 1989, Kim Il Sung supported the Chinese military crackdown on the movement. Fearing that reforms in other similar countries could have a negative impact on the regime stability and trigger the demise of communism in the country, North Korea did not want either Soviet-style *glasnost* or the Chinese model of reform, but wanted to develop their own type of reform and development based on their own method and *Juche* ideology.

To maintain the regime stability, Kim Jong Il promoted the "military first policy" (*son'gun chongch'i*) that gives priority to the military and places the Korean People's Army at the front as a pillar of the socialist revolution and construction. This policy not only augmented his power as the supreme leader of the military but also helped him to balance between the older generation revolutionaries and the younger generation technocrats. However, the "military first policy" is not a military dictatorship or rule by the military, but a policy based on the premise that the model of military organization should be followed by the party and the society to promote the spirit of revolutionary army in the society.[62] The "military first policy" does not necessarily downplay the role of the party or downgrade the party below the military[63] as the KWP is the ruling party which is completely intertwined with the military and the state in the leadership system and power structure. "The party is the very army and the army is the very party."[64]

Kim Jong Il is himself Secretary General of the Korean Worker's Party (KWP). Kim's latest speeches and the editorials in North Korean newspapers do not downgrade the role of the party – the KWP is presented as "the core driving force of socialist society," "the vanguard advancing the most correct lines and policies in each period of the revolution's development," "the only guiding force of the masses," "the fundamental source in creating new heroic achievements," and "the most formidable force for carrying out any task." The armed forces are also viewed as the vanguard "in carrying out the tasks of the Party." The KWP's predominant role in the DPRK can be seen not only on the propaganda level but also on the practical level. The party continues to have a Military Committee, which supervises the daily activities of the armed forces.[65] Every level of the military command has been penetrated by party committees and political departments modeled on the Soviet Army. The party apparatus, through its organic networks over all sectors of the state and the society, continues to constitute one of the most important pillars that Kim Jong Il can use to maintain political stability and dictatorial rule.

Kim Jong Il has attempted to maintain a balance and check between the party and the army using "divide and rule tactics" aiming to facilitate the division and mutual competition of the ruling elite. Thanks to his balancing act among political forces, power elite remains cohesive and loyal to the junior Kim, which helps to maintain a high degree of stability even in a state of economic crisis.[66] The emphasis on the regime survival and stability has defined the scope, content, pace, and direction of economic transition in North Korea although the regime has implemented some market-oriented economic reforms and open door policy in the past two decades. Therefore the gradualism of reform has been the best choice for Kim Jong Il's regime to maintain political, economic, and social stability.

VIETNAM

Vietnam's *doi moi* has resulted in a market-based and multi-sectoral economy that leaves some economic areas beyond the reach of the party and creates many ideological inconsistencies between Marxist-Leninist doctrines and market reform practices. The central question the leadership has been concerned with is how the communist party can maintain its power and leadership in the process of reform. At the heart of the issue is the question of the relationship between economic and political reform and between reform and stability. The Vietnamese leadership has regarded Vietnam as having a more satisfactory balance between economics and politics and between reform and stability.[67]

In late 1989, in the wake of the collapse of communism in Eastern Europe, reformers pushed for democratic reforms and moved the country towards a multi-party system, which sparked off a fierce debate within the party. This led to the removal of reformist leader, Tran Xuan Bach, from the Politburo in March 1990, and the removal of many other reformers such as Duong Thu Huong (a writer), Bui Tin (a former army colonel and editor of the party newspaper Nhan Dan), Nguyen Khac Vien (a well-known intellectual), and Hoang Minh Chinh (director of an official think tank). "Books were banned, publishing houses were closed and editors sacked, and in early 1992 tough new guidelines were issued to control publications."[68]

On the other hand, the VCP leadership responded to these challenges by taking some measures, including secret ballot voting procedures, broader participation in the selection of leaders both within and outside the party, rejuvenation of the party-state leadership, efforts to separate the functions of party and state institutions, and declaration of the party policy being subject to the law made by the National Assembly. These measures are superficial and very similar to those adopted in post-Mao China. But, the collapse of communism in East Europe has made the party leadership more cautious about any liberal challenges to the system and the VCP leadership.[69]

At the Seventh Party Congress in June 1991, party conservatives gained the upper hand in the Politburo, with the more conservative leader Do Muoi taking over the position of General Secretary and a majority of the Politburo seats taken by conservatives.[70] The military-security leaders have emerged as a large bloc in the Party Central Committee since then, thus emphasizing the Party's concern for maintaining stability in the country. This group as a collective conservative voice has retained its influence in determining political, social, and economic policies.[71]

At the Eighth Party Congress in 1996, Le Kha Phieu, who succeeded Do Muoi as Party General Secretary was also a conservative leader who sought to protect the *doi moi* course from being sidetracked from socialism. *Nhan Dan*, the mouthpiece of the VCP, warmed the Party that "hostile forces are implementing their 'peaceful evolution' strategy against our country in a bid to do away with Marxism-Leninism and Ho Chi Minh's thought, undermine the ideological single-mindedness within our Party and among the people, negate our Party's leadership, attempt to get rid of the socialist regime in our country... and cause our socioeconomic system to sidetrack from the socialist orbit."[72] However, the reformists, rallying behind Former Prime Minister Kiet, advocated party reform and a more open approach to the functioning of the party to fight against bloated bureaucracy, corruption, inefficiency, and waste. Although this proposal was largely unsuccessful, the reformists had the upper hand when parts of the draft economic document, which was referred to as the promotion of the state sector to 60 percent of GDP, was removed from the resolution of the Eighth Party Congress. The resolution was a compromise or a deadlock. The party rejected political pluralism, but left many fundamental issues unresolved. Such issues as economic pluralism, public administration reform, SOE reform, and integration into the global market were accepted without clear implementation details and schedules. The various factions in the VCP agreed on three broad policy areas: the need for political stability, the need for openness to the outside world through foreign trade and investment, and the need for Vietnam to reform at its own pace. Because each faction could interpret these policy issues differently, further discussions are required. As a result, the implementation of reforms was slow and partial. All factions agreed on the need for reform, but the problem was how much the VCP should risk in its commitment to deeper reforms? The pace of reform was the main point of contention. Gradualism was the result of compromise between various factions within the VCP leadership.[73]

At the Fourth Plenum in December 1997, the party endorsed the "gradual" restructuring of SOEs. The Plenum stressed the mobilization of domestic capital and encouraged foreign investment, but was cautious about the opening-up of Vietnam's capital market. The various plenum meetings between 1998 and 1999 (Fifth, Sixth, Seventh, Eighth) had been convened to tackle urgent economic problems in the face of the Asian crisis, but the meetings were dominated by the main concerns of ideology, stability, party unity, and party building. The VCP continued to stress stability over reform and use the gradual "learning by doing" approach to economic reform as its counterpart, the CCP, did in post-Mao China throughout its reform process.[74] Since the Eighth Party Congress in 1996, the Politburo has been deadlocked, as internal conflict between conservatives and reformers has prevented an agreement on the direction of the reform program. "The VCP consists of not one but many groups or 'factions' jockeying for power and other interests. This struggle impacts on the party's ability to achieve consensus."[75]

At the Ninth Party Congress in 2001, although former General Secretary Le Kha Phieu was replaced by a more reform-minded leader, Nong Duc Manh, this change in leadership is regarded as a compromise choice between the differing "tendencies" within the party, particularly with regard to the pace and depth of economic liberalization.[76] Despite the differences, both conservatives and reformers have agreed on the fundamental need of maintaining political stability as the prerequisites for economic reform and growth because both factions are fearful of instability and believe that changes and reforms can also bring down the regime if not controlled. Therefore, the VCP leadership has firmly turned its back on any significant political reform and is determined to maintain party-state power and control, while adopting the idea of a "socialist oriented market economy" as the direction of the economic reform program. SOE reform continued to be a contentious issue that divided the VCP leadership between those wishing to retain state control of the economy and those wishing to let market forces take the lead.

At the Third Central Committee Plenum in August 2001, the VCP adopted a resolution on "Continuation of the Reorganization, Renovation, and Development of State-Owned Enterprises," which signaled the continuation of SOE reform. However, the VCP leadership also viewed SOE reform as a sensitive political issue that was closely related to social and economic stability, and therefore, as General Secretary Nong Duc Manh pointed out at the plenum, "SOEs should continue serve as a tool in the hands of the state to regulate the economy, ensure adherence   to the socialist path, and maintain political, economic, and social stability."[77]

Therefore, much as in China, the gradualism of reform is also determined by the conflict and compromise between conservatives and reformers within the leadership over the political direction, the pace of reform, and the determination to maintain the party control over the transition process and the political order of this country.[78] The objective of reform is not to undermine but to strength the credibility of the communist party-state as the legitimate leading force for change and development. Economic reform, globalization, and their consequential impact on the party-state capacity and the economic development have propelled the communist leadership of Vietnam to be concerned with the system stability and coherence. Many economic issues are considered as "politically" and "socially" sensitive, which has prevented the leadership from taking a bolder move, but instead has made the choice of "muddling through" as the way to resolve the problems.

LAO PDR

Reform was reaffirmed at each party congress from 1986 to 2001. However, stability has also become a primary concern of the Lao People's Revolutionary Party as economic reforms have brought about many problems that may threaten the party-state rule. An important objective of reforms is to strengthen the credibility of the party-state as legitimate forces of change rather than to undermine it. The fear of losing control over the changes brought about by economic liberalization has dominated each party congress since the 1990s. Each party congress reaffirmed the one-party state and emphasized the importance of building up institutions to secure it.[79] The party-state structure, rather than weakened, has been institutionalized and strengthened by cross leadership appointment and dual leadership system from top to bottom. As many of the Politburo members have their background in the army, the military has played an important role in shaping the agenda, policy, pace and direction of reform and economic change in Lao PDR.

After the collapse of communism, some debates over the draft of constitution led to criticism of the LPRP leadership and its policies causing corruption and increasing social and economic inequality. Some dissent voices even advocated that Laos should move toward a multiparty system. Latsamy Khamphoui, a former vice minister in the State Planning Commission, voiced his criticism of the party policies in his letter to the government. Thongsouk Saisangkhi, another vice minister of Science and Technology, submitted his resignation from the party, accusing the leaders of creating a "communist monarchy" ruled by the "dynasty of the Politburo." He called for the establishment of a "multiparty system in order to bring democracy, freedom, and prosperity to the people." Both of the party officials and another official in the Justice Ministry who had been outspoken in his criticism of the constitution were arrested without legal representation. These arrests followed similar purges in Vietnam and Cambodia that attempted to silence the dissent voices and reinforce the dominance of the communist parties.[80]

To maintain the party control over the transition process and strengthen the party leadership, the LPRP economic policy followed the path of Chinese and Vietnamese transition, rather than that of the Soviet Union and Eastern Europe. This means that the goal of reform was to strengthen the party leadership, the state domination, and the socialist orientation while introducing market competition, material incentive, de-collectivization, trade liberalization, SOE reform, and open door policy for foreign investment. "As long as Laos' policy makers regard maintaining social, economic, and political stability as paramount, this policy approach is likely to remain unchanged."[81]

CAMBODIA

Reforms in Asian communist states were carried out within the framework of the one-party dictatorship. In Cambodia, although the Paris agreement in the early 1990s brokered a political transition from Vietnamese-backed communist rule to a domestically elected coalition government, a July 1997 coup by the communist party's co-prime minister Hun Sen purged his royalist co-prime minister Norodom Ranariddh and returned the country to the communist party rule. The former communist party-state apparatus has remained politically dominant, as formalized by the 1997 coup. Both political life and economic administration have remained highly personalistic and elitist in Cambodia.[82]

Among the major obstacles to democracy are ideological conflict between the major contending parties, anti-democratic cultural values, and asymmetrical power relations among the political factions.[83] The opposition parties sought to undermine the ruling party CPP by accusing its leaders of continuing to adhere to communist totalitarianism or communist type system, where the ruling party structures and state structures are intertwined as the party-state. The CPP continue to exercise exclusive control over the most powerful ministries of defense, interior, justice, foreign affairs, and military and security forces despite its power sharing with other political parties in other areas.[84] The CPP also controls local governments (communes) since 1979. The local level provides the CPP with the base for national chains of patron-client networks that ensure the accumulation and extension of power throughout the country.[85] The CPP continued to be dominant at the local level after the 2002 local election.

Hun Sen's government "pursued its economic goals in an environment of political uncertainty, both in terms of the Khmer Rouge insurgency and the political infighting among the leaders of the governing coalition."[86] The case of Sam Rainsy illustrated that the ruling party in the coalition government would continue to suppress the challenges and criticisms that might cause a direct threat to its power and control over the transition process. Sam Rainsy's outspoken criticisms and efforts to fight against corruption caused a storm of protest from politicians, business interests, and the armed forces, and he was removed from the Cabinet of Hun Sen's government, and then ousted from the National Assembly and the National United Front for an Independent, Peaceful, Neutral, and Cooperative Cambodia (FUNCINPEC) party in a government crackdown against dissent. Two editors of the newspaper *Voice of Khmer Youth* were also arrested and sentenced to jail for publishing so-called false and defamatory articles that allegedly undermined people's confidence in the government and its leaders and caused damages on political stability.[87]

On Thursday, February 3, 2005, Cambodia's National Assembly achieved the two-thirds majority it needed to overturn rules protecting Sam Rainsy and his colleagues Cheam Channy and Chea Poch from prosecution. Their parliamentary immunity was thus stripped. As a result of the decision, the three men could face a series of defamation charges – which could force them to pay hefty fines or even spend time in jail. Hours after the decision, Sam Rainsy left the country to Paris. Cheam Channy was taken into custody by police on Thursday afternoon, and has reportedly been charged with starting an anti-Hun Sen militia. Chea Poch is thought to be in hiding. In this way, Hun Sen's party, supported by FUNCINPEC, has kicked out the opposition voice out of the coalition government.[88] The current government, an uneasy coalition between socialists and royalists, seems to find some common interests in preserving and extending their power and maintaining order and stability at the expense of freedom and democracy. The stability that Hun Sen and his CPP obtained in Cambodia has been achieved by suppressing all opposition forces through the exiling or killing of those who dare to oppose him and his party. Even the King and royalist party now side with Hun Sen.

The Relationship Between Socialist Principles and Market Reforms

In socialist reforms, the primary actors initiating reforms are the party-state elite and the direction of those changes is determined by their perceptions and visions on reform, which are expressed in different interpretations of Marxism-Leninism. It is in this context that the debate on overall or particular reform policies has taken place. The primary barriers to reform and change are the official ideology, and therefore the removal of ideological barriers allows reforms to move to the next stages and spread from one area to the other. The first hotly debated ideological issue in communist countries has to do with the relationship between plan and market. The leadership's different understanding of the plan-market relationship has largely determined the pace and scope of economic reform. The second has to do with ideological commitment and regime identity, in which the corner stone of socialism is identified with public ownership and therefore must be preserved in market-oriented reform.

CHINA

In China, an important ideological debate was the compatibility between plan and market, and this shaped and constrained the reform process from the very beginning. During the late 1970s and the early 1980s, an initial step of reform was to encourage experimentation with household contracting (*baogan daohu*) in agricultural farming, which led to the abandonment of people's communes and the introduction of the household responsibility contracting system. This meant no more collective farming and production targets. Households were given the use rights of a piece of land and allowed to sell any surplus on the market after delivery of a certain amount of grain to the state at set prices.[89] Important consequences of this were the increasing role of the market and independent decision making on the part of peasants, which generated a serious debate within the party on the relationship between plan and market. The debate ended with an official resolution by the CCP that the market mechanism be considered a useful supplement to socialist planning.

During the 1980s, no breakthrough was made in terms of the relationship between two of the most important concepts in the political economy of state socialism – plan and market. For the conservative or moderate reformers, the market was equal to capitalism while the plan was equal to socialism. For the conservatives, the market was seen as a bird in the cage of the socialist plan, which was called "birdcage economy," in which "the state guides the market and the market guides the enterprises." For the radical reformers, the plan was not considered as the fundamental principle of socialism. Both plan and market were just two different means for allocating social and economic resources and, therefore, not attributed to the nature of a political economy.[90] The debate ended with a compromise at the 13th Party Congress in 1987: the CCP adopted the concept "Socialist Planned Commodity Economy" that combined planning and market mechanism.

Since 1992, the radical reformers gained the upper hand on this issue with the support of Deng Xiaoping. Since then the CCP has adopted the concept "Socialist Market Economy" based on the idea that the market mechanism was merely an instrument of resource allocation and not a defining feature of an economic system. The market was considered compatible with both capitalist and socialist economies. The socialist nature of the economy would be maintained as long as the CCP ruled and the public ownership (the state and the collectives) occupied a predominant position in the economy. Since then, China has made the transition from a centrally planned economy to a market-based mixed economy with public ownership occupying the predominant position.

The reform process in China suggests that different views of the relationship between plan and market have played an important role in shaping the reform objective model, from "a planned economy with some market adjustment," to "a planned commodity economy based on the combination of plan and market," and now to "a socialist market economy" which enables the market to play a central role under the state's macroeconomic control.[91] It took fourteen years (1978-1992) for China to switch from the initial reform objective model to the current economic model.

Another important ideological conflict arising from the reform process is the compatibility of a market system with those principles of socialism. Although China's post-Mao leaders are devoted to reform, they also remain committed to socialism. Many reform measures conflict with socialist principles and ethics in China. Reforms call for an increase in the private sector, the role of market forces, and the maximization of profit, but socialist ethics demand the predominance of public ownership, the role of state planning and control, and the social need of production. The tension between the reformist spirit and the socialist ethic has been the foundation of the debate over economic reform that has continued throughout the post-Mao era. While the moderate reformers have placed a greater emphasis on maintaining a socialist economic system that embodies traditional socialist values, the radical reformers have been more flexible with the definition of socialism, embracing the ideas of market competition, private interest, and even a certain degree of economic inequality.[92]

Although the Third Plenum of the Eleventh National Congress of the CCP Central committee held in 1979 initiated China's economic reform, reformers within the party disagreed on one key issue: what is the nature of the socialist economy? More than three decades of experience with the traditional planned economy had exposed serious problems and made the post-Mao leaders aware of the need for reform. The question was in what direction. Throughout the 1980s, the moderate and radical reformers debated the nature of the socialist economy, which would set the direction for China's reform. Obviously, the answer to the question had important implications for the reform strategy to be adopted. Within the political context of Chinese socialism, this was a central question. For the moderate reformers, the socialist economy at the primary stage of communism was a commodity economy based on public ownership, which could coexist with other types of ownership, and therefore, economic reform must conform to the principle of developing the commodity economy through the conscious utilization of "the law of value." For the radical reformers, the socialist economy was a type of market economy based on a mixed structure of ownership, with the market playing a central role in the economy, and therefore, economic reform must move in that direction. The debate between these two groups was not resolved until the Fourteenth National Congress of the CCP Central Committee in 1992, which defined the nature of the socialist economy as the "socialist market economy," and this marked the victory of the radical reformers in the debate. Hence, the market mechanism was viewed merely as an instrument of economic development and not a defining characteristic of an economic system, and it was compatible with either a capitalist or socialist economic system.

Further reform in the 1990s called for a breakthrough in ownership theory. The debate on the nature of shareholding cooperative system was raging during the early 1990s, with a primary focus on whether the shareholding cooperative system was public or private in nature. The result of the debate is the retention of the state sector with the concomitant creation of a parallel non-state sector. The Chinese officials made the distinction between "privatization" and "corporatization" and view the conversion of SOEs into shareholding companies and the subsequent sale of such shares on a security market as ideologically compatible with "socialism with Chinese characteristics." The strategy has not been to privatize the state sector and hand over control and equity to private hands, but rather to bring private savings and foreign capital into state controlled shareholding enterprises within the state-controlled parameters of "market socialism" in order to serve the state's financial needs, ensure the state's priority in access to investment capital, and maintain the dominant position of the state as majority shareholder. That is to say, corporatization has not been to allow private entities greater ownership and control over enterprises, but allow the state to exercise greater ownership and control over a vast pool of private capital hidden in the non-state sector. Shareholding reform has been limited by ideological constraints: the quota system regulating the number of SOEs allowed to be listed on a security market only recently abolished, the type of enterprises (state, not private, enterprise) allowed to be listed on a security market, and the percentage of shares (a minority) in listed enterprises allowed to be privately owned and traded.[93] The reform pace and direction have been shaped by a decade long disagreement, debate, and compromise between reformers and conservatives, which has resulted in a gradual, phased, experimental and dual-track pattern.

NORTH KOREA

In North Korea, in January 2001, before and after Kim Jong-Il visited China, North Korean media carried his remarks on renovation in thought and way of thinking, launching a "new thinking campaign" for changing the out-of-date manner of work and thinking in the past and for refashioning the national economy. Noteworthy was the emphasis on a fundamental innovation in ideological view, way of thinking, outlook, conception, and technological reconstruction to adjust its economy to the changing international environment and to carry out economic management efficiently and in a profit-oriented manner.[94] As Kim Jong-Il said on his way back from China to Pyongyang, "All the officials must discard the outdated thought, follow the new and bring about a radical innovation in the method of work."[95] The "new thinking" ideological campaign was viewed as a sign that North Korea began to embrace the kind of controlled economic reforms which have allowed China and Vietnam to attract foreign investment and revitalize the economy with its political system intact. But, Kim Jong-Il has maintained that innovation and economic development should be made within the framework comprised of socialist ideologies, principles, and military strength. Therefore, his "new thinking" is not comparable to that of Gorbachev who combined both economic restructuring (*perestroika*) and political openness (*glasnost*).[96] However, it is clear that North Korean leadership has made efforts to "rebuild its economy by introducing market mechanisms."[97]

Kim's *Juche* idea is the ideological foundation of the North Korean system and the guiding principle of the economic reform. A major dilemma for the DPRK leadership is how to reconcile the ideology of *Juche* self-reliance with the pragmatic approach to the economic reform and opening policy that seeks trade and investment relations with other countries based on the rules and practices of market economy. On the one hand, the *Juche* idea is a guiding principle of the party and state, and adhering to the principle of self-sufficiency in the economy means building an economy which is free from dependence on others, which is considered essential for guaranteeing the political independence and sovereignty of the country. On the other hand, the economic reform will require that the DPRK leadership must seek foreign aid and investment on terms acceptable to the international community based on commonly accepted market practices and rules. This means that there will be inevitably increasing level of dependence on other economies and deepening economic interdependence with other countries. To solve this dilemma, the *Juche* idea is "destined for the same creative re-interpretation as the ideologies of the Communist Parties in China and Vietnam have undergone in recent years."[98] That is to say, the North Korean leadership has to revise the *Juche* doctrine to meet the new challenges and practical needs in the economic reform and opening. North Korea now calls this reform and opening policy as "*silli* socialism" (*silli* means "profit" or "practicality") – "practical socialism," which is now included in the concept of *Juche*. The change suggests that North Korean leadership has concentrated on the practical matters in the current situation rather than the long-term goal of "complete success of socialism." *Juche* has been redefined on the basis of practicality rather than utopianism. In this way, North Korea has provided the ideological justification for the reform policy under Kim Jong Il.[99] Although North Korea also claims the reform is not an acceptance of a free market economy of capitalism, it has recognized that socialism can coexist with capitalism and planning can coexist with markets, and the reform is practical application of the socialist framework. These two facades – blending of elements of socialism and capitalism or socialist planning and markets – are indeed a reflection of the core idea of market socialism, which will be thoroughly discussed in Chapters 5 and 6.

Finance Minister Mun Il-bong's speech at the SPA session of March 26th 2003 resembles the Chinese concept "Three Represents" "Our people, holding high the Great Leader's ideology of nation-building (*konguksasang*) after liberation, have built a new democratic Korea upon the rubbles, those with strength (him) using strength, those with knowledge (*chisik*) using knowledge, and those with money (*ton*) using money."[100] In the Chinese context, the "Three Represents" provides a solution to the problem of how to integrate newly emerged market and capitalist elements into market socialism, in which the Chinese Communist Party does not only represent the working class but also the newly emerged entrepreneurs, thereby attempting to bring them under the umbrella of the party-state, while resolving contradictions between reality and ideological theory in the reform. In the DPRK context, "strength" stands for the workers and farmer's, "knowledge" stands for the intellectuals – all three well known and represented in the emblem right on the *Juche*-Tower in Pyongyang (hammer, sickle, brush). But "money" is a new component, and it stands for those individuals and entrepreneurs in economic and business activities being integrated into the socialist society.[101] As Ch'oe Hong-kyu, Bureau Director in the State Planning Commission, put it, "Kim Jong-Il stresses that all the outworn and dogmatic 'Soviet-type' patterns and customs should be renounced in the fields of economic planning, financing and labor management... He also points to the fact that foreign trade should be conducted in accordance with the mechanism and principles of capitalism."[102]

The ideological backing for change is provided by the *Juche* ideology itself, in particular its creative principle, which was originally meant to provide justification for modification on Marxism and Leninism and some independence from Moscow and Beijing; now, it serves as a justification for economic reforms that embrace the market, which is no longer considered as something related to capitalism and can be utilized under both capitalism and socialism. Embracing markets is considered as the provisional character of a socialist society – as the transitional stage towards communism – and due to this transitional character, there is a relationship between commodities and money which requires markets to supplement the role of the state, both of which constitute the dual, hybrid structure of the socialist economy. However, for North Korean leaders, markets play a supplementary role under socialism to increase the efficiency of state-directed production and distribution, not to replace them, and markets exist only temporarily until their functions will be gradually taken over by the state.[103] The ideological constraints on the market reform and the resolutions to the contradictions between theory and reality have partially determined the speed and scope of the market reform – on the one hand, North Korea has gradually and partially introduced some elements of capitalist market economy into its reform and opening policy while on the other hand it has continued to adhere to the basis principles of the socialist economic system. Thus, the transition pattern is similar to that of China – gradual, partial, dualist, and experimental.

VIETNAM

In Vietnam, the leadership's perception of the relationship between plan and market has also shaped the reform agenda and the fundamental issue of what is permissible and what is not within socialism. At the Sixth Party Congress which set the guidelines for *doi moi*, the Vietnamese leadership recognized the problems of the central planning system and the advantages of the market. However, the problem is how to balance the two and use the plan as an indicator of general direction.[104] Reformers viewed the coexistence of plan with market and of the state sector with the market sector as the way to salvage the inefficient state sector and to relieve the state of heavy burdens to the society. Conservatives, on the other hand, contended that market-oriented economic liberalization and relaxed state control over the economy undermined the existing socialist programs and also blamed corruption, social problems, and the failure of land reform in the South on market reforms.

The strategic choice of reform policies in Vietnam was also shaped by the debate on the relationship between socialist principles and market reform practices. Market reforms have brought about many changes that contradict the doctrines of Marxism-Leninism. It is in this context that the debate on overall or particular reform policies has taken place. The function of party ideology is to provide reforms with a theoretical framework or basis, and what is more, direction. Therefore, Vietnam's party must balance socialist principles with market reforms and insure that the identity and legitimacy of its ruling status will not be undermined during economic transition.

As early as the 1980s, a theoretical issue emerged in Vietnam: can Vietnam bypass the stage of capitalist development? The political debate leading to the Seventh Party Congress raised a fundamental question concerning the applicability of socialism in Vietnam. The Seventh Party Congress rejected the idea of a stage of capitalist development in Vietnam, especially as a political system and ideology, but its contributions to developing forces of production were considered as a "consequence of the intellect of humanity" which could be used for promoting socialist construction in Vietnam.[105] General Secretary Nguyen Van Linh warned against two deviations from the party's reform policy: one was the tendency that merely saw the corrupt aspects of a capitalist society without recognizing its progress in technology and management organization, and the other was the tendency that only saw its good aspects without recognizing its bad aspects.[106]

Another theoretical question loomed: how can socialism encompass the aspects of capitalism without losing its identity? The answer is that reform and renovation "do not negate or dismiss the socialist principles because they are the boundaries between communists and noncommunists, socialist and nonsocialist societies, and revolution and reformism"[107] In defending socialist principles, Nguyen warned that "whoever in the name of 'creativity' or 'doi moi' says they accept Marxism-Leninism but in their actions erase its revolutionary and scientific principles, they are sinking deep into the morass of rightist or 'leftist' opportunism."[108] The landmark of socialism is identified with the public ownership of the means of production and land.

Vietnam did not follow a comprehensive reform plan which would spell out each of the stages from beginning to end, but moved forward in a step by step manner.[109] The first step of reform was in the northern rural sector where both collective farms and state enterprises were allowed to engage in a wide range of "experiments," which included contracting between individual farmers and collectives. Collectivization in the south was temporarily abandoned with only one-third of collective production teams still in existence. By the early 1980s, most agricultural households were operating individually under "production contracts" that stipulated for each household a quota for delivery of food grains to the state, and allowed above-quota sales at a negotiated price with the state agency.[110] However, this reform was not part of a longer-term plan, and peasants could not count on them, because cooperatization or collectivization remained on the party agenda. In December 1982, the Third Plenum of the Fifth Party Congress declared that the cooperatization of the southern region should be "basically completed" by the end of 1985, and in 1984 an effort to renew a "collectivization drive" was made by the Fourth Plenum. The Sixth Party Congress in December 1986 fully endorsed the move towards a market economy from a planned economy. But, it was only after the adoption of Politburo Decree No. 10 in April 1988 that the peasant family was clearly understood to be the basic unit in the agricultural sector and the contracting system became the basis of a long-term tenure system granting user rights of land and freedom to sell products on the open market. The user rights in the contracting system were not private ownership of land. The contracting system is similar to the one adopted in China.[111]

The Seventh Party Congress in June 1991 continued to reject privatization of land and endorse the role of cooperatives in managing common matters and assuring equity. The cooperatives have not been abandoned, but their role has changed from one of administrative responsibility over production to one of responsibility for the distribution of inputs, provision of irrigation and other services, collection of taxes and fees, and procurement of outputs. Cooperatives also continue to own capital equipment, such as tractors and trucks, but management has been contracted to individual operators. The actual role of the cooperative in the south is more limited but remains powerful in some respects, having decisive influence over certain crucial matters such as the leasing of land.[112]

In the 1990s, SOE reform began to emerge as a hotly debated issue in the VCP leadership. The conservatives rejected the attempt to privatize the SOEs and were not at ease with the development of the private sector. For them, the corner stone of socialism was identified with public ownership and therefore SOEs and state control must be preserved in market-oriented reform. The reformists advocated a parallel development of private and public sectors and a reduced role of the state in the economy. For them, the development of private sectors would not undermine the predominant position of public sectors and would be beneficial to the improvement of living standards for the Vietnamese people. The result of the debate was a compromise: the Vietnamese leadership began to allow private enterprises to develop in some areas, eliminate most plan targets, emphasize the financial accountability and autonomy of state enterprises, and initiate credit and price reforms. However, "SOEs are cosseted and indirectly subsidized by preferential access to land usage rights, tax concession, and priority treatment on matters of bank finance, transport, and licensing."[113] In the 1990s, the reform of SOEs followed a very similar pattern of Chinese reform. Although the number of SOEs has been reduced, they have been restructured into a score of state conglomerates, each associating a significant number of enterprises in a particular industrial sector, such as rubber, steel, transport, and cement.[114] These new state companies have also taken advantage of new business opportunities provided by reform at all levels of the party-state to expand into new areas, including foreign and domestic trade, joint-ventures, real estate, banking, tourism, and entertainment. In these new areas, they have benefited a great deal from various forms of monopoly or oligopoly control.[115]

As late as August 2001, at the Third Plenum of the Ninth Central Committee, the VCP continued to declare that "the state sector of the economy (in which state enterprises are the main pillars) shall occupy a leading role and this role is closely associated with the country's move towards socialism and stable economic and social development."[116] The Ninth Party Congress in 2001 did not make any breakthrough in economic reform objectives and only reaffirmed the policy direction laid down at the Sixth and Seventh Party Congress. Before the Ninth Party Congress, party documents declared that it was the long-term policy of the VCP to develop a "commodity-based multi-sectoral economy operating in accordance with the state-managed and socialist oriented market mechanism." The Ninth Party Congress merely condensed this long sentence into a single phrase – "develop a socialist-oriented market economy." At the First Plenum, the VCP leadership, as its counterpart did, began to grapple with the complicated question of whether businessmen should be allowed to join the party since plenty of businessmen were already party members from the party-state organizations or SOEs, but it failed to come up with a detailed policy. The private sector is now allowed to develop, but still barred from "sensitive" industries. The boom in private companies stem almost entirely from small, family-run and privately-financed firms. To grow into bigger businesses however, those ventures will require resources that mainly go to SOEs. The country has a fledgling stock market exchange, in Ho Chi Minh City, but all the listed companies are state-owned. In 2001, the Vietnamese government promised foreign donors that it would sell some 300 state outfits, but only managed half that number, because the VCP continues to preserve a significant public sector as the corner stone of socialism.[117] As Nong Duc Manh acknowledged at the Third Plenum that SOE reforms were "sensitive political issues that are closely related to social and economic stability," and therefore SOEs "should serve as a tool in the hands of the state to regulate the economy, ensure adherence to the socialist path, and maintain political, economic and social stability."[118]

The continuity in Vietnam's economic policy is largely a result of the compromise and balance between reformers and conservatives in the VCP leadership. Reformers wanted to scrap the inefficient state sector and free up the private sector, while conservatives contended that the collapse of the state sector could lead to mass unemployment and political unrest. The state sector was considered as the backbone of the socialist economy and must be maintained as the dominant role in the economy. Therefore, the effort should focus on making the SOEs efficient and profitable. The VCP leadership has not been able to resolve the debate between the liberal and conservative positions and form a consensual policy.[119] A middle-road between the two groups has been sought and reaffirmed at the Third Plenum of the Ninth Central Committee. In the foreseeable future, the direction of economic policy will be most likely to muddle through on this middle road.[120]

LAO PDR

Similar reforms were undertaken in Laos in 1979 when economic reform began with agricultural liberalization, the collectivization was temporarily abandoned, and the emphasis shifted to cooperatives or "mutual aid teams." At the Fifth Party Congress in 1991, the policy of cooperatization was abandoned and "the farmers household economy" was promoted as the basic unit in Laos agriculture. The new policy was market-oriented and aimed at shifting subsistence production to commodity production. As in China and Vietnam, all land still belongs to the state. Land legislation focuses on user rights of land rather than formal ownership. Peasants are allowed to lease or sell their user rights and their children can inherit the right to use the land.[121] Industrial reform began with leasing and privatization of some SOEs, management reform in the public sector, grant of full autonomy to SOEs to set prices (except public utilities), encouragement of private enterprises, and liberalization of foreign trade and investment. All these measures are taken gradually and initially on an experimental basis as a result of a new party policy known as the "New Economic Mechanism" (NEM) adopted in 1986. So far, nearly all private firms are in Laos are small- and medium-sized enterprises, while SOEs retain the dominance in all key and strategic industries. The thrust of this NEM was to liberalize markets and decentralize economic decision making.

Market-oriented reforms contradicted the doctrines of Marxism-Leninism and generated serious concerns within the party about the nature of socialist reform, which called for theoretical justification and self-legitimization. In response to this concern, Former Secretary-General of the party and Prime Minister, Kaysone Phomvihane, found its theoretical justification from Lenin's New Economic Policy in the early 1920s:

> Lenin stressed that under conditions in which administrative power is in the hands of the people, we are not afraid that free trading will develop. On the contrary we can prevent capitalism from developing along the path of state capitalism and create necessary and firm conditions for turning state capitalism into socialism in the future. The capitalist economy is still useful to production and social life ... we are fully capable of using its positive characteristics in our production and social life, and of checking and limiting its negative sides without being afraid that when capitalism is fully developed it will override socialism.[122]

The political reports to the delegates of Party Congresses have always reiterated that the party and Laos will adhere to Marxist-Leninist principles and socialist orientation. These principles are considered as the fundamental to the socialist nature of Lao PDR. The change fell short of expectations for those hoping for the political system to open up and new leadership to emerge in Laos.[123]

However, according to some scholars, Lao PDR has developed a unique economic system which blends some elements of Marxism, Capitalism, and Buddhism, as the leadership of the LPRP realized the integral role of Buddhism in the way of life of the majority of Lao people and the utility of capitalist market economy for the Lao economy. "From the perspective of the Lao leadership, pure capitalism and pure Communism are both too extreme, and the Lao mix of Adam Smith, Karl Marx, and the Buddha represents an interesting and innovative attempt at political economy, which may be called 'Laoism'."[124] Laoism suggests that Lao has pursued its own path of development while it is also mindful of the experiences and mistakes of reforming Asian economies. This approach would have to blend different elements, which might be contradictory in practice and gradualist in character.

CAMBODIA

In Cambodia, as in the rest of Indochina, reform began with agricultural liberalization – the extreme form of collectivism practiced by the Khmer Rouge was replaced by a three-tiered structure of collectivized groups or solidarity groups (*krom sammaki*) consisting of a number of peasant families. The *krom sammaki* agricultural system has undergone important changes since its introduction in 1979, particularly regarding the degree of collectivization. By 1987, the lowest level of *krom sammakis* – farmers family economy – were the dominant form of agricultural organization and production throughout rural Cambodia. Farmers are required to sell only a portion (10 percent or less) of their harvest to the state at a price lower than the market price and deliver a certain quantity to the state as a "patriotic contribution" (essentially an agricultural tax). Farmers may sell all that remains of their production in the free market. In 1989, collectivization was formally abandoned as state policy and recent reports indicate that the *krom sammaki* has disappeared in a formal or organized sense.[125] Today, peasant family economies have developed into a dominant form of production in all three countries of Indochina, and peasant families have direct access to land through some kind of constitutionally guaranteed long-term tenure, with an entirely new relationship to the market. They may, by and large, grow what they choose to subsist or to sell in the market, with prices negotiated between the parties.[126] However, the legal framework to grant land titles was not fully implemented, and only 1% of rural households have full legal rights to their agricultural land.[127]

In Cambodia, ownership reform has moved the country toward an economy with different kinds of ownership. At the initial stage of reform, three types of economic organization were recognized: state, cooperative, and family; after the Fifth Party Congress in 1985 a fourth, private sector, was allowed to develop, and in 1989 a fifth sector comprising state-private joint ventures. Until 1985-1986 all state industries were centrally planned and financed. Beginning in 1986-1987 a certain degree of decentralization was instituted, both in planning and finance. A certain amount of private industry was also allowed and incorporated into the constitution as a new economic sector.[128]

Conclusion

This chapter has examined three key variables that have shaped the strategic choices of reform policy and therefore the pattern of Asian transition from state socialism. The reform pace and direction have been shaped by a decade long disagreement, debate, and balance between reformers and conservatives along the three main dimensions, which has resulted in a gradual, phased, experimental and dual-track pattern of transition. Chinese and Asian transition from state socialism confirms the following temporary generalizations that can be found in the literature on Asian economic transition from socialism.

First, there is a direct causal relationship between elite strategic choice and pattern of transition and an antecedent relationship between structural factors, policy choices, and patterns of transition. The entire process of reform has been shaped and determined by the tensions between moderate and radical reformers and the interaction of their reform strategies.

Second, if the reformers are in a relatively weak political position, then support for reform can be obtained by introducing step-by-step partial reforms directed at areas where possible and where there will be a quick payoff such as in agriculture. The initial success would then strengthen the political support for reform and more difficult reforms can be attempted. Therefore, the timing and priorities of reforms are often dictated by economic feasibility and political sustainability perceived by the leadership.[129]

Third, because the party's ideology blocked macro-systemic change, reform started with micro-economic reform of agricultural organization and industrial enterprise management.[130]

Fourth, governments always face political constraints or the need to overcome potential opposition from various groups when elaborating reform proposals. Political constraints vary, depending on the regime type or the type of society, under an authoritarian regime or under a parliamentary democracy.[131]

A reform-minded government faces constraints of political acceptability at each period. Radical, large-scale reforms involve greater aggregate and individual uncertainty about the outcome than gradualist reforms. Gradualist, partial reforms make reforms easier to start because it gives an additional option of early adjustment at a lower cost of trial and error after partial uncertainty resolution. This advantage of gradualism explains why Asian leaders take a gradual approach. If partial reforms are unstable, the choice at each stage of transition is between accepting the next reforms or reversing the previous ones. If the initial reforms have been a success, it will thus create momentum by strengthening the support for the next reforms. In contrast, starting transition with the more painful reforms undermines popular support and may unnecessarily lead to reform reversal.[132]

Many empirical studies on China's reforms have confirmed the important idea of political constraints of reform in shaping the choice of reform policy, such as or state-owned enterprise reform through a "profit contracting system" was chosen over "comprehensive reform" and price liberalization through the dual-track price reform was chosen over one-step price reform in the mid-1980s.[133]

For all transitional economies of communist states, when designing politically acceptable structural reforms, governments always face a tradeoff between the budgetary cost of the reform and its degree of allocative efficiency: massive reduction of redundancies might yield rapid efficiency gains, but at a great budgetary cost, whereas gradual reforms involve less in terms of compensation payments, but imply a slower move towards allocative efficiency.[134]

Early economic reform has followed a political logic in which policies that distributed benefits to localities (such as internal decentralization and external opening) prevailed over policies that attempted to launch a swift marketization (such as price reform or hard budget constraints) (Shirk, 1993).

Asian transition from communism has suggested some major lessons. If the reformers are in a relatively weak political position, then support for the reform can be obtained by introducing step-by-step partial reforms. A partial reform policy has the advantage that the initial reforms can be directed at areas where there will be a quick payoff such as in agriculture. The initial success then strengthens the political support for reform, and more difficult and painful reforms can be attempted. This suggests that a strong pro-reform government can succeed with a big-bang reform strategy while a weak reforming government can consider a partial, phased, and gradual reform strategy. Second, the timing and priorities of reforms are often dictated by economic feasibility. Some policies, such as more material incentives and autonomy of enterprises, produces an instant result, while others, such as development of market institutions, are slow to take effect.[135]

Notes

[1] Stanley Fischer and Alan Gelb, "The Process of Socialist Economic Transformation," *Journal of Economic Perspectives*, vol. 5, no. 4, 1991, p. 104.

[2] Harry Harding, *China's Second Revolution: Reform after Mao* (Washington, DC: The Brookings Institute, 1987), p. 77.

[3] Ibid., p. 46.

[4] Ibid., pp. 78-83.

[5] Wing Thye Woo, "The Economics and Politics of Transition to an Open Market Economy: China," *Technical Papers*, no. 153, OECD Development Centre, October 1999, p. 34.

[6] Harry Harding, p. 83.

[7] Wing Thye Woo, p. 34.

[8] Harry Harding, pp. 83-85.

[9] Wing Thye Woo, p. 37.

[10] Harry Harding, pp. 86-90.

[11] Gao Shangquan, *Two Decades of Reform in China* (Singapore: World Scientific,1999), p. 34.

[12] Wing Thye Woo, p. 54.

[13] Ilpyong J. Kim and Jane Shapiro Zacek, *Reform and Transformation in Communist Systems* (New York: Paragon House, 1991), pp. 301-302

[14] Hy-Sang Lee, "The Economic Reforms of North Korea: the Strategy of Hidden and Assimilable Reforms," *Korea Observer*, vol. 23, no. 1, Spring 1992; Doowon Lee,

"North Korean Economic Reform: Past Efforts and Future Prospects," in John McMillan and Barry Naughton, eds., *Reforming Asian Socialism: The Growth of Market Institutions* (Ann Arbor, MI: The University of Michigan Press, 1996), pp. 322-323, 327-329; Young-Sun Lee, "The Kim Jong-Il Regime and Economic Reform: Myth and Reality," in Chung-in Moon, ed., *Understanding Regime Dynamics in North Korea* (Seoul, Korea: Yonsei University Press, 1998), p. 187; Myung-bong Chang, "A Study of Changes in Economic Articles of North Korea's Amended Socialist Constitution in 1998," *Tongil Kyungje* 46, October 1998, pp. 40-54.

[15]   Jeong-Ho Roh, "Making Sense of the DPRK Legal System," in Samuel S. Kim, ed., *The North Korean System in the Post-Cold War Era* (New York: Palgrave, 2001), pp. 139-156.

[16]   Ruediger Frank, "North Korea: 'Gigantic Change' and a Gigantic Chance," http://nautilus.org/fora/security/0331_Frank.html

[17]   Asia Intelligence Monitoring Centre: North Korea, accessed at the website "North Korea Studies" http://north-korea.narod.ru/AsiaInt_economy.htm

[18]   Myung Chul Cho and Hyoungsoo Zang, "The Present and Future Prospects of The North Korean Economy," http://www.ier.hit-u.ac.jp/COE/Japanese/discussionpapers/DP99.3/99_3.html

[19]   Ibid.

[20]   Jung-Chul Lee, "The Implications of North Korea's Reform Program and Its Effects on State Capacity," *Korea and World Affairs*, vol. 26, no. 3, 2002, pp. 357-364.

[21]   Kim Jong-il, "The 21st Century is a Century of Great Change and Creation," *Rodong Sinmun*, January 4, 2001, p. 2.

[22]   *People's Korea*, "Kim Jong-il's Plan to Build a Powerful Nation," January 31, 2002, http://www.korea-np.co.jp/pk/174th_issue/2002/013101.htm

[23]   *People's Korea*, "New Economic Policy Enforced in DPRK: Seeking Maximum Profits while Maintaining Principles, August 17, 2002, http://www.korea-np.co.jp/pk; "Let us Fully Demonstrate Dignity and Power of DPRK under Great Banner of Army-Based Policy," New Year Joint Editorial of *Rodong Sinmun*, January 11, 2003, p. 2.

[24]   http://www.vyapaarasia.com/n.korea/eco.asp

[25]   Doowon Lee, pp. 330-331.

[26]   Ilpyong J. Kim and Jane Shapiro Zacek, eds., *Reform and Transformation in Communist Systems* (New York: Paragon House, 1991), pp. 301-302.

[27]   Doowon Lee, p. 331.

[28]   Chung-in Moon and Yongho Kim, "The Future of the North Korean System," in Samuel S. Kim, ed., *The North Korean System in the Post-Cold War Era* (New York: Palgrave, 2001), pp. 234-237; Jei Guk Jeon, "North Korean Leadership: Kim Jong Il's Balancing Act in the Ruling Circle," *Third World Quarterly*, vol. 21, no. 5, 2000, pp. 761-779.

[29]   Thai Quang Trung, *Collective Leadership and Factionalism* (Institute of Southeast Asian Studies, Singapore, 1985).

[30]   Quan Xuan Dinh, "The Political Economy of Vietnam's Transformation Process," *Contemporary Southeast Asia*, vol. 22, no. 2, August 2000, pp. 365-366. James Riedel and William S. Turley, "The Politics and Economics of Transition to an Open Market Economy in Viet Nam," *Technical Papers*, no. 152, OECD Development Centre, 1999, pp. 35-36.

[31]   Communist Party Vietnam, *Tang cuong xay dung dang trong hop tac xa tieu cong nghieh va thu cong nghiep* (Strengthen party construction in artisanal and light industrial cooperatives), Hanoi: NXB Su That, 1979; "Phuong huong, nhiem vu phat trien cong nghiep tieu dung va cong nghiep dia phuong" (Directions and duties in the

development of consumer goods industry and regional industry), *Nhan Dan,* October 6, 1979; *Ve phuong huong, nhiem vu phat trien cong nghiep hang tieu dung va cong nghiep dia phuong* (On the directions and duties in the development of consumer goods industry and regional industry), Hanoi: NXB Su That, 1979; Nguyen Duy Trinh, *Ve hoi nghi 6* (On the Sixth Plenum), *Nhan Dan,* January 19, 1980; Nguyen Lam, *Phat trien cong nghiep hang tieu dung va cong nghiep dia phuong* (Develop consumer goods industry and regional industry), Hanoi: NXB Su That, 1980; "May van de ve tu tuong chinh sach kinh te hien nay" (Some current problems in thoughts about economic policy), *Tap Chi Cong San* (Communist Studies), no. 3, 1980.

[32] Adam Fforde and Stefan de Vylder, *From Plan to Market: The Economic Transition in Vietnam* (Boulder, CO: Westview Press, 1996), p. 131.

[33] Ibid.

[34] Ibid., pp. 126-127.

[35] Ibid., pp. 127, 149.

[36] James Riedel and William S. Turley, "The Politics and Economics of Transition to an Open Market Economy in Viet Nam," *Technical Papers*, no. 152, OECD Development Centre, 1999, p. 19.

[37] Adam Fforde and Stefan de Vylder, pp. 254-255.

[38] Zachary Abuza, "The Lessons of Le Kha Phieu: Changing Rules in Vietnamese Politics," *Contemporary Southeast Asia*, vol. 24, no. 1, April 2002, pp. 127-128

[39] For a detailed discussion on factional struggles and new developments, see James Riedel and William S. Turley, pp. 35-41.

[40] Russell Heng Hiang Khng, "Leadership in Vietnam: Pressures for Reform and Their Limits," *Contemporary Southeast Asia*, vol. 15, no. 1, 1998, pp. 104-105.

[41] James Riedel and William S. Turley, p. 10.

[42] Quan Xuan Dinh, p. 372-383.

[43] Transition Newsletter, "Interview with Vietnam's Prime Minister Phan Van Khai," http://www.worldbank.org/transitionnewsletter/aprmayjun03/boxpg35.htm

[44] Martin Stuart-Fox, "Laos at the Crossroads," *Indochina Issues*, no. 92, March 1991, pp. 1-4.

[45] Yves Bourdet, *The Economics of Transition in Laos: From Socialism to ASEAN Integration* (Cheltenham, UK: Edward Elgar, 2000), pp.2-3.

[46] Yves Bourdet, "Laos in 2001: Political Introversion and Economic Respite," *Asian Survey*, vol. 42, no.1, 2002, pp.108-109.

[47] David Roberts, "From 'Communism' to 'Democracy' in Cambodia: a Decade of Transition and Beyond," *Communist and post-Communist Studies*, vol. 36, no. 2, 2003, p. 247.

[48] David Roberts, "Political Transition and Elite Discourse in Cambodia, 1991-99," *Journal of Communist Studies and Transition Politics*, vol. 18, no. 4, 2002, pp. 101-118.

[49] David Roberts, 2003, pp. 247-248.

[50] Ibid. p. 248.

[51] Dylan Hendrickson, "Globalization, Insecurity and Post-War Reconstruction: Cambodia's Precarious Transition," *IDS Bulletin*, vol. 32, no. 2, 2001, pp. 101-103.

[52] David Roberts, 2002, pp. 101-118.

[53] Sorpong Peou, "Hun Sen's Pre-Emptive Coup: Causes and Consequences," *Southeast Asian Affairs*, 1998, pp. 99.

[54] George Gilboy and Eric Heginbotham, "China's Coming Transformation," *Foreign Affairs*, vol. 80, no. 4, 2001, pp. 27-28.

55   Kalpana Misra, "Neo-Left and Neo-Right in Post-Tiananmen China," *Asian Survey*, vol. 43, no. 5, 2003, p. 718.

56   Al L. Sargis, "Ideological Tendencies and Reform Policy in China's Primary Stage of Socialism," *Nature, Society, and Thought*, vol. 11, no. 4, 1998, pp. 391-398.

57   Kalpana Misra, pp. 731-740.

58   Bruce Gilley, "Communist Party Grapples with Reform," *Far Eastern Economic Review*, vol. 164, no. 19, May 17, 2001, p. 26.

59   "Intimation of Mortality," *Economist*, vol. 359, no. 8228, June 30, 2001, pp. 21-24.

60   Andrew G. Walder, ed., *China's Transitional Economy* (New York: Oxford University Press, 1996), p. 24.

61   Jei Guk Jeon, "North Korean Leadership: Kim Jong Il's Balancing Act in the Ruling Circle," *Third World Quarterly*, vol. 21, no. 5, 2000, p. 774.

62   Young Chul Chung, "North Korean Reform and Opening: Dual Strategy and 'Silli (Practical) Socialism," *Pacific Affair*, vol. 77, no. 2, Summer 2004, p. 291.

63   Jei Guk Jeon, p. 778, endnote 23.

64   Ibid., p. 768.

65   DPRK Report No. 14 on The Global Beat, http://www.nyu.edu/globalbeat/asia/cns1098.html

66   Jei Guk Jeon, pp. 771, 776.

67   David W. P. Elliott, "Dilemma of Reform in Vietnam," in William S. Turley and Mark Selden, eds., *Reinventing Vietnamese Socialism: Doi Moi in Comparative Perspective* (Boulder, CO: Westview, 1993), p. 73

68   Russell Heng Hiang Khng, p. 100.

69   Ibid., p. 101.

70   Ibid., pp. 101-102.

71   Derek Tonkin, "Vietnam: Market Reform and Ideology," *Asian Affairs*, vol. 28, no. 2, 1997, p. 193.

72   Ibid.

73   Quan Xuan Dinh, pp. 367-368.

74   Ibid., pp. 369-372.

75   David Koh, "The Politics of a Divided Party and Parkinson's State in Vietnam," *Contemporary Southeast Asia*, vol. 23, no. 3, 2001, p. 535.

76   Allen Jennings and Michael Karadjis, "Vietnam: Communist Party Resolves to Stay on Socialist Path," *Green Left Weekly* (online edition), http://www.greenleft.org.au/back/2001/447/447p21.htm

77   Carlyle A. Thayer, "Vietnam in 2001: The Ninth Party Congress and After," *Asian Survey*, vol. 42, no. 1, 2002, p. 8; "General Secretary Addresses Third Plenum of Communist Party," *Voice of Vietnam* (VOV), Hanoi, August 13, 2001. "Party Chief Nong Duc Manh Delivers Closing Speech at Party Plenum," *Nhan Dan*, English-language website, August 25, 2001, at http://www.nhandan.org.vn/.

78   Peter Wolff, *Vietnam – the Incomplete Transformation* (London and Portland: Frank Cass, 1999), pp. 124-127.

79   Yves Bourdet, 2000, p. 2.

80   Martin Stuart-Fox, pp. 3-4.

81   Nick J. Freeman, "Laos: Exiguous Evidence of Economic Reform and Development," *Southeast Asian Affairs*, 2004, p. 133.

82   Edwin A. Winckler, ed., *Transition from Communism in China: Institutional and Comparative Analysis* (Boulder, CO: Lynne Rienner, 1999), pp. 46, 249.

83   Sorpong Peou, "The Cambodian Elections of 1998 and Beyond: Democracy in the Making?" *Contemporary Southeast Asia*, vol. 20, no. 3, 1998, p. 279.

[84]   Ibid., pp. 291-296.

[85]   Kheang Un and Judy Ledgerwood, "Cambodia in 2001: Toward Democratic Consolidation?" *Asian Survey*, vol. 42, no. 1, 2002, p. 101.

[86]   Ronald Bruce St John, "The Political Economy of the Royal Government of Cambodia," *Contemporary Southeast Asia*, vol. 17, no. 3, December 1995, p. 276.

[87]   Ibid., p. 275.

[88]   http://news.bbc.co.uk/2/hi/asia-pacific/4231771.stm

[89]   Barry Naughton, "Distinctive Features of Economic Reform in China and Vietnam," in John McMillan and Barry Naughton, eds., *Reforming Asian Socialism: The Growth of Market Institutions* (Ann Arbor, MI: The University of Michigan Press, 1996), p. 275.

[90]   Gao Shangquan, p. 3.

[91]   Gao Shangquan, p. 42. According to Gao Shangquan, one of the most important architects of China's economic reform, "The Socialist Market Economy is a market economy within the context of the socialist system, effecting the operation of the market under socialist conditions." He rejects the view that the market economy is equivalent to privatization and capitalization by further clarifying the definition of the concept: "The essence of the socialist market economy is that public ownership forms its basis." Gao Shangquan, *China's Economic Reform* (New York: St. Martin Press, 1996), pp. 5-6.

[92]   Harry Harding, p. 100.

[93]   Lan Cao, "Chinese Privatization between Plan and Market," *Law and Contemporary Problems*, vol. 63, no. 4, 2000, pp. 13-16.

[94]   Young-Ho Park, "North Korea in Transition?" *Korea and World Affairs*, vol. 25, no. 1, 2001, pp. 24-36; Yinhay Ahn, "North Korea in 2001: At a Crossroads," *Asian Survey*, vol. 42, no. 1, 2002, pp. 46-55.

[95]   *Pyongyang Times*, January 27, 2001.

[96]   Young-Ho Park, p. 29.

[97]   Lim Hyun-Chin and Chung Yong Chul, "Is North Korea Moving toward a Market Economy?" *Korea Focus*, vol. 12, Issue 4, July-August 2004, p. 50.

[98]   Bradley O. Babson, "Economic Cooperation on the Korean Peninsula," www.nautilus.org/DPRKBriefingBook/economy/issue.html

[99]   Young Chul Chung, "North Korean Reform and Opening: Dual Strategy and 'Silli (Practical) Socialism," *Pacific Affairs*, vol. 77, no. 2, Summer 2004, pp. 300-302.

[100]   *Rodong Sinmun*, March 26, 2003, http://www.kcna.co.jp/calendar/2003/03/03-27/2003-03-27-002.htm

[101]   Frank, Ruediger, "Economic Reforms in North Korea (1998-2003): Systemic Restrictions, Quantitative Analysis, Ideological Background," *Journal of the Asia Pacific Economy*, vol. 10, no. 3, pp. 278-311.

[102]   *People's Korea*, "Kim Jong Il's Plan to Build Powerful Nation," January 31, 2002, http://www.korea-np.co.jp/pk/174th_issue/2002/013101.htm

[103]   Ruediger Frank.

[104]   David W. P. Elliott, p. 71.

[105]   David W. P. Elliott, p. 64; Nguyen Kien Phuoc and The Gia, "Affirming the Continuation of *Doi Moi* and the Advance to Socialism," *Nhan Dan*, May 5, 1991.

[106]   *FBIS-EAS*, October 3, 1989, p. 7.

[107]   *FBIS-EAS*, October 3, 1989, p. 70.

[108]   *Nhan Dan*, December 12, 1990

[109]   David W. P. Elliott, p. 73.

110   Chu Van Lam, "Doi Moi in Vietnamese Agriculture," in William S. Turley and Mark Selden, 1993, pp. 153-155.

111   Börje Ljunggren, "Market Economies under Communist Regimes: Reform in Vietnam, Laos, and Cambodia," in Börje Ljunggren, ed., *The Challenge of Reform in Indochina* (Cambridge, MA: Harvard University Press, 1993), pp. 67-68.

112   *Ibid.*, pp. 68-71.

113   Derek Tonkin, p. 189.

114   *Ibid.*, 191.

115   M. Gainsborough, "Beneath the Veneer of Reform: the Politics of Economic Liberalization in Vietnam," *Communist and Post-Communist Studies*, vol. 35, no. 3, September 2002, pp. 353-368.

116   "Thong bao Hoi nghi lan thu ba Ban Chap hanh Trung uong Dang khoa IX" (Communique of the Third Plenum of the 9th Central Committee), *Lao Dong*, August 23, 2001. http://www.laodong.com.vn/pls/bld/folder$.view_item_detail(12867)

117   "Reluctant Capitalists," *Economist*, March 16, 2002, p. 46.

118   "Party Chief Nong Duc Manh Delivers Closing Speech at Party Plenum," *Nhan Dan*, August 25, 2001, http://www.nhandan.org.vn

119   Zachary Abuza, pp. 129-130.

120   David Koh, "The Politics of a Divided Party and Parkinson's State in Vietnam," *Contemporary Southeast Asia*, vol. 23, no. 3, December 2001, pp. 542-543.

121   Börje Ljunggren, pp. 72-73.

122   Quoting Kaysone in Bernard Funck, "Laos: Decentralization and Economic Control," in Börje Ljunggren, ed., *The Challenge of Reform in Indochina* (Cambridge, MA: Harvard University Press, 1993), p. 130

123   Yves Bourdet, 2002, p. 114; Joshua Kurlantzick, "Laos: Still Communist after All These Years," *Current History*, March 2005, vol. 104, issue 680, pp. 114-120.

124   Gerald W. Fry and Manynooch Nitnoi Faming, "Laos," in Patrick Heenan and Monique Lamontagne, eds., *The Southeast Asia Handbook* (London and Chicago: Fitzroy Dearborn Publishers, 2001), p. 154.

125   Börje Ljunggren, pp. 74-75.

126   Börje Ljunggren, pp. 76-77.

127   Cambodian Development Resource Institute (CDRI), *Policy Brief: Land Ownership, Sales and Concentration in Cambodia* (Phnom Penh: CDRI, March 2001), p. 1.

128   Micheal Vickery, "Notes on the Political Economy of the People's Republic of Kampuchea (PRK)," *Journal of Contemporary Asia*, vol. 20, no. 4, 1990, pp. 442-450.

129   John McMillan and Barry Naughton, eds., *Reforming Asian Socialism: The Growth of Market Institutions* (Ann Arbor, MI: The University of Michigan Press, 1996), p. 14.

130   Barry Naughton, *Growing Out of the Plan: Chinese Economic Reform, 1978-1993* (Cambridge: Cambridge University Press, 1995)

131   Marthias Dewatripont and Gerard Roland, "Economic Reform and Dynamic Political Constraints," *Review of Economic Studies*, vol. 59, no. 4, 1992, p. 703.

132   Marthias Dewatripont and Gerard Roland, "The Design of Reform Package under Uncertainty," *The American Economic Review*, vol. 85, no. 5, 1995, pp. 1208-1209.

133   Susan L. Shirk, *The Political Logic of Economic Reform in China* (Berkeley, CA: University of California Press, 1993); L. Lau, Y. Qian, and G. Roland, "Reform without Losers: An Interpretation of China's Dual-Track Approach to Transition," Discussion Paper, CEPR, London.

134   Marthias Dewatripont and Gerard Roland, 1992, p. 704.

135   John McMillan and Barry Naughton, p. 14.

Chapter 5

The Nature of Asian Transition from Communism

The transition from state socialism towards market-oriented economies has been one of the most significant historical developments in the final quarter of the 20th century. The former state socialist economies in Asia have made enormous progress in market reform. However, the state of transition in these Asian countries suggests a mixed picture that reflects the complexity of transition process and the variations in the degree of economic liberalization to the market system. This chapter will assess the nature of changes in these countries – what direction and how far with regard to some key indicators or important empirical elements of a market economy – socialist market economy or capitalist market economy, in other words, market socialism or market capitalism.

After more than two decades of economic reform, commercial, labor, real estate, and stock markets have emerged and many other elements of a market economy have come into being in most of Asian communist and post-communist states. However, the questions are: To what degree has a market economy been established in the Asian transition economies? What is the nature of the economic reform in these transition economies? Has the post-communist reform process transformed their centrally planned economy into a free market economy of capitalism or its equivalents? To answer these questions, we must focus on the ownership system, because the ownership system, rather than the market mechanism, is fundamental to the economic transition. Moreover, it is in this most important domain of the socialist economic reform that the dispute over the nature of economic reform – capitalism or socialism – has centered in their political and ideological discourse. However, some studies in the transition literature tend to equate the market or marketization with capitalism or privatization, and consider the market as the defining feature of capitalism and planning as the defining feature of socialism, which can be formulated as a simplistic definition: market = capitalism; state planning = socialism.

However, this equation makes no distinction between capitalism and socialism and contradicts the modern empirical world in which capitalism embraces state planning while socialism utilizes the market mechanism. What is meant by a market economy? A free market economy is the most efficient system in which the market is the invisible hand that ensures resources being allocated to their most productive uses in line with the principle of consumer choice and utility maximization.[1] The basic case for a free market economy is "the achievement of the conditions of a competitive environment in which market prices reflect relative scarcities, and enterprises and individuals make decisions mainly in response to *undistorted* market signals."[2] The very foundation of a free market economy is the private ownership or the "impersonalization" of property rights. According to Kornai, the state-owned enterprises in socialist countries are characterized by the "soft-budget constraint" – as the economic theory of property rights would put it: "the residual income that emerges as the difference between receipts and expenses does not pass into the pockets of natural persons, and the losses are not covered by the same natural party."[3] This embraces the central thesis of the property rights approach: that it is only the natural-personal owners who control and direct production and distribution of residual income, and that it is only based on this condition that modern capitalist economies have developed. The impersonalization of property rights is the very foundation of the free market economy.[4] "The fundamental difference between a socialist and a capitalist market is the form of ownership."[5] What distinguishes capitalism and socialism is the type of ownership which generates property rights and residual income rights by owning the means of production and exchange, defines the core of the relations of production, and determines the nature of an economic system.[6]

Socialism is an economic system in which the means of production and exchange is publicly owned and major economic activities are performed by governmental, societal, or public agencies, while capitalism is an economic system in which the means of production and exchange is privately owned and major economic activities are performed by private organizations.[7] However, as the history of modern socialist movements has suggested, socialism does not presuppose public ownership of *all* the means of production and exchange, but is compatible with the existence of private ownership in some economic fields, for instance in agriculture, handicrafts, retail trade and small and middle sized industries. Socialist countries not only differ on the method of socializing the economy but also vary greatly in the degree to which their economies are socialized because of the widely different political cultures of these countries.[8] Even then, however, the single most essential trait of ownership is sufficient to allow these countries to be placed in a common classification.

Therefore, sensible assessment of economic transition requires a coherent analytical framework for developing conceptual and empirical indicators as measures to evaluate the state of economic transition in these countries, examine the trends, directions, achievements, and limits of the reform in these Asian countries, and determine what has changed and what has not, in degree or in kind.

Conceptual Framework and Indicators

In the history of economics, Adam Smith and Karl Marx presented two ideal types: "free market economy" of capitalism and "planned command economy" of communism. In a free market economy, it is private citizens or private firms who own the private property or the means of production, and therefore control their own factors of production, determine what should be produced, and have the right to the residual income from their asset. It is the "invisible hand" of the market forces that establishes the exchange value while the state plays a passive role allowing private actors to operate freely in the market and prevent private actors from doing violence to each other or violating the rights of others. In a planned command economy, it is the state who owns the means of production, and therefore controls and runs the economy, and determines what to produce and who will receive what products at what levels according to the state plan. It is the state who sets the official values for all exchanges of goods and services.

Table 5.1 Two ideal-type political economies

Key Points	Free Market Economy	Planned Command Economy
1. Control of factors of production	Private citizens or private firms own the means of production and therefore controls their own factors of production	State owns the means of production and therefore controls factors of production
2. Production decisions	Private actors determine what to produce, how to distribute products, and have the right to the residual income from their assets	State determines what to produce and who will receive what products at what levels according to detailed state plan
3. Value established	"Invisible hand" of the market forces establishes exchange value for goods and services	State sets official values for exchanges of goods and services
4. Role of the state	The state plays a passive role, enforces rule, and provides protection to economic actors	State owns, dominates, plans, controls, and regulates economic activities

Source: Modified on the table in Robert J. Jackson and Doreen Jackson, *A Comparative Introduction to Political Science* (New Jersey: Prentice Hall, 1997), p. 160.

However, there are many mixed types of political economy in between because states and markets play their different roles in the economy throughout the world. Even within the same type of political economy, such as the market economy of capitalism (i.e. market capitalism), there could exist many variations and significant differences in the operation of those political economies, such as the United States, Great Britain, Japan, and Germany. They do not exhibit the key characteristics of market capitalism to the same degree, and some of the characteristics are barely present at all in one or another of the systems, because of the widely different traditions and political contexts. Even then, however, there does retain sufficiently similar defining characteristics to allow them to be placed in a common classification. Similarly, the same situation may occur in any other systems. "State capitalism" and "market socialism" are the two most important hybrid types. Although these models may not be a perfect reflection of the real world, these four types attempt to simplify and generalize a diversity of modern economic systems and they can be presented along the left-right spectrum (see Figure 5.1).

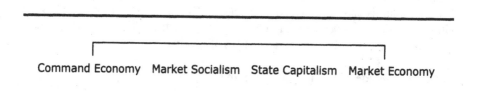

Command Economy   Market Socialism   State Capitalism   Market Economy

Figure 5.1 Linear left-right spectrum

This model locates ownership and control at some points between two extremes. It does provide a general picture of mixed political economies between the two ideal-types as a result of different combinations of ownership and control between states and markets. However, this model tells us no clear direction and the extent to which the particular change occur because the change may not come in the linear form. A command economy may not necessarily make a transition toward a market economy in the linear form, or could end in a mixed political economy, such market socialism or state capitalism without moving further toward market economy of capitalism. A two-dimensional spectrum can be used to further illustrate the key points of these four ideal types (see Figure 5.2).

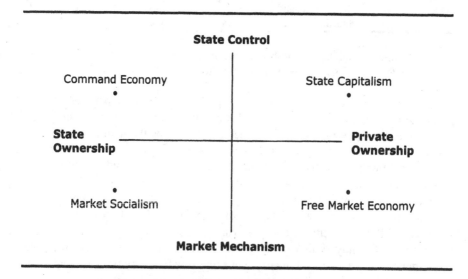

Figure 5.2 Two dimensional spectrum

In this spectrum, the horizontal axis indicates the ownership dimension with state ownership at one extreme and private ownership at the other while the vertical axis measures the role of state and market in the economy with state and market at opposite extremes. Thus, the differences and similarities between the four ideal types can be clearly illustrated.

State ownership with state control is a planned command economy (USSR and Mao's China). State ownership without state control is market socialism (Yugoslavia and Hungary). Private ownership with state control is state capitalism (Taiwan and South Korea). Private ownership without state control is a *laissez-faire* market economy (UK in the 19th century and US prior to the New Deal).[9] Therefore, ownership and control are the two most important indicators that distinguish one type of political economy from the other and thus constitute a feasible analytical framework against which to examine and evaluate the transition from communism in these Asian countries.

In what follows, we will compare the Asian transitions along these two dimensions to solve the following questions: What is the nature of the economic reform? What is the goal of the economic reform? To what extent is the party-state playing a role in the economic reform? Why and how is the reform process in these Asian countries similar to or different from one another? Why and how is this reform process different from what happened in Eastern European countries? What are the trends, directions, and limits of the reform in these Asian countries? Has the economic reform transformed state socialism into market capitalism, state capitalism, or market socialism? These questions are important and contentious. Its purpose is to show to what extent these reforms and changes have transformed the economic system. The answer to the question of whether any of these economies is a market economy depends on what one means by the term "market economy." Therefore, key concepts will be defined and empirical indicators will be established as a theoretical framework for the assessment of reform achievements in these Asian countries as compared to those in Eastern European countries. Therefore, road maps will be provided for readers to compare and understand the transition outcomes across the two regions. In this chapter, we will first define the key concepts and construct key indicators along two dimensions: public vs. private ownership and market vs. state control. Then, we will examine what has changed and what has not in China, North Korea, and Indochina – a brief conclusion for each country under study – what direction and how far. Finally, we will put the Asian transition in comparison with that of Eastern Europe to determine the nature of changes in Asian countries and make some analytical generalizations. To begin with, we must define three key concepts – market, ownership and control – which are used in the study of economic transition from state socialism before we can operationalize them into key indicators for measurement.

- MARKET: refers to economic institutions dominated by individual self-interest and invisible hand of demand and supply, mechanisms of allocating scarce resources and factors of production among those economic institutions to their most productive and efficient uses, and "a competitive environment in which market prices reflect relative scarcities, and enterprises and individuals make decisions mainly in response to undistorted market signals."[10] An economy that meets these three basic conditions is called "market economy" although there have existed different kinds of market economy in modern history.

- OWNERSHIP AND CONTROL: Having simultaneous legal "title" to a resource, good, or commodity and the ability to determine how the resource, good, or commodity is used. Ownership means that having legal title. Control means having the ability to determine use. Ownership and control generally come as part of the same package in a market-oriented capitalist economy. You buy a good, you own the good, you decide how to use it. You own a resource, you have the resource, you decide who can buy it. Ownership and control is a direct consequence of the institution of private property underlying capitalism. When someone has legal ownership of a resource, good, or commodity, then that someone usually has control over how the resource, good, or commodity is used. Combined ownership and control is important to the efficient allocation of resources. However, in some cases ownership comes without control and control comes without ownership. In those circumstances efficiency is not as easily attained. While it would seem as though ownership and control of resources, goods, or commodities always go together, such is not necessarily the case. In some circumstances ownership is absent of control and control exists without ownership. Let's run through a few examples of ownership without control: Corporate stock is one example in which control is not necessarily attached to ownership. For many who own corporate stock, and thus the assets of the corporation, control is often relinquished to corporate officers. The other side of corporate stockholders having ownership without control is the corporate officers who have control without ownership. Government is another example, on an even larger scale. Citizens, taxpayers, and the public, in principle, own government property and assets, but have almost no control over how they are used. And the other side of the public having ownership of government assets without control is government officials having control over these resources without ownership.[11]

- PUBLIC AND PRIVATE OWNERSHIP: public ownership, in Asian socialist states, consists of state owned enterprises, collective owned enterprises, and rural collectives or cooperatives. It refers to the means of production that are not owned and controlled by any individual but owned by any public or collective entity. Private ownership consists of private or individually owned property or the means of production, and refers to the property relations that are independent of the state or public entity.

- MARKET CONTROL: The ability of buyers or sellers to exert influence over the price or quantity of a good, service, or commodity exchanged in a market.

Market control depends on the number of competitors. If a market has relatively few buyers, but a bunch of sellers, then the buyers tend to have relatively more market control than sellers. The converse occurs if there are a bunch of buyers, but relatively few sellers. If the market is controlled on the supply side by one seller, we have a monopoly, and if it is controlled on the demand side by one buyer, we have a monopsony. Most markets are subject to some degree of control.[12]

- STATE CONTROL: An economy in which in which government uses its coercive power to command, regulate, direct, order, or dictates) the resource allocation decisions. A full state control is the real world version of the idealized theoretical pure command economy. While in this real world version some allocation decisions are undertaken by markets, the vast majority are made through central planning. The contrasting economic system is a market-oriented economy, in which resource allocation decisions are achieved primarily through voluntary market exchanges although some government control is used to address the issues and questions of resource allocation. To achieve the allocation in absence of market exchanges, command economies make use of central planning. While central planning exists to some degree even in market-oriented capitalist economies, the level of detail needed command economies is extensive. Every input, every output, every intermediate good, every worker, every resource is allocated based on a predetermined plan. Such planning is inherently less flexible and less efficient that markets.[13]

An ideal type of the market economy does not exist in real world, but we may agree upon certain basic principles which can be observed in a market economy in real world and can be used as a reference point for developing measure or key indicators of market economy. In studying transitional economies, Stanley Fischer and Alan Gelb, De Melo et al. and other scholars developed a cumulative liberalization index as a combined indicator of the depth of market reform while the European Bank for Reconstruction and Development (EBRD) developed cardinal measures of the status of reform as "transition indicators." Some other quantitative research projects by IMF and World Bank also developed equivalent indicators as measures of the state of economic transition. Despite the considerable differences between the transition experiences in different countries, there are some shared core features characterizing both the objectives of this process and the type of reforms required to attain them. The key elements of the transition process required to attain these objectives have been identified early on in the transition process of the centrally planned economies of Central and Eastern Europe. Despite variations in the measurement schemes, these studies have agreed upon the basic requirements or definition of a market economy. They include price and market reforms (aimed at allowing the market mechanism to determine relative prices in accordance with the relative scarcity of different inputs and outputs), enterprise restructuring and privatization (aimed at subjecting enterprises increasingly to market forces and transferring the ownership and control of the means of production from the public to the private sector), and redefining the role of the state (from being the main direct participant in the production of goods and services to establishing and safeguarding the institutional infrastructure which allows markets to function properly).[14]

This study attempt to distinguish the hardcore features from operative features of a market economy in which the former defines the nature and dynamics of an economy while the latter accounts for the functioning and operation of the economy. The hard core features – public or private ownership and state or market control – are the most fundamental and provide the basic defining characteristics of a political economy while other operative features – such as rate of inflation, fiscal deficit, and physical infrastructures – may exist in all political economies. Based on this fundamental distinction, this study attempts to develop a measurement scheme that includes 10 indicators along the two major dimensions, which are derived from the basic definition and requirement of a market economy and constitute the most important defining components of institutional arrangements of a typical market economy. This measurement scheme assumes that, in transition from centrally planned economy, the less the public ownership controls the means of production and exchange, the smaller the government's role in the resource allocation, the closer the economy is to the market economy. Therefore, the degree of liberalization or transition from centrally planned economy to a market economy of capitalism can be measured by these key indicators along the two major dimensions. Examination of economic changes using this measurement would tell us how closer the economy is to the market economy. However, since the transition in different countries does not necessarily move toward a market economy of capitalism, and states and markets play their different roles in the transitional economies, the transition may not come in the linear form, but demonstrate a more complicated and mixed picture – a hybrid economy that falls between command economy and market economy.

Table 5.2 Key indicators of market economy along the two dimensions

Public versus Private ownership	
Public/private share of GDP	Non-public share of GDP is predominant.
Public/private share of national assets	Non-public share of national assets is predominant.
Public/private share of industrial output	Non-public share of industrial output is predominant.
Privatization	Large and medium-size SOEs and land are privatized.

Market versus State Control	
Prices	Prices are determined by market forces of demand and supply.
Factor markets	Including land, capital, labor, industrial, and consumers markets.
Control of resources	Major economic resources are privately owned and controlled.
Financial institutions	Major financial and credit institutions are privately owned
Monetary policy	Floating exchange rate and monetary policy governed by rule of law
Trade Policy	Free trade regime and all economic sectors are free to trade.

The key empirical indicators in Table 5.2 could serve as road maps for readers to compare and understand the nature and outcomes of the Asian transition from communism across the countries. In what follows, we will assess the nature of changes in these countries – what direction and how far – with regard to the key indicators or important empirical elements of a market economy along the two dimensions.

Examination of Key Empirical Dimensions of Asian Transition

CHINA

Public Sector Share of GDP

Since the market reform, the pattern of ownership has developed into multi-sectoral structure in which multiple types of ownership co-exist, with the public ownership occupying a predominant position. Chinese economic sectors are now divided into several categories: state-owned enterprises and enterprises with controlling shares held by the state; collective-owned enterprises; individual-owned enterprises; private enterprises, joint ventures, joint-stock companies, limited-liability companies, and foreign owned enterprises. Therefore, economic sectors can also be classified into two major categories: public sector and non-public sector. Public sector includes SOEs, enterprises or firms with controlling shares held by the state, and urban and rural collectives with government-oriented characteristics, such as the role of government finds its expression "in the authority to appoint managers, the authority to examine and approve major decisions made by enterprises, and the authority to exercise external supervision and policy constraint over the operational activities of managers."[15] Non-public sector includes the remaining sectors in which the role of government is limited to policy restrictions and regulations although the local government often finds its way to influence the operation of enterprises. Figures for the public sector differ sharply depending upon source and accounting method. Xinhua News Agency reported that the public sector share for FY2001 was 37% of GDP.[16] However, PriceWaterhouseCoopers (PWC) reported that China's public sector accounted for 40% GDP by mid-2002.[17]

Private Sector Share of GDP

As of 2000, the number of registered private business proprietors totaled 3.9535 million; private firm totals were 1.7618 million. As of 2002, with a combined capitalization of 1.33 trillion Yuan, the privately registered companies employed 20.1 million workers, with 2,470 billion registered capital.[18] As of mid-2003, private sector employed nearly 200 million workers, including more than 100 million peasants. Furthermore, eight out of ten new jobs are created by private small-and-medium ventures.[19] Although the percentage is small, these figures will be most likely to increase with wider liberalization, private investment, FDI and WTO commitments.[20] China's private sector has surged in the past five years. Moreover, its presence in the Chinese economy will no doubt continue to increase both in scope and importance. What is in dispute, however, is the actual share – as expressed in percentage – of the private sector in China's GDP. This likely reflects the provenance of the data and the accounting standards (Chinese or Western) used to produce it. As such, dual sources will be provided herein. In March of 2002, the Xinhua News Agency reported that the private sector had accounted for 33% of GDP.[21] However, PWC economists, using data provided by the Asia Development Bank, reported that China's private sector contributed about 60% of GDP in 2002.[22] The method by the latter is misleading, because what it really suggests is a non-state sector which includes collectives, private, foreign, joint-ventured, and individual businesses as a whole. However, collectives, by nature a form of public ownership, rather than private ownership, constitute the largest portion of China's non-state sector.

Privatization Policy

The CCP has constantly rejected a large scale privatization and continued to emphasize the predominant position of public ownership in the economy as the most important socialist criteria and reform principle. Therefore, major SOEs are corporatized into giant conglomerates or "enterprise groups" through "capitalization" in the stock market while small SOEs have been allowed to lease, merge, and sell off depending on different situations. From 1995 to 2000, the number of small SOEs was reduced by more than half, from 72,000 to 34,000, mostly due to privatization and liquidation. Most of small SOEs were sold to "insiders" of enterprises under the name of "joint stock cooperatives," in which shares were distributed among workers either equally or in favor of the management at preferential prices. "Outsider" could obtain minority shares in some cases. However, despite the substantial reduction, the total number of small and medium-sized SOEs in all sectors remains large, over 180,000 in 2000.[23] China's structural reforms are less advanced among the transitional economies in the degree of liberalization as measured by the cumulative liberalization index used by some economists or the transition indicators developed by European Bank for Reconstruction and Development (EBRD), and China lags significantly behind in the majority of reform areas relative to the more advanced transition economies. China is particularly lagging behind in the areas of privatization of large scale public enterprises and banking sector.[24] China has sought to improve SOE performance and financial capacity not through privatization as in other transition economies in Russia and East Europe, but through corporatization as means of improving corporate governance, management, fund raising, intra-group cross-financing, and retaining the continued domination of state ownership. As a matter of fact, corporatization has been used by the CCP as an alternative to avoid a large scale privatization. The formation of "enterprise groups" has put together vertically and horizontally linked SOEs to promote rationalization of production structure, optimization of resource allocation, technological development, intra-group cross-financing, and create large conglomerates, modeled on the Korean chaebols, with the scale economies, resources, and critical mass to compete internationally.[25]

Stock or Shareholding Companies

The stock market emerged in response to the urgent need to finance SOEs with private savings in the market reform when the share of government in national saving declined from 38.5 percent to 17 percent during the period of 1978-1995, while the share of private saving rose from 11.6 percent to 56.3 percent and became the main source of national saving. However, the government has rejected any possibility of a major scale privatization. Instead, government policy is formulated in such a way to maximize state ownership and control in the corporate sector in shareholding reform through the corporatization of SOEs, the controlling share of stock companies, and raising fund from private savings from the stock market.[26] A high degree of concentrated state ownership is a key feature of the Chinese stock exchange. By the end of 1997, 97 percent of companies listed in the Shanghai and Shenzhen stock exchange markets were either state-owned, state-controlled, or with significant state shareholding. About 75 percent of total shares were held directly or indirectly by the state. Of all the companies listed in the Shanghai stock exchange, only five did not have state or legal person shareholding.[27] More recent securities reform could promote diversification of share ownership, but will not fundamentally change the continued domination by the state ownership. In the transition process, banks and stock markets have replaced the budget as the main source to finance SOEs. Many of large SOEs are listed and registered on the Hong Kong stock market and on the U.S. market to raise foreign capital. When SOEs are transformed into joint ventures or listed in the stock market, the existing state equity holdings are not sold. Because SOEs are capitalized with non-state equity investments, their ownership structure becomes diversified in that the state is no longer the sole owner. Ownership transformation of this kind shares certain common features with the reform in Bolivia in the 1990s, known as "capitalization" rather than traditional privatization. However, small SOEs have been made exception when the CCP leaders decided to "grasp the big and let go the small."[28]

Prices

Prices are claimed by the government as largely determined by free market forces; that is to say, supply and demand. However, Beijing still places strictures and measures on investment and capital flow, public ownership continues to dominate the economy, and the government continues to control over the key resources. Therefore, prices are not totally free, but subject to the government manipulation and intervention. WTO obligations may incrementally phase out such phenomena.[29] Despite price reforms in past years, not all prices are decided by market forces. Prices of many key commodities and materials, such as energy, raw materials, and construction materials, are decided by the government. Prices of many commodities directly affecting residents' lives, such as grains and meat, are supervised by the government. Therefore, since the prices of so many basic inputs are set by the government, and all the key aspects, industries, resources, and "commanding heights" of the national economy, which seriously affect the market formation process, are still determined by the government and state agencies, it is really hard to assess what percentage of the economy is truly adjusted by the market force, even though Chinese officials are claiming that 90 percent of the products in the Chinese economy have prices at least partly determined by the market. With energy, raw materials, land, and key resources controlled by the government, the cost of production of goods in China often bears little resemblance to their actual market cost of production.

Factor Markets

Factor markets have come into being in China. The commercial market is probably the first market developed in China since market reform. The labor market is very active, and even SOEs have to compete for labor forces on the market. However, managerial job markets do not exist in the state sector because appointments to managerial positions, both in SOE and companies with state controlling shares are ultimately politically determined.[30] The land market is emerging as real estate markets are booming and land use rights are allowed to transfer. But, this does not change the ownership. What is on market is use rights not ownership. The ownership of land belongs to the state and the collective. The stock market has become instrumental for the government to push for market-oriented reform and for the state sector to raise money from different sources in the society to fund production and investment.[31] China is currently the economic darling of the world, attracting vast sums of investment and FDI. However, there is much concern about the debt-ridden, state-funded domestic financial markets (particularly state banks with low-performing loans) as well as a vast labor market that is unemployed and unskilled (particularly in rural areas like Northeastern China).[32]

Control of Resources

State and collective sectors continue to dominate the economy and the state sector continues to control all the key aspects, industries, resources, production factors, and "commanding heights" of the national economy. The state obtains resources through various forms of revenues, including tax revenues, surtax revenues, government capital funds, special-item revenues, revenues from all kinds of administrative fees and levies at all levels of government, currency-minting revenues, extrabudgetary revenues, and nonbudget revenues. The state also controls natural resources, such as land, mine deposits, forest resources, water resources, and so forth. While most geological resources are state owned, the Chinese government also controls imported foreign resources, specifically iron, steel, copper, oil, electricity and natural gas. The government continues to manage and control most of health and social resources although local community and private sectors are encouraged by the government through continued economic reforms.

Financial Institutions

The state continues to dominate the financial institutions and markets and use this leverage to advance its policy goal in promoting economic reform while maintaining financial and economic stability. State-owned banks constitute major banks of China. People's Bank of China, being the central bank of China, is China's highest financial organ. Its main duty is to formulate and implement state financial policy, regulate and control the scale of credit and the amount of money supply of the whole society, manage the state treasury and public funds, issue state bonds, represent the government to participate in the related international financial activities, control foreign currency and gold reserves, and assume the leadership, administration, coordination, supervision and audit work of the specialized banks and other financial institutions in China. China also has some large state-owned specialized or commercial banks, such as Industrial and Commercial Bank of China, People's Bank of China, Bank of Communications of China, Agricultural Bank of China, China Construction Bank, and Bank of China. Major decisions are typically made by the state central bank in concert with the Party Politburo and rubberstamped by the National People's Congress. Pursuant to WTO entry terms, Beijing espouses continued economic liberalization in financial reforms but progress is made at a slow pace. Banks in China, though largely owned by the state, collective, joint-ventured and foreign branches are now allowed with restrictions.[33]

Monetary Policy

China is increasingly developing a liberal monetary policy so as to meet WTO protocols, compete internationally and meet domestic and international demand. On taxes, Beijing had set the corporate income tax at a quasi 33%. In practice, a series of preferential policies reduces the tax paid by foreign-invested enterprises: a 15% rate is applied in special economic zones, and a 24% reduced rate is applied in 14 coastal (open) cities. (Investments in Western China and transport infrastructure attract favorable tax rates, too).[34] China has strategically pegged the Yuan vis-à-vis the U.S. Dollar at 8.2781. In 2005, Beijing began to peg the Yuan to a basket of currencies. While creating tension between Beijing and Washington, the peg – similar to that used by both Hong Kong and Japan – has helped catapult Chinese exports (to the American market, now its largest) to the degree that the U.S. now has its biggest trading deficit with China. Inversely, China runs a deficit with its neighbors (particularly Japan & South Korea) who have assisted in and indeed prospered from China's economic boom. Beijing's prodigious foreign reserves have given it the wherewithal to affect change in the markets. For example, China's vast sum of foreign reserves (world's second largest in purchasing parity) allowed the government to recapitalize or bail-out state-backed banks.[35]

Trade Policy

China gained entry to the WTO in December 2001. Today, all enterprises in China are granted access to foreign trade though not without restrictions. China's WTO agreements require China to reduce a wide range of other trade and investment barriers. As of January 2003, average tariffs on imported industrial goods fell from 11.7%-10.6%; average tariffs on agricultural goods fell from 18.5%-17.4%; and tariffs on more than 110 products were recently eliminated. Further obligations require China to eliminate the enforcement of foreign exchange balancing requirements, local content and export performance offsets, and technology transfer requirements. China also lifted a moratorium on the transfer of state-owned and corporate shares of listed firms to foreign investors. State-owned and corporate shares, in principle, could be transferred to overseas investors through public bidding. Moreover, qualified foreign investors may establish joint-venture trading companies. Foreign investors are permitted 25%-49% share of joint-venture trading companies, and the minimum allotted capital for a joint-venture trading company is 50 million Renminbi (30 million Renminbi for central and western areas). Solely foreign owned enterprises also emerged recently in areas carefully defined and regulated by the government. Those areas that are considered by the government as the strategic sectors or the "commanding heights of the national economy" are still not open to foreign investors or selectively used by the government to attract advanced cutting-edge technology to modernize the key industries. But, this effort has not made a significant progress due to the US policy that places restrictions on the export of "sensitive" high tech products to China. The US policy has also affected the trade policy of its allies, NATO, EU, Japan, Israel, Taiwan, South Korea, Australia, etc. Hong Kong – treated as a separate entity, having entered the WTO first – will be granted unfettered & free access to China's markets before other WTO member states.[36] As of 2002, foreign direct investment was growing at 12.5% per annum and reached a record high of U.S. $52.7 billion. As such, China surpassed the United States as the world's number one place for foreign direct investment. Moreover, by the end of 2002, 424,196 foreign companies were doing business in China, bringing aggregate stock of FDI to U.S. $447.9 billion.[37] The following data represents Chinese export destinations for 2002: United States (21.5%), Hong Kong (18%), and Japan (14.9%). Inversely, the following data represents Chinese import origins for 2002: Japan (18.1%), Taiwan (12.9%), and South Korea (9.7%).[38] Table 5.3 is a summary of the key indicators along the two dimensions.

Summary Remarks

The overarching goal of China's reform is to create a "socialist market economy with Chinese characteristics." This will be an economy in which public ownership, including state and collective sectors, would maintain a predominant position in the economy while allowing multi-sectors, including private, foreign, and joint-ventured enterprises to develop, and economic sectors of all ownership types would have to seek to maximize profits in response to market forces while the state would retain effective macro-economic control over the economy. Reforms in various areas have accomplished some major tasks in establishing such a market-based economy, including transforming the SOEs into a modern enterprise system, restructuring and reorganizing the strategic or pillar industrial sectors into modern enterprise groups to achieve economies of scale, developing the financial, legal, and other institutions and rules for the functioning of a market economy, opening the domestic economy to the world economy, and allowing the private sector to grow to promote the production of commercial goods, etc.[39] So far, a market-based economy with Chinese characteristics has come into being. However, the question is what direction and how far. In what follows, we will examine several important dimensions of China's economic reform to determine what direction China is heading and how far China has moved toward that direction.

First, the SOE reform has been the most essential in defining the nature of China's economic reform since SOEs constitute the foundation of the traditional centrally planned economy. The fundamental purpose of the SOE reform since the 1990s is to strengthen and revitalize the medium-size and large SOEs while allowing smaller SOEs to be converted into other forms of ownership through leasing, contracting, sale, joint venture, joint stock, merger, etc. The former measure is called "corporatization" that aims to transform SOEs from sole state

Table 5.3 Key indicators along the two dimensions (China)

Public vs. Private ownership	
Public/private share of GDP	Public sector share of GDP = 1/3, private sector share of GDP = 1/3, and other mixed forms = 1/3
Public/private share of national assets	Public sector = over 60%
Public/private share of industrial output	Public sector share of industrial output = 85%
Privatization	Lease (long term), joint-venture, and sale (small-medium scale) of non-strategic sectors. Private property right and its legal status are formally recognized.

Market vs. State Control	
Prices	Prices are claimed by the government as largely determined by market forces of demand and supply. But, the state continues to control and supervise many prices of strategic goods, raw materials, and key commodities and retains the freedom to intervene at its pleasure.
Factor markets	Restricted land market, restricted capital market, but relatively free labor market
Control of resources	Government control of land, power, natural resources, and the "commanding heights" of the economy
Financial institutions	State banks dominate, with a few joint-ventures
Monetary policy	Managed floating exchange rate, with a monetary policy subject to political influence of the party policy
Trade Policy	Partly liberal – reduced tariff and quantitative control, but informal barriers, quotas, internal priority lists, restrictive licensing control, export subsidies, etc. are employed.

proprietorships controlled by the state agencies at various administrative levels to modern corporation with a Western-style corporate governance structure. The majority of the shares in most corporatized enterprises are held by the state or business entities controlled by or affiliated with the government or other SOEs. The public nature of the corporatized enterprises could remain unchanged, because "corporatization" does not necessarily change the nature of ownership as long as the state hold the controlling share and make major decisions in management control and allocation of resources. "Corporatization," by nature, is diversification of ownership structure through inclusion of non-state parties as shareholders, without losing its own share or privatizing its assets into private hand. Therefore, "corporatization" is different from "privatization" which is defined as "the sale of state-owned assets" such that "management control (the right to appoint the managers and board of directors) passes to private investors.[40] In contrast to many Eastern European countries where outright privatization is the dominant form, privatization in China is limited to small SOEs.[41] The main strategy is to corporatize and commercialize the large- and medium-size SOEs. The emphasis on large enterprises and key sectors represented a substantial shift from earlier reform strategy that were aimed at improving the performance of the entire SOE sector to the current strategy that emphasizes downsizing the overall scope of state activity while concentrating state resources and efforts on those areas that are considered "strategic" industries or "commanding heights" of the national economy. In addition to these central efforts to reorganize SOEs, provincial governments are also encouraged to develop their own policies for strengthening larger SOEs under their control. Provincial and municipal governments have identified additional 2,600-odd SOEs to be restructured into thousands of regional and local enterprise groups.[42]

One of the important measures to maintain the predominant position of SOEs was to conglomeratize or corporatize the large-and medium-scale enterprises (LMEs). The sales and profits of the 300 largest SOEs were responsible for more than 50 per cent of the total SOEs sales and profits, although these major enterprises were only one per cent of the total SOEs.[43] "SOEs are still responsible for a substantial share of the economy, but the government's control of the economy goes far beyond those enterprises it directly owns. State-issued economic plans set policy on all ventures, including private and foreign-owned ones."[44] The total value of the state assets, rather than decreasing, had actually more than doubled since the late 1980s, among which the LMEs had 75 per cent of the total state assets and contributed 60% of total profits and tax revenue.[45] The LMEs in the Chinese SOEs are at the heart of China's traditional state socialism and the reforms of LMEs should represent the core of China's overall economic systemic transformation.[46] The same logic would be that the abandonment of the "Four Cardinal Principles" should represent the core of China's overall systemic transformation. Even after the wave of corporatization of SOEs into joint-stock companies, the majority of these corporatized firms have the state as the dominant owner and, more crucially, the essential features of their governance structure (soft budget constraint, government intervention, and the employment relationship) have remained intact.[47]

Second, ownership structure is a key measure of the economic transition that determines the nature of change. In China, SOEs and collectives together, as the public sector, continue to comprise 60-70 percent of the economy in almost every key respect, despite the fact that the non-public sector has increased considerably in terms of its percentage of China's GDP, industrial assets, labor force, and industrial output value. In the nonpublic sector, we also have to recognize that share-holding corporations and joint-ventured enterprises are not private-owned but mixed economies, including state and collective funds, which comprise about one third of the non-state sector. These enterprises are the fastest growing sector since shareholding reforms. Their ownership is not controlled by any individual or private organization but shared by different economic elements. Table 5.1 illustrates some quantitative changes in the Chinese ownership structure.

The result of ownership reforms has suggested that, among the major economic sectors, the state sector has indeed shrunk in the past two decades. However, the state sector continues to dominate, control and monopolize the "commanding heights" of the national economy in China, which include infrastructure industries

Table 5.4 Shares of different economic sectors in GDP, selected years (%)

	GDP		Industrial Assets		Labor Force		Industrial Output	
	1979	2000	1985	2000	1985	2000	1985	2000
SOEs	56	29	74	67	41	38	64	47
COEs	42	39	24	8	49	34	32	20
Others	2	32	2	25	10	28	4	33

Source: *China's Statistical Yearbook*, various years; *China Economic Information Network*, January 31, 2000.

Note: SOEs = state-owned and state-shareholding enterprises
        COEs = collective-owned enterprises, including urban and rural cooperatives
        Others = share-holding, joint-ventured, foreign-owned, private-owned, and
        individual-owned enterprises

(energy, raw materials, and transportation), pillar industries (mechanical, metallurgical, electrical, chemical, building, machinery, petroleum, natural gas), high tech industries (information, telecommunication, biological technology), financial and banking systems, foreign trade and international economic cooperation, and new material technology As the *Economist* observes, "the state sector tends to contain industries that are the most capital-intensive and often the largest in scale, and financing them absorbs a large share of national resources, especially financial resources."[48] Some Chinese scholars called for more reduction of SOEs in national economy based on the argument that the nature of socialism would remain unchanged if SOEs could control these key industries and commanding heights of national economy, even if the share of SOEs would decrease to 20-odd %.[49] According to Jinglian Wu, one of the most important Chinese economists, although the state sector produces about one third of overall GDP today, it is still the major user of China's economic resources. Reform of SOEs has been far from satisfactory, and the old system maintains its influence and continues to impede the establishment of a new market economic system. Therefore, "we cannot say that the market has started to operate as the primary allocator of economic resources."[50] The resources that are actually controlled by the government include the following major types:

- Resources obtained through various forms of revenues, including tax revenues, surtax revenues, government capital funds, special-item revenues, revenues from all kinds of administrative fees and levies at all levels of government, currency-minting revenues, extrabudgetary revenues, and nonbudget revenues which are largely nontransparent and collected under concealed circumstances.

- Accumulated stock of state-owned and state-holding assets, with the original principal value of state-owned fixed assets being 73 percent of the total assets of the society in 2000.

- Natural resources controlled by the state, including land, mine deposits, forest resources, water resources, and so forth.

- Nonstate assets controlled through various administrative methods. From the perspective of ownership, these resources are owned by enterprises that are not owned by the government. However, their deployment is actually subject to the direct control of the government and therefore they become resources actually controlled by the government – through its authority to review and approve investment projects, operation licenses, stock and bond issuing, through maintaining state stock-controlling status, through the allocation of loans and credit capital by state bank, through setting up administrative barriers and state monopolies, and so forth.[51]

Third, market and state control over the resources is another key dimension of economic transition. In China, what has emerged is a fledgling and distorted market with a predominant state sector and intervention. Under the new ideological convention, the market mechanism is merely an instrument of economic development and not a defining characteristic of a social system; the socialist character of the economy is preserved by the predominant ownership of the public sector (including the state and the collectives) over the means of production. The market system is therefore considered fully compatible with either capitalist or socialist systems. Therefore, the objective model of the post-Mao economic reform is to transform the economy from a predominantly central planning system to one in which market mechanisms play an important role.[52] The main task of planning will be to set rational strategic targets for national economic and social development, to forecast economic development, to control total supply and total demand, to readjust the geographical distribution of industries, and to master the financial and material resources necessary for the construction of important projects.[53] As Zheng Peiyan, the Commissioner of the State Development and Planning Commission (SDPC), put it, "the government restructuring does not mean any weakening of the functions of the SDPC but brings the new functions of the SDPC in line with the requirements of the socialist market economic system,

... and enables us to make a flexible use of economic and legal means as well as the necessary administrative means."[54]

It is true that economic activities are more responsive to the market today, but still deeply involved in and constrained by *the controlled interdependence* of economic, social, cultural, administrative, and political institutions. Compared with the situation in Mao's era or in the 1980s, the level of government intervention in economic activities has been significantly reduced. But the government intervention of all forms has not been removed. *The state is not withdrawing from its role in the economy, but merely redefining it.* Most of China's enterprises and economic activities actually remain within the scope of government administrative or non-administrative intervention and adjustment, since the dominant position of the public sectors have remained unchanged. Extensive state intervention, which remains commonplace in post-Mao China, inhibits the market efficiency and competition. Bureaucratic inspections and tedious appraisals and examinations still divert much of enterprise leaders' attention from their management work. Random policy changes, fees, fines and taxes imposed upon state enterprises and other economic organizations under various pretexts also increase enterprises' production costs, and discourage their production initiative. At present, most public enterprise leaders, including state-owned, collective-owned, and state- or collective-predominant cooperatives and shareholding companies, are appointed by their superiors, rather than being elected or chosen through modern employment mechanism. Their promotion or demotion sometimes depends not on their performance, but on their superiors' likes and dislikes. All such administrative interventions have greatly inhibited fair, free and efficient competition of the marketplace.[55]

According to Chen Xiaolong, who has conducted an in-depth examination on the current situation and the tendency of China's economy, in the reality of the Chinese economy, the planning administration is weakening, while administrative intervention from the government and monopolistic state economic institutions has rather than been reduced but more strengthened and "randomized" along with the decentralization of administrative power to local governments. The post-Mao economy is not the one dominated by the market but a "dual track" system with a half market exchange and a half "randomized" administrative intervention. In socialist states, after the abdication of commanding planning, a commodity market could develop rapidly. But such a marketizing process of commodity exchange does not necessarily bring about the marketization of resources allocation. A non-market allocation of resources can coexist with a commodity market, thus developing a "dual track allocation of resources" under a decentralized command economy.[56] His study also suggests that the economic marketization has been developed in the context of socialist sociopolitical structure and systemic culture and the two bases of China's planning economy have remained: the organizational structure of the giant party-state apparatus and the monopolistic state economy has not been disintegrated but only rearranged or renamed, and its potential power of intervening daily economic activities has never been abolished; more than ten million party-state cadres and twenty million employees in monopolistic state economy continue to enjoy their political and social status, and their capacity for maneuver is enormous and goes even farther than before.[57]

Zhang Haoluo, Vice Director of the State Restructuring Commission, admitted that the "dual track" system was the major barrier to the marketizing reform in China.[58] The combination of state socialism and a commodity market economy has randomized local administration intervention in daily economic activities and greatly expanded the space of "rant-seeking" in the form of "money-power exchange." The "dual track" system with the combination of the fledgling market and the government intervention can hardly suggest the domination of the market mechanism in economy. The expansion of non-state economic sectors has encountered various systemic barriers and heavy financial burdens, and their capacity for capital accumulation has been limited.

Administrative intervention is also extensive in business operations and bank financial activities. Even today, after more than two decades of economic reforms, when business disputes occur, many of the concerned parties have not been turning to the law, but to administrative authorities for solution. Administrative authorities also encroach upon the normal business operation of commercial banks. Commercial banks sometimes grant loans, not according to the profit-maximizing principle, but in compliance with administrative orders from government organs. This is one of the main causes for the preponderance of bad debts in state commercial banks.[59] At present, the People's Bank of China exercises its administration over grassroots financial institutions through its branches at the provincial level, which could hardly be immune from the influence of local governments. Their financial activities are always motivated by the interests of local governments or departments, rather than governed by the economic laws of the marketplace.[60]

Financial reform has replaced the monobank system with a multilayered system, and created asset management companies, recapitalized banks, restructured trust and investment corporations, and small and medium-sized financial institutions. Stock, bond, and money markets have also come into being.[61] However, almost all banks are still owned by the state. The financial sector comprises state commercial and policy banks, joint-stock and city commercial banks, urban and rural credit cooperatives, and trust and investment corporations. State commercial banks (SCBs), including the Bank of China, the Agricultural Bank of China, the Construction Bank of China, and the Industrial and Commercial Bank of China, remain the backbone of the financial system, with total assets in the range of $300-500 billion and a total of 120,000 branches all over the country, accounted for two thirds of total assets of the entire financial system. The SBCs have been the primary source of financing for large SOEs. Joint-stock commercial banks (JSCBs) and city commercial banks (CCBs) accounted for 10 percent of the total assets of financial system at the end of 2001. The JSCBs have diverse ownership structures, with SOEs and local governments as their main shareholders, and finance smaller SOEs and nonstate firms. CCBs have been created by the merger of urban credit cooperatives since the mid-1990s, which also have diverse ownership structures. Their equity is held by urban collectives and local governments. China's policy banks, including the Agricultural Development Bank, the China Development Bank, and the Export-Import Bank of China, accounted for 10 percent of system assets. Policy banks fund themselves through central bank loans, government deposits, and the issuance of government-guaranteed bonds held by commercial banks. Policy banks primarily extend long-term loans for infrastructure projects, development in the poorer western and central regions. Urban and rural credits cooperatives (UCCs and RCCs) provide small scale banking services and finance small, collectively and individually owned enterprises. The lending operations, normally financed by deposits, have been funded increasingly by central bank loans, with assets equivalent to 14 percent of the system total assets in 2001. International trust and investment corporations (ITICs) were established by provinces and cities to mobilize foreign funds through the issuance of bonds to finance local companies and infrastructure projects, which accounted for 3 percent of financial system assets.[62] According to the same study, the state ownership of the financial system reduces incentives for good corporate governance and the banks also lack incentives to exert market discipline over borrowers, particularly the large SOEs, since the bulk of bank lending goes to SOEs. The direct loans to the nonstate sector constituted only 5-6 percent of total lending in 2001. A recent survey suggested that private firms primarily relied on self-financing.[63] "Many listed companies have had to provide financial assistance to smaller and weaker enterprises in exchange for being allowed to list."[64] As Li Rongrong, SETC Director, pointed out, "the SOEs still encounter a number of in-depth issues and problems in their reform and development, and those problems have not been fundamentally solved.[65]

Based on the above discussion, we can conclude that China has attempted to build up a modern "socialist market economy with Chinese characteristics," i.e. a market-based economy characterized by the predominance of public ownership. "This is a new model of economic development, which is different from both Western market economies and formal plan economies. It is the model that China innovates with a wish to show its success and benefits for the world."[66] This is the Chinese-type "market socialism" which is innovated and developed by the Chinese communist regime to avoid both ideological and practical difficulties of privatizing SOEs. The key characteristics of the Chinese-type market socialism include:

- The goal of restructuring property rights is to enhance the role of the market and improve productivity while maintaining the party-state control in the process of marketization and reinforcing the predominant position of public ownership in quality and quantity, rather than moving the Chinese economy toward capitalism.

- State and other public-sectors have continued to dominate the economy and control all the key aspects, industries, resources, production factors, and "commanding heights" of the national economy while on the other hand other economic sectors have gained considerable importance in GDP, employment, industrial output, production of commercial goods and service.

- Large and medium SOEs have been corporatized into joint stock and shareholding companies with a rearranged pattern of public ownership.

- The core of socialism remains but coexists with market relations. The decision-making of public and non-public owned enterprises has become market-oriented or market-based, but being subject to the state interference and influence due to the state control over the resources and the various constraints of party-state political context in which the economy operates. Many elements of market economy, such as factor markets, real estate market, stock market, etc., have come into being, but are weak and distorted.

- Decollectivization without privatizing land. Peasants have only use rights not ownership rights, and therefore these rights are often constrained by the power of state agencies and cooperative organizations. The state can often limit what peasants can do with the land through administrative means although use rights are transferable for benefit according to land lease system.

- The party-state control system remains effective and state intervention remains extensive. The core of the party-state defines the nature and functioning of the Chinese politics and the parameters within which the state economic policy can be initiated and implemented and the entire economy can move around.

More than two decades of market socialist reform have brought about a rapid and steady economic growth, by which China has gained prominence in the world economy.

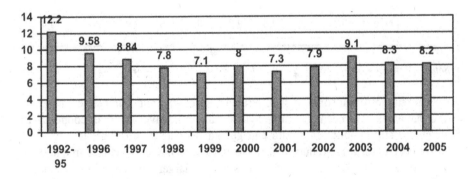

Figure 5.3 Real GDP growth by year in China (%)

Sources: China Statistical Yearbook; China Monthly Economic Indicators; Asian Development Outlook; CIA World Factbook (various issues).

NORTH KOREA

Public Sector Share of GDP

Data is uncertain given the isolated and reclusive nature of North Korea. However, the public sector still dominates all economic areas.[67] Public ownership, in North Korea and other Asian socialist states, consists of state owned enterprises, collective owned enterprises, and rural collectives or cooperatives. It refers to the means of production that are not owned and controlled by any individual but owned by any public or collective entity. Like any market socialist economy, North Korea never abandoned this principle. However, since the 1990s, the state sector shrunk to around 30 percent of GNP in North Korea, and it demonstrates a significant departure from the pre-reform command economy (see Table 5.5).

Table 5.5 State sector in GNP in North Korea (%)

		94	95	96	97	98	99	2000	2001	2002
1st Industry	State sector	29.5	27.6	29	28.9	29.6	31.4	30.4	30.4	30.2
2nd Industry	State sector	42.6	42.1	38.7	36.1	34.8	36.2	37.1	37.8	38.2
3rd Industry	(mixed)	27.9	30.3	32.3	35	35.6	32.4	32.5	31.8	31.6
	State sector	18.6	20.7	22.5	25.1	25.3	22.8	22.6	22.2	22
	Non-state sector	9.3	9.6	9.8	9.9	10.3	9.6	9.9	9.6	9.6

Source: Bank of Korea, 2003.

This suggests that some of state farms in agriculture and small state enterprises in urban areas have been "downgraded" to rural collectives or urban cooperatives, which are still "public" in nature and guided by state policy. This is a result of recent decentralization, reduced state subsidies to SOEs, and changes in enterprise management. The collectives now constitute a larger portion of the economy, though state sector continue to be dominant in the economy. Both state sector and collectives account for the most of the economy activity in North Korea.

Private Sector Share of GDP

In 2000, the private sector reportedly accounted for 3.6 percent of its $16.79 billion gross domestic product (GDP), with 5 percent of industrial output attributed to private enterprises.[68] The expansion of the private sector and the so-called "second economy" has brought into being a new social class who pursue private interests and profits in competitive markets. "Most visitors to North Korea today are struck by the growth of small shops and restaurants that have been tacitly (if not explicitly) approved in the wake of the reforms initiated in July 2002."[69]

The extension of kitchen gardens to 1,300 square meters and the experiment with the family farming system are significant moves. Both measures have given individuals and families greater control of the land and its products. So far, however, the family farming system seems to remain in the experimental stage. Though other reforms increase farmers' incentives, they fall short of the land reform measures taken by China in 1979 and especially by Vietnam in 1988-89.

Privatization Policy

Although North Korean economy is still largely state-owned and controlled, the government has implemented some economic reforms in the past years such as phasing out of rations; tolerance & promotion of limited entrepreneurship (small businesses & farmers' markets); wage increases; a new pricing system and the development of economic zones (in concert with Beijing & Seoul). More significantly, constitutional revisions in 1998 gave more freedom and autonomy to state and cooperatives and recognize the legal status of private businesses. Farmers' markets have mushroomed and developments of free trade zones in Rajin-Seonbong, Sinuiju, Kaesong, and Mt. Kumgang have increased private sector and foreign share of GDP and industrial output. Since the end of 2003, farmers' markets are now just called "markets" to reflect the fact that not only agricultural goods but also industrial and commercial goods are traded.[70] As the Economist Intelligence Unit reports, "de facto private enterprise is emerging to complement or supplant the failing formal economy."[71] Though such developments do not necessarily represent an embracing of privatization, they do, however, seem to indicate Pyongyang has begun to tolerate some private ownership.

Stock/Shareholding Companies

At present, no domestic stock or shareholding companies exist in North Korea, particularly those with international exposure and meaningful capitalization and marketization. Any business would likely be done through cooperatives and state-rune conglomerates and entities. However, Seoul, as part of its Sunshine Policy, has achieved a modicum of rapprochement to the degree that South Korean companies – in particular, the Hyundai conglomerate – have been allowed to establish an economic zone at Kaesong, near the DMZ.[72]

Prices

In 2001, Pyongyang allowed agricultural cooperatives greater autonomy to determine production and to sell (one third) of their output at a price determined by the cooperative.[73] Furthermore, in collective farms in the north, farmland is allocated to individual farmers for cultivation.[74] In 2002, North Korea launched sweeping price reform. Pyongyang used to buy rice at 0.8 won from farmers, and sell it at 0.08 won to consumers. After reform, rice is bought at 40 won, and sold at 44 won. In the case of rice it meant a nominal increase of 55,000%. Prices of other goods also soared such as those for utility, bus/train services, and rent.[75] Prices in farmers' markets (now "markets") and in SEZs are determined by demand and supply.[76] Moving toward a free floating exchange rate, Pyongyang banks now pay around 900 North Korean won for the dollar, near the black market rate, and far above the fixed rate of 2.1 won to the dollar in 2002.[77]

Factor Markets

Factor markets are mostly non-existent in North Korea, with the exception of farmers' markets and SEZs. However, SEZs are the area where factor markets are encouraged as foreign firms compete for labor, land, and capital. However, the government can intervene at its wishes as it is suggested by a recent plan of the government to deport 500,000 residents out of Sinuiju special economic zone and replace them with 200,000 model workers.[78]

Foreign visitors increasingly see evidence of a grass-roots market economy. Large market halls have been built in Pyongyang and in most of the major cities and towns. There, people buy and sell vegetables, grain, shoes, clothes and cosmetics at largely free-floating prices. The markets legalize what was a flourishing black market and make up for the state's inability to maintain its food and clothing rationing system. Increasingly, farm managers choose their crops and individuals now make money repairing bicycles and renovating apartments. Government-run companies won more freedom to invest their foreign exchange earnings in production. Private groups increasingly are leasing from the state restaurants, hotels and shops.[79]

Reports also indicate the recent reforms have led to a proliferation of small markets dealing with farm and non-farm goods.[80] These appear to represent an active hybrid sector of the economy with both private and public players, though representatives of SOEs may have become predominant sellers in many of the markets. Market forces are clearly operating in these establishments, though the government appears to be setting some price guidelines.

Control of Resources

Markets have come into being and played an increasingly important role in people's business and daily life. There are growing private and joint-ventured enterprises in non-strategic sectors, consumer goods, and "special open-door areas." Collective farming has been reduced to smaller units or the collective land has been assigned to households for production. Individual farmers can now decide on what to produce and sell extra output on free markets after delivering a certain quota to the government. In 2002, the amount of agricultural revenue to be ceded to the state was reduced from 30-40% to 18%.[81] Even so, the majority of resources are controlled by the state. Despite recent market reforms, all natural resources, land, energy, capital, education, and information are controlled by the state.

Financial Institutions

North Korea's financial institutions (banks and non-bank financial institutions) are completely controlled by the state.[82] In 2003, there were a total of 18 financial institutions: 50 percent (9) were controlled by the government; 28 percent (5) by the Korean Workers' Party (KWP); 17 percent (3) by the Department of Defense, and 5 percent (1) by the Department of Post.[83]

Monetary Policy

North Korean price and wage reforms in 2002 were followed by a more liberal monetary policy. Pyongyang revised the official exchange rate of the North Korean won from 2.15 to the dollar to 150. The black market rate is more than 800 won for the dollar.[84] Moving toward a free floating exchange rate, Pyongyang banks now pay around 900 North Korean won for the dollar, near the black market rate, and far above the fixed rate of 2.1 won to the dollar in 2002.[85]

Trade Policy

Since 1984, North Korea began to adopt a more liberal trade policy in order to stimulate economic growth. As early as 1984, the Foreign Joint Venture Law was adopted to attract foreign investment, but resulted little due to North Korea's low credibility within the international community and unattractive terms of the Law. Throughout the 1990s, more free trade or special economic zones were established to attract foreign investment and promote trade.[86] However, these efforts achieved limited success.

Although the 2002-03 reforms are mainly aimed at changing the domestic economy, the designation of Sinuiju, Gaesung, and Mt. Gumgang, in addition to the Rajin-Sunbong area, as economic "special open-door areas" is part of the open-door policy. Pyongyang granted each of the special economic zones strong economic autonomy under the guidance of market economy principles. However, the North Korean open-door policy has been constrained by U.S. containment that prohibits economic exchanges with North Korea on the basis of the "Trading With the Enemy Act" and the resolution of the nuclear issue that prevents economic cooperation between North Korea and Western countries. The prospect for improvement in foreign relations is further clouded by North Korea's resumed nuclear program. The credibility of the government is still questionable to foreign investors, particularly from the Western world. As a result, the North Korean government has largely failed to attract substantial foreign investment developed capitalist countries, and the special economic zones have not been as successful as expected. This is mostly due to the external world's strong skepticism on whether the North Korean internal environment can guarantee business activity sufficiently and if there is profitability in doing business with the North.[87]

Measured by GDP growth, FDI, and other economic indexes, North Korean success has been limited and reforms have lagged behind its counterparts in East and Southeast Asia. However, the degree of success in reforms in respect to economic growth and other economic indicators does not determine the nature of transition. It is the defining features of a political economy that determine if North Korea has departed from the traditional command economy toward a market-based socialism. Table 5.6 is a summary of the key indicators along the two dimensions.

Summary Remarks

North Korea launched a sweeping price reform in 2002. Victor D. Cha provided a lucid overview of North Korea's economic reforms since 2002. According to his testimony before the US Senator Committee on Foreign Relations, the July 2002 market liberalization undertaken by North Korea was the most significant sweeping reform in the DPRK's history. The reform measures are generally associated with four major measures. The first is an attempt to monetize the economy by abolishing the coupon system for food rations, relaxing price controls, thereby allowing supply and demand to determine prices. In order to meet the rise in prices, the government also hiked wage levels – for some sectors by as much as 20-fold (110 won/month to 2000 won/month) and for other "special" wage sectors by as much as 60- fold (government officials, soldiers, miners, farmers). Small-scale markets have sprouted up all over North Korea and the public distribution system has broken down. Second, the government abandoned the artificially high value of the North Korean won, depreciating their currency from 2.2 won to US$1 to 150 won to US$1. This measure was aimed at inducing foreign investment and providing export incentives for domestic firms. The "unofficial" value of the currency has depreciated further since the reforms (some estimate 700 won or even lower). Third, the government decentralized economic decisions. Measures entailed cutting government subsidies, allowing farmers markets to operate, and transplanting managerial decisions for industry and agriculture from the central government into the hands of local production units. Enterprises have to cover their own costs. Managers have to meet hard budget constraints. Fourth, the government pressed forward with special administrative and industrial zones to induce foreign investment. The Sinuiju Special Administrative District is a proposal for an open economic zone for foreign businesses designed to exist completely outside DPRK regular legal strictures. The Kaesong Industrial District is another project designed in particular to attract small and medium-sized South Korean businesses, and the Kumgang Mountain site provides hard currency from tourism. All three projects sought to avoid the mistakes and failures of the first Rajin-Sonbong project attempted by the North in 1991, although these projects are still hampered by the lack of adequate infrastructure among other problems.[88]

Table 5.6 Key indicators along the two dimensions (DPRK)

Public vs. Private ownership	
Public/private share of GDP	Public sector share of GDP varies from industry to industry ranging between 20 and 40, private sector share of GDP is about 3.6%, and the data is uncertain.
Public/private share of national assets	Public sector is dominant. No specific data is available
Public/private share of industrial output	Public sector is dominant. 5% of industrial output is attributed to private enterprises
Privatization	No privatization policy is observed, but private property right and its legal status are formally recognized.
Market vs. State Control	
Prices	Prices are brought to the level of free markets after the sweeping price reform in 2002. But, the state continues to control and supervise many prices of strategic goods, raw materials, and key commodities and retains the freedom to intervene at its pleasure.
Factor markets	Factor markets are mostly non-existent, with the exception of farmers markets and SEZs.
Control of resources	Government control of land, power, natural resources, and the "commanding heights" of the economy
Financial institutions	All financial institutions are controlled by the State.
Monetary policy	North Korea has a more liberal monetary policy, moving toward a free floating exchange rate since 2002.
Trade Policy	North Korea also has a more liberal trade policy, creating free and special economic zones to attract foreign investment and promote trade, but with limited success.

Decentralization has been a major aspect of economic transition in North Korea because Pyongyang is determined to maintain the dominant position of public ownership in the economic liberalization. By decentralizing decisions, and separating the local economy from the central economy, local governments and counties can set their own production levels and prices, which encourages competition. State-owned enterprises have incentives now to meet government production targets and then sell surplus on the open market for profit.[89] Visitors to North Korea note a new, albeit limited, spirit of entrepreneurship. Caritas and other international relief organizations report small-scale markets with kiosks selling drinks, cigarettes, and cookies as the public distribution system has basically broken down.[90] While DPRK propaganda still maintains anti-capitalist rhetoric and spurns market economic principles, the regime now admits flaws in the socialist style economy as the source of the problem. "The socialist economic management method is still immature and not perfect... If we stick to this hackneyed and outdated method, which is not applicable to the realities of today, then we will be unable to develop our economy."[91]

Table 5.7   Major economic reforms in North Korea, 1 July 2002 (Unit: North Korea Won)

	Before July 2002 (A)	After July 2002 (B)	Price Increase (B/A, Times)
Commodities			
Rice (kg)	0.08	44	550
Corn (kg)	0.07	33	471
Beans (kg)	0.08	40	500
Beer (per bottle)	0.5	50	100
Diesel Oil (kl)	1	38	38
Electricity (kwh)	0.035	2.1	60
Subway fare (per sector)	0.1	2	20
Train Fare	50	3,000	60
Wages			
For a laborer (per month)	110	2000	18
In the personal service industry (per month)	20–60	1,000–1,500	50-25
For a military lieutenant (per month)	95	2,970	31.3
Exchange rate			
U.S. $ equals	2.15 DPRK *won*	150 DPRK *won*	69.9

Sources: People's Korea, 17 August 2002, www.korea-np.co.jp; Peter Gey, "Nordkorea: Reform sowjetischen Typs und Erosion der Staatswirtschaft," *Internationale Politik und Gesellschaft*, no. 1, 2004, p. 127; Hong Ihk-pyo, "A Shift toward Capitalism? Recent Economic Reforms in North Korea," *East Asian Review*, vol. 14, no. 4, Winter 2002, p. 96.

The central government now plans only strategically important departments, while letting each enterprise and factory plan by itself. SOEs are allowed to trade a part of its production and materials between themselves in a new market called "socialist goods trading market." They can sell or export their products by themselves, and earn the capital necessary for their plan. Here, the prices can be set between the traders, within 10-15% of the prices set by the government. In production, such indicators as cost and profit are also emphasized and SOE are expected to be self-financed, shutting down highly inefficient ones. They are also expected to focus on their specialties of their production. SOE also started to restructure their organization, firing many of managers (Party members) who were enrolled for political reasons.[92]

Farm reforms allow farmers the right to cultivate a piece of land, while the government retains owning the land. Farmers can distribute their product according to the amount of their labor, after paying the fee, 15% of their product. Furthermore, in collective farms in the north, farmland is allocated to individual farmers for cultivation. Here again, the prices can be set between the traders, within 10-15% of the prices set by the government.[93]

Although North Korea claims the reform is not an acceptance of a free market economy, it is recognition that socialism can coexist with capitalism, and it is a practical application of the socialist framework. North Korea has used "*silli* (practical) socialism" to re-define *Juche* and provide the ideological justification for the reform policy under Kim Jong-il.[94] Kim Jong-il himself attempted to justify his new economic reform policy by saying that "things are not what they used to be in the 1960s. So no one should follow the way people used to do things in the past ... We should make constant efforts to renew the landscape to replace the one which was formed in the past and to meet the requirements of a new era."[95] North Korean official, Ch'oe Hong-kyu, a bureau director in the State Planning Commission, also explains, "Kim Jong-il stresses that all the outdated and dogmatic 'Soviet-type' patterns and customs should be renounced in the fields of economic planning, finance, and labor management... Foreign trade should be conducted in accordance with the mechanism and principles of capitalism."[96]

According to South Korea's central bank, the North Korea's real GDP growth registered 2 percent in 2005 and marked the seventh consecutive year of positive growth and expansion since 1999. The bank attributed the North's overall gain to growing inter-Korean trade and strong agricultural and industrial performances following its 2002 economic reform measures.[97]

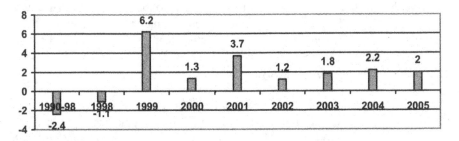

Figure 5.4 Real GDP growth by year in North Korea (%)

Source: Bank of Korea; The Washington Times.[98]

Politically, a mixed picture of continuity and change can also be observed. In light of political continuity, the Leninist Party-State remains intact, the ideology of *Juche* continues to permeate all spheres of social, cultural, economic, and political life, and Kim Il Sung's legacy remains intact. However, some political changes have taken place: new constitution was passed at the 10th SPA, the power and status of the Central People's Committee were dismantled, the institution of the President was abolished, the NDC was made the supreme state body and Kim Jong Il as a de-facto supreme leader, private ownership was allowed, more powers were decentralized to local governments, and state-sanctioned revival of religions allowed people to practice Christianity and Buddhism.

The key features of market reform measures are a combination of state planning and commodity-market relations through the introduction of costs, prices, profits, and material incentives in the state-owned enterprises, the revitalization of commodity exchange in the rural area, and the establishment of a special economic sector as an open-door window to attract foreign capital and new technology. What has emerged in North Korea is a "dual structure" or "hybrid system" combining state and market roles and blending market and socialist principles in reform practice. As repeatedly stated in a DPRK official newspaper, *People's Korea*, "we should manage and operate the economy in such a way as to ensure the maximum profitability while firmly adhering to the socialist principles."[99] Such reforms are comparable to those measures introduced in other Asian socialist economies such as China in the early and mid-1980s. The North Korean-type market socialism can be summarized as follows.

- The goal of economic reform and opening policy is to embrace the role of the market and improve productivity and people's living standards while maintaining socialist principles and reinforcing the predominant position of public ownership in the economy, rather than turning to a capitalist economy.

- The reform is the application and renovation of *Juche* ideology in a transitional stage of DPRK socialist society toward communism in response to new challenges and changes in a new era.

- Market relations exist in a socialist society due to the transitional character as socialism is the transitional stage toward communism. Therefore, North Korean socialist economy is a dual structure that combines state and market roles and market and socialist principles, with socialist principles as the guiding forces of the economy.

- The core of socialism remains but coexists with market relations or something similar to market relations. But, markets play a supplementary role in the economy to improve the productivity of public sectors, not to replace the state role in guiding the economy. The decision-making of public and non-public owned enterprises is becoming more market-oriented or market-based, but being subject to the state interference and influence due to the state control over the resources and the various constraints of party-state political context in which the economy operates. Many elements of market economy, such as factor markets, real estate market, stock market, etc., have come into being, but are weak and distorted.

- The party-state control system remains effective and powerful and state intervention remains extensive. The core of party-state system defines the nature and functioning of the Chinese politics and the parameters within which the state economic policy can be initiated and implemented and the entire economy can move around.

VIETNAM

Public Sector Share of GDP

The Vietnamese state sector accounted for 38.7 percent of GDP production share in 2003, and this represents 12.4 percent growth from 2002.[100] However, figures differ slightly from different sources. The United States Department of Commerce reported that the Vietnamese state sector accounted for 40 percent of GDP and 42 percent of industrial output.[101] The Mekong Vietnam Investment put state sector production of GDP at 39 percent [102] while the Economist Intelligence Unit reported that the state sector generated 41 percent of industrial output.[103]

Private Sector Share of GDP

The nonstate sector, including collective, households, mixed, private domestic enterprises, and FIEs, accounted for about 61 percent of GDP in 2001. However, private domestic manufacturing is still relatively small, accounting for less than 4 percent of GDP, 6 percent of manufacturing output, and about 3 percent of total employment. Private sector's growth has been slow, but shown a positive tendency. Most of the private enterprises are concentrated in food processing, wood products, garments, and ceramics and glass products, and are usually located in Hanoi or Ho Chi Minh City.[104] Different sources have provided different statistical figures due to the use of different accounting standards and methods. Vietnam's Industry Minister estimated that the domestic nonstate sector accounted for 25.1 percent of GDP production share in 2003, and this represented growth of 18.7 percent from the previous year. Foreign-invested enterprises accounted for 36.2 percent of GDP, and this represents growth of 18.3 percent in 2003.[105] However, the Mekong Vietnam Investment put domestic nonstate sector production of GDP at 48 percent and foreign sector production of GDP at 13 percent.[106]

Privatization Policy

Vietnam has committed itself to the development of a market socialist economy and begun to implement cautious market reform and liberalization since the *doi moi* reforms. The Company Law, Law on Private Businesses, and Law on Encouragement of Domestic Investment have had a profound impact on the development of the private sector in Vietnam. The laws assure the business activity of private enterprises and private property ownership, and encourage their investment in trade, production, and other commercial activities.[107] Since then, 72,000 enterprises are registered.[108] However, the registration process is often lengthy and expensive. There is a 30 percent limit of foreign owned enterprises, and the government is considering raising the ownership limit to 40 percent to aid the stock exchange.[109] The 9th National Party Congress in 2001 announced that the government would streamline the registration process for new businesses in order to "create a new strength for economic sectors to improve their productions and businesses in various forms of ownership."[110] However, the application of privatization seems to be more out of necessity than ideology, given the success of its neighbors, especially China.[111] Despite efforts to encourage private sector, the state maintains a base of 700 large state-owned enterprises and controls shares in another 2,000 major companies.[112] One of the central SOE reform plans is to corporatize and transform SOEs into joint-stock companies as its neighboring country China does. This is an effort by the government "to encourage diversification of ownership forms and make use of all latent capital sources in society."[113]

Stock/Shareholder Companies

Stock exchange was established in July 2000 in Ho Chi Minh City with only 2 companies. By November 2002, 19 companies were listed. As of 2004, the stock market has 24 listed companies with combined capitalization of $245.2 million, and listed government bonds with a total value around VND 15.7 trillion.[114] The stock exchange is operated and regulated by the State Securities Commission.[115] The Vietnamese stock exchange is the smallest in Southeast Asia, with company listings mostly from Vietnam and its ASEAN partners.[116] Though small in stature and volume (especially when compared to the Hong Kong and Singapore markets in the near region), the Vietnamese stock market is increasingly becoming an accepted and expected way of raising private capital, promoting free market values, and propagating corporate transparency.[117] The legal limitations on foreign ownership of listed companies have restricted those foreigners willing to invest. Therefore, Decision 36 of the Prime Minister of March 11th 2003 removed some of the restrictions and provided them with greater access to the stock market. However, this does not alter the fact that foreigners can only invest in those sectors set out by the government policy nor does it enable foreign investors to be involved in management of the company in which they invest.[118] While the reform of equitizing small and medium SOEs is gaining momentum, it is likely that the state will retain ownership of the large SOEs and corporatize them into stock holding companies as China does.[119]

Prices

Price reform was one of the earliest reforms undertaken during the *doi moi* to set prices according to the laws of demand and supply.[120] However, the state continues to control the price as it sees necessary. The state sets rates for electricity, petroleum, telecommunications, water, and fares for train and air travel. Price controls also exist on natural monopolies. Prices are usually set higher for foreigners, but the dual track pricing system has been officially removed.[121] Domestic prices that are set higher than the international market include: cement, 115 percent; printing paper, 127 percent; urine-fertilizer, 131 percent; steel, 125 percent; and sugar, 140 percent.[122] Since the Asian financial crisis, Vietnam has been keen to control both prices and investment. The government can impose a direct price control through "price stabilization measures" by the Price Management Office and the Ministry of Finance.[123]

Factor Markets

Factor markets have come into being since the *doi moi*, and the government promised to build greater capital, property, and labor markets.[124] The industrial market accounted for 37.8 percent of GDP in 2001, following an increase of 10.1 percent in 2000 and 9.7 percent in 2001.[125] The land use rights market does exist, and buyers are given the actual land use certificate under the Land Law, since the state retains the land ownership.[126] But individuals can transfer land use rights if they move, set up a new business, or lose ability to work on the land. All transfers, however, are subject to the approval of state authorities at different levels. The government leases land and grants land use rights to individuals and firms. In a survey of four rural communes, 10-32 percent of the households have engaged in renting-in land activities and 0-8 percent have engaged in renting-out land activities. Those who have exchanged land use rights range from 0-38 percent, and much of this activity happens underground to avoid the restrictions on transfer of use rights. In urban areas, hundreds of real estate businesses have started, and foreign companies can obtain land use rights through contractual arrangements regulated by the law. This indicates that a regulated land market has emerged along with other changes since the amendments of the Land Law in 1993.[127] But, registration is required for the mortgages of land use rights.[128] The capital market is dominated by the state banks and non-bank financial institutions. The government controls the flow of capital, for example, foreign currency must be deposited in designated, licensed banks. Since the government approved "equitization" in 1992, the stock market has become instrumental for the state sector to raise fund and attract capital for investment. But, the development is slow, and total capitalization of market is $130 million, of which private sector accounts for 24-25 percent of annual investment capital throughout the country.[129] The government has taken steps to lay down principles and practical details on the conditions under which enterprises should remain in state ownership, on how to sell shares, what proportion of shares to be sold, who is eligible to buy stocks, and so on.[130] The labor market might be the most "free" of factor markets in Vietnam because the state sector employs 10 percent of labor force while other economic sectors could compete in the labor market.[131] The number of registered domestic companies has more than doubled in the past two years. Roughly 35,000 enterprises have registered since 2000, and their aggregate capital is about 9 percent of Vietnam's annual GDP.[132]

Control of Resources

According to a report by Le Phu Cuong, a member of Planning and Statistics Department of Ministry of Trade of Vietnam, since Vietnam started the transition to a socialist-oriented market economy, the situation of monopoly and oligopoly has little changed. The monopoly business in Vietnam can be classified into two categories: state monopoly or administrative monopoly, which is created by the administrative regulation of the state, and the natural monopoly. However, there are not many differences between state and natural monopoly because all the natural monopoly industries are in the hand of the State. The administrative monopoly can be granted to one SOE, which can be identified as absolute monopoly or enterprise monopoly, and to a number of SOEs, which is called as oligopoly. The monopoly private firm has not emerged so far due to their small scale, and low level of technology. The monopoly of the foreign invested enterprises (FIEs) also has not emerged yet because these FIEs are still required to enter a joint-venture or business cooperation contracts (BCC) with local companies. Besides, in some provinces, there is also the so-call "local monopoly" resulted from the administrative provisions of the local authority, in which the product manufactured by the monopoly enterprise of a province is solely consumed within the territory of that province, including the products such as beer, sugar, construction material. Some local administrative provisions provide the local firms special trading rights (such as purchasing rice) in the local market. These local provisions distort the market conditions and place the competing firms in adverse position in the market.[133]

The state-owned corporations have been granted monopoly status and supported by the state budget and preferential financial aid from both domestic and foreign loans. These businesses are protected by the administrative barriers from the entry of any other enterprises, including joint-venture with foreign firms, local private firms and even other state-owned enterprises. In addition, other forms of restrictions are also in place such as business license regulations, price mechanism (electricity price, telecommunication charges, and airfare) and even the behavior of governmental bodies in tendering, quota allocation, etc. In Vietnam, these SOEs have not been supervised by laws, but the governmental statutes, decrees, or documents prepared by the very monopoly agency.[134]

The state enterprise monopoly sectors, where the monopoly SOEs normally occupy over 80% of market share, include the following industries: aviation; telecommunication; sea transportation; railways; electricity; energy; financial and banking; stock exchange center; construction and operation of ports, port services, passenger car stations, bridge and roads, etc.; international trade of newspapers and books; production and distribution of film; production and distribution of cigarette; water supply, etc. The oligopoly sectors, where the monopoly sectors are controlled by more than one SOE, include petroleum product distribution, insurance, commercial banking, production and distribution of cement, steel, sugar, etc. The monopoly sectors are mostly the "commanding heights" of Vietnam economy, especially in the services sector (transportation, telecommunication, banking, etc.).[135]

More recently, the resolution of the Third Plenum of the Central Party Committee (IX Section) has provided the major guidelines on SOE reform, and the monopoly issues have been addressed as well. Since then, the government has allowed the entry of new firms in some monopoly sectors, such as telecommunication. The most recent effort to address monopoly issues, which is pushed by Vietnam's integration into the regional and world markets, particularly accession into WTO, is to draft "Competition Law." However, the drafted law only applies to private businesses, and organizations and associations in general, not the enterprises engaged in public utility or in the field of state monopoly.[136] Therefore, the government controls the key resources and industries while, as the General Statistical Office of Vietnam reports, resources under private sector control are mostly consumer goods, such as tea, salt, porcelain, glass products, bricks, water pumps for agriculture, crude oil, etc.[137]

Financial Institutions

Vietnam's financial institutions are mostly state-run. However, the banking system was recently reformed into a two-tier system, thereby separating the central state bank from commercial banks; this act has opened the financial sector to private actors.[138] In 2001, Hanoi adopted banking reforms that relied on market-based actions and implementation of state enterprise reform. The program is comprised of three areas: restructuring joint stock banks; restructuring and commercialization of state-owned banks; and improving regulatory framework and enhancing transparency.[139]

The State Bank of Vietnam is the central bank that has the authority to set the monetary policy, provides a national network of banking services, and supervises the operation of the state banking system. Other state-owned commercial banks deal with specific sectors, including Bank of Foreign Trade of Vietnam (foreign currencies and international banking business), Industrial and Commercial Bank of Vietnam (personal savings, loans, securities, and investment), Vietnam Export-Import Commercial Joint-Stock Bank (banking transactions for export and import productions and operations), Vietnam Agricultural Bank (banking support for agriculture), etc. These commercial banks hold 80 percent of total bank assets of

Vietnam, and control 72 percent of outstanding loans as of 2001.[140] Among the "five state-owned commercial banks, VBARD currently tops the list with total registered capital of $285 million, followed by BIDV with $175 million, Vietcombank and Vietincombank with $162 million, and MHB with $51.9 million."[141] Although state banks number few, they control the majority of assets that is the key to policy control and resource control in Vietnam. Although the commercialization of the central bank has made it easier for private firms and individuals to borrow, but at least 2/3 of bank lending goes to SOEs.[142] At present, there are 27 foreign bank branches, 4 joint-venture banks, 3 finance leasing companies under joint-venture or wholly-foreign investment, and 42 representative offices operating in Vietnam.[143]

Monetary Policy

Vietnam's monetary policy is purposefully structured to be cautious and conservative. Specifically, it endeavors to keep interest rates at moderate levels, allowing for sustained investment and borrowing within inflationary parameters. In an attempt to promote exports, Vietnam has eliminated multiple exchange rates and replaced them with a single rate reflecting free market forces. However, Hanoi also implements foreign exchange controls, export-import controls, and control of commercial credit for import. The government also controls foreign borrowing more strictly, including both government and private borrowing, because it relates to the debt service capacity of the economy.[144]

An austere monetary policy has been adopted to control inflation. Controls still apply to all transactions in money market, capital instrument derivatives, commercial credits, and direct investment. The government still uses direct monetary instruments like credit plans to control and allocate credit, as part of the investment plan made by the State Planning Commission. Other formal and informal controls over commercial banks still restrict their scope and flexibility. However, the government has removed interest rate control on lending, allowing banks to grant loans to the emerging private sector, while retaining control over long-term interest rates.[145] As the deputy governor of Bank of Foreign Trade of Vietnam said, the state bank would continue to intervene when necessary to maintain a reasonable exchange rate between the dollar and the dong in order to prevent any shocks to the domestic market.[146]

Trade Policy

Vietnam has adopted a strategy of gradual and phased-in integration with the international economy. Vietnam has committed – under the ASEAN Free Trade Agreement (AFTA), the United States Bilateral Trade Agreement (BTA), and agreements with the World Bank and IMF – to liberalize its trade and investment rules, abolish quantitative restrictions on all but five items, lower tariffs and gradually develop transparent trading and investment systems as a prerequisite for entry into the WTO.[147] Both tariff and non-tariff barriers have been substantially reduced and/or incrementally eliminated. 52 percent of tariff lines are between 0 and 5 percent. Import duties have been significantly lowered while many export products enjoy a tax rate of zero with only 12 export products subject to tax up to 5 percent. Tax reductions or exemptions are provided to companies that produce export goods. Most commodities and goods are now freely imported into and exported from Vietnam.[148] By the end of 2003, all quantitative restrictions on imports were abolished with the exception of sugar and petroleum.[149]

As early as 1997 with the adoption of the Trade Law, Vietnamese businesses have the right to direct export/import business within their registered scope of operation or could act as sale and purchasing agents for domestic and foreign firms. Moreover, foreign trading companies are permitted to establish branches and/or representative offices in Vietnam to conduct and promote trade.[150] However, there are still many problems with the trade: protection given to SOEs; the absence of a quantifiable and transparent legal system; abstract taxation and investment laws; corruption in infrastructure projects; a highly regulated import system symbolized by the ad hoc levy of tariffs; and the relatively porous state of the financial system.[151]

Vietnam has made the departure from the centrally planned economy and transitioned towards a market socialist economy. What has emerged in Vietnam is a "dual structure" or "hybrid economic system" combining state and market roles and blending market and socialist principles. Such reform efforts are comparable to those measures introduced in China. Table 5.8 is a summary of the key indicators along the two dimensions.

Summary Remarks

Since 1986 the VCP has committed itself to economic reform (*Doi Moi*), a transition from a centrally planned economy to a socialist-oriented, multi-sectoral market economy. The government has abolished price control, devalued the Dong, legalized private ownership, freed the private sector, withdrawn subsidies from some loss making state enterprises, opened up the country for foreign investment, begun to introduce a modern legal framework, and pursued monetary and fiscal policies. The goal of these reforms is to double Vietnam's GDP and to become an industrialized nation by 2020.[152]

The study suggests that, while having achieved a great progress in its market-oriented reform, Vietnam has not moved toward a free market economy of capitalism. "No doubt, a market mechanism exists in Vietnam but is unlike the markets associated with Western capitalism."[153] The Vietnamese economic system is described in Article 15 of the 1992 Constitution: the state develops a socialist-oriented multi-sectoral commodity economy driven by the state-regulated market mechanism. The multi-sectoral structure of the economy with diversified types of production and business organization is based on ownership by the entire people along with collective and private ownership, of which the public ownership are the

Table 5.8 Key indicators along the two dimensions (Vietnam)

Public vs. Private ownership

Public/private share of GDP	The state sector accounts for 38 - 41 percent of GDP, while the non-state sector, including collective, mixed, foreign owned, households and private owned enterprises account for 60%, but, domestic private enterprises only account for 4 percent of GDP.
Public/private share of national assets	Public sector is dominant. No specific data is available
Public/private share of industrial output	Public sector share of industrial output is dominant. 6% of industrial output attributed to private enterprises
Privatization	Lease, joint-venture, sale (small scale) of non-strategic sectors. Private property right and its legal status are formally recognized.

Market vs. State Control

Prices	Prices are claimed by the government as largely determined by market forces of demand and supply. But, the state continues to control and supervise many prices of strategic goods, raw materials, and key commodities and retains the freedom to intervene at its pleasure.
Factor markets	Restricted land market, restricted capital market, but relatively free labor market
Control of resources	Government control of land, power, natural resources, and the "commanding heights" of the economy
Financial institutions	State banks dominate, with some foreign bank branches and joint-ventures
Monetary policy	Managed floating exchange rate, with a monetary policy subject to political influence of the party policy
Trade Policy	Partly liberal – reduced tariff and quantitative control, but the ad hoc levy of tariffs, informal barriers, restrictive licensing control are employed.

cornerstone.[154] The Ninth Party Congress in 2001 continued to emphasize the leading role of party organizations in the SOE to ensure the implementation of party lines and policies and the correct direction of enterprise business development.

While the state-run sector will maintain its dominant role in the economy, shares of other forms of ownership including private sector will be allowed to invest and operate in those production and businesses not prohibited by law or where the state does not need to hold 100 percent of capital. However, as the political report at the Ninth Party Congress pointed out, the socialist path with a multi-sectoral market economy "requires a long period of transition with many transitional stages and forms of socio-economic organization... In the period of transition, there are many forms of ownership of the means of production, many different economic sectors, classes and social strata... therefore there inevitably remain class contradictions and class struggle."[155]

Ownership structure and market and state relations are two most important dimensions that allow us to determine the nature of change and to what extent a free market economy has been established. The Land Law enacted in 1987 and amended in 1993 did not establish private property, but granted individual households long-term use rights over land and freedom over production in the rural area. Land remained owned by the state, reverting back to the authorities when a household moved or stopped farming. The commune authorities were entrusted with the power to decide how the land was to be allocated and how much land could go to any one household. The land Law also prohibited voluntary re-contracting of land-use rights after the decollectivization.[156] Urban land is more tightly controlled by the government. The state continues to own all land although households can transfer the usufruct rights. Although the nonstate sector is growing faster than the state sector and now provides the largest share of employment and output in the economy, SOEs continue to dominate capital share and key industries. Enterprise reform has lagged behind in Vietnam and has been implemented in a gradual trial-and-error process. Since 1992, a small number of SOEs out of more than 12,000 have been corporatized into state-holding joint-stock companies, others have been merged or closed. SOEs continue to maintain advantages over private enterprises because of their control over land, buildings, and physical assets, and greater access to credit, loans and trade licenses.

Since 1988, Vietnam's monobank system, consisting solely of the State Bank of Vietnam (SBV), has been transformed into a two-tier financial system. The new system includes its central bank, the SBV, which is given greater monetary policy and regulatory roles, and four state-owned commercial banks that are charged with financial intermediation responsibilities. On the other hand, the financial institutions also include foreign banks, domestic joint-stock banks that are primarily state-owned, credit cooperatives, people's credit funds, and insurance companies.[157] Like in China, the Vietnamese financial system has been dominated by the state-owned commercial banks – 80% of state ownership in financial market structure – which have given SOEs privileged access to loans and credits according to government policies and directives. Although private banks are allowed to operate in Vietnam, "the unwillingness of the authorities to undertake a thorough reform of the financial sector, at least so far, is a natural result of their continuing desire for a 'market economy with a socialist orientation" in which the state occupies the 'commanding heights' of the economy."[158]

The state sector has in fact grown rapidly although the non-state sector has growth fast, particularly in agriculture where the non-state sector has become predominant. Overall, the state sector has not diminished but flourished since reform (*doi moi*). Although the number of SOEs and employment has decreased, SOE industrial output has recovered and increased. The share of output produced by the state sector has increased while the share of output produced by the non-state sector has decreased since 1990. Table 5.4 and Table 5.5 suggest that the state ownership continues to be predominant while the non-state appears to lag behind the state sector. State enterprises continue to enjoy many advantages through their close relationship with the bureaucratic agencies and they can find their way through the maze of regulations and obtain licenses, permits and other privileges that private enterprises would not obtain easily. This gives the state sector monopoly power in many areas under the new, market-oriented economy while it puts the private sector in a disadvantageous position and inhibits its growth. This also explains why foreign investment in Vietnam usually takes the form of joint ventures with state enterprises.[159] Contrary to what one may believe, a more recent official picture of SOEs, according to the enterprises census on April 1, 2001, suggests that more than 75 percent of SOEs were profit-making in 2000, particularly those larger, strategic SOEs.[160] This demonstrates that the state sector remains a key contributor to economic growth in Vietnam. The data in Table 5.9 and Table 5.10 suggest that the transition has been taking place gradually and the state sector still holds a prominent place in the economy, which has become a mixture of state-owned and privately owned sectors.

Table 5.9 Industrial output by types of ownership (%) – selected years

	1990	1995	1996	1997	1998	1999	2000	2001	2002	2003
State Sector share	67.6	50.29	49.25	47.96	45.93	43.38	41.8	41.1	40.26	39.09
Non-state sector share	32.4	49.71	50.75	52.04	54.07	56.62	58.2	58.9	59.74	60.91
Private owned firms	23.3	23.99	23.44	22.55	21.52	21.3	21.59	22.9	23.67	24.31
Foreign owned firms	------	25.09	26.73	28.92	31.98	34.68	35.94	35.3	35.43	36.05
Joint ventures	9.1	.63	.58	.56	.57	.64	.67	.69	.64	.55

Sources: Data on 1990 from Jose L. Tongzon, *The Economies of Southeast Asia*, 2nd ed. (Northampton, MA: Edward Elgar Publishing, Inc., 2002), p. 204; Data on 1995-2003 calculated from statistics published by General Statistics Office of Vietnam: http://www.gso.gov.vn/default_en.aspx?tabid=470&idmid=3&ItemID=1806.

Table 5.10 Investment share by ownership in Vietnam, 1995-2001 (%)

Ownership	1995	1996	1997	1998	1999	2000	2001
State	42.0	49.1	49.4	55.5	58.7	57.5	58.1
Non-state	27.6	24.9	22.6	23.7	24.0	23.8	23.6
Foreign	30.4	26.0	28.0	20.8	17.3	18.7	18.3

Source: General Statistical Office, Statistical Yearbook 2001.

Despite the large numbers of private enterprises in Vietnam, SOEs dominate the economy. For example, in 1998, fully owned SOEs accounted for almost half or 46% of economic output. SOEs are also joint venture partners in about 70% of foreign invested enterprises, which produced 32% of industrial output in the same year. Joint ventures with foreign partners provide SOEs with much needed access to capital, management and marketing skills, better technology, and know-how. While SOEs as a whole dominate economic output, the individual performance of state-owned firms varies. A number of SOEs are loss-markers, to improve the SOE productive capacity and competitiveness, and to better ensure the financial stability of Vietnam's development process, Vietnam started corporatization of SOEs under the State's SOE Equitization Program, in which some SOEs have been merged or dissolved and others are being equitized or be forming joint ventures with foreign companies[161] However, the most significant result of the SOE restructuring effort is that the total number of SOEs decreased from 12,300 in 1990 to 5,700 in 2001, but the total capitalization increased from VND 29 trillion in 1990 to VND 165 trillion in 2001 and gross revenues of SOEs increased from VND 2,672 billion to VND 423,000 billion from 1990 to 2001.[162] Like its counterpart in China, the SOE reform in Vietnam has strengthened rather than weakened the state financial capacity.

There are many obstacles to the development of the private sector in Vietnam. Ideologically, the government still believes in state-led growth and therefore it has not done enough to create a favorable environment to foster private business development, such as lack of adequate institutions and legal infrastructure, confusing government policies and regulations, and limited access to investment capital.[163] Like their counterparts in China, the Vietnamese financial institutions have been dominated by a few large state-owned banks, which give SOEs privileged access to loan and credit according to government policies and directives while other financial actors are either weak in financial resources or unfamiliar with private enterprises, which lead to limited access to investment capital for private firms.[164]

The planning system has not been abolished but restructured although some functions of planning output targets and distributing materials and equipment have disappeared, which allow all inputs to be traded at market prices and all enterprises to make decisions on production. The State Planning Committee (SPC) has changed its name to the Ministry of Planning and Investment (MPI) in a new market-oriented economy while the internal departmental structure is barely changed. Some of the important functions include gathering data, forecasting trends, suggesting priority areas for development and foreign investment, ensuring coordination between ministries and provinces, planning public investment program, etc. which provide "state guidance" in the context of a socialist market-oriented economy. While functions of the central planning have changed dramatically to meet the requirements of market reforms, there are also clear continuities in the way it operates, including the continued use of administrative methods, such as quotas and approval procedures, to achieve its planning objectives and maintain macroeconomic stability.[165]

The goal of *doi moi* is not to create a capitalist market economy but a socialist-oriented market economy in which the Leninist party-state remains in place and public ownership of the means of production remains a dominant position. The transition from state socialism in Vietnam has created a hybrid economic form – a mixed ownership structure in which the state sector continues to play a substantial role, with 64 percent of contribution to gross industrial output in 1995, while non-public sectors dominates agricultural and domestic trade.[166] Since 1989, government policy has encouraged the development of non-public sectors, such as family, individual, and private sectors, to soak up the unemployed and contribute to the economic growth. However, although non-public sectors could enter into joint ventures but were restricted from entry into some areas of production and services which remained under state monopoly, including publishing, printing, gold and precious stones, alcohol, cigarettes, port and long distance transport, etc. Many other products were closely monitored and sanctioned by the state.[167] Law on Companies allows individuals to establish limited liability and shareholding companies. However, Article 11 requires approval from the state authority for the establishment of companies proposing to conduct business in certain economic sectors. Article 13 requires the company to give priority to the use of domestic labor. Article 20 requires another application to be submitted to the People's Committee if a company wants to establish a branch office outside of the province where its head office is located. Similarly, Article 21 further requires that the company must notify the planning committee which issues its certificate of business if the company decides to change its objective, area of business, charter capital, or any other items on its business registration. All these measures allow the government to maintain control over the operation and area of business. Law on Private Enterprises allows individuals to establish private enterprises and the private owners are free to make independent decisions in relation to their business activities. However, as with the Law on Company, the economic freedom provided by the law is limited. In addition to the specific requirements for the application to the People's Committee that grants licenses, Article 9 requirements restrict private owners from making several important decisions on the area of business, operation of business outside the location where head office is located, and changes in business. Article 24 further requires approval from the People's Committee for the sale or merger of private enterprises. The Temporary Regulation on the Issuance of Bonds and Stocks of State Owned Enterprises allows SOEs to issue bonds and stocks, but they have to obtain approval from the state authority and meet some specific requirements. These state firms must assure that the "total value of state stocks" would "not be less than 30 percent of the total capital of the enterprise. Therefore, although these laws, together with other provisions and regulations concerning bankruptcy, corruption, and procedures for breaches, provide a necessary legal framework for market reforms and development, they also limit and control the degree and scope of market reforms.[168]

In the process of reform, the state has continued to maintain tight control over the main resources, the key industries, the infrastructure, the Internet, the media, and foreign trade, and extensive regulation of the economy. However, factor markets, such as labor, capital, and land, have come into being due to continued economic liberalization, market reforms, growth of non-state sectors in the economy, legal reforms, banking reforms, wages reform, etc.

The *doi moi* policy has produced good results. Despite the adverse impacts of the recent regional economic crisis, Vietnam's GDP doubled during the 1990–2000 period. Vietnam's economy has experienced very strong growth over the past decade with GDP averaging 7.5%, even though growth in the last few years has not been quite so high. The share of GDP by economic sectors is changing positively. Agriculture's share of total output has decreased markedly while output in the industrial and services sectors has increased.[169] Inflation dropped from three digits in the 80s to less than 10% since mid 90s. The exchange rate with the US dollar has remained relatively stable. State revenue rose from 15.2% of GDP in 1990 to 27.2% in 2000. Domestic saving and investment also increased from 14.4% and 13.2% in 1991 to 27% and 22.1% of GDP respectively in 2000.[170] The private sector has also been growing rapidly.[171] More than two decades of economic reform have made a great progress toward market-oriented economy, which itself is an important factor in contributing to rapid and steady economic growth rates.

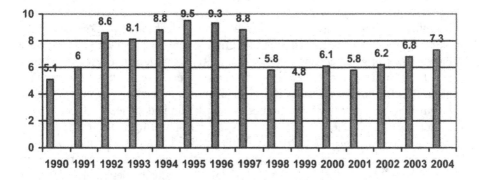

Figure 5.5 Real GDP growth by year in Vietnam (%)

Sources: Statistical Yearbook of General Statistical Office of Vietnam; Asian Development Outlook; CIA World Factbook (various issues).

LAOS PDR

Public Sector Share of GDP

Public sector share of GDP (2001) was 20%.[172] The number of SOEs has been reduced from more than 800 in the early 1990s to about 90. However, the privatization program has not made further progress. Thirty-two major SOEs are currently excluded from the privatization process and will remain under state control for "strategic" reasons. The Sixth Party Congress in 1998 emphasized that different forms of economic ownership were permitted, but stressed boosting the efficiency of state enterprises. Foreign investment should be accepted only in areas the government regarded as necessity or priorities.

Private Sector

In the area of private sector, some progress has been made to streamline approval procedures for the establishment and operation of foreign inverted enterprises and simplify the regulations and procedures for establishing businesses in Laos. However, private sector statistics are murky at best. The following official statement by the Mekong Capital Group symbolizes this evident fact. "We can find little reliable data on the size of Laos' private sector."[173] The private sector consists mainly of small family trading and food-related businesses. The government still views the emerging private sector as potential threat to the party-state authority to control the economy.[174]

Privatization Policy

Officially, the Laos PDR has recently encouraged greater economic openness and liberalization, but the preservation of political stability and one-party rule remains top concern for the party leadership. Vientiane has promoted gradual economic liberalization through the policy, New Economic Mechanism (NEM). Under the NEM policy Laos has moved carefully from a centrally planned economy to a more market-oriented economic system. In 1991, Laos adopted a new constitution, which legitimized the creation of a market-oriented economy and provided protection for foreign and domestic investment and property.[175] Foreign investors could own their own businesses, but were still limited to lease of land. Such strategic sectors as electricity, water, gas, air transport, logging/forestry, mining, and the pharmaceutical industries are still protected from privatization although some noncore state assets are sold or leased out in the reform. Investors in these sectors must pay additional taxes which are individually determined for each contract with the Committee for Investment and Foreign Economic Cooperation (CIFEC). Vientiane is also wary of outright sale of SOEs, fearing that low sale prices could turn into high profit for buyers at the loss of the state. Therefore, most of SOEs are leased out rather than sold out or "privatized." Leasing does not change the ownership but the management.[176] In 2003, following the lead of

Vietnam, the amendments to the constitution formally recognized private property and its legitimate status on an equal footing with the state sector.[177]

Stock or Shareholding Companies

Laos does not have a functioning stock market, and seems unlikely to have one in the near future. Moreover, its state and private enterprises are not currently listed on international markets for reasons of high taxation, access to credit and lack of maturity. Like Cambodia, its companies have yet to establish an international and even domestic reputation for transparency, reliability, profitability and sustainability.[178] Therefore, "the use of a stock market as a platform to publicly sell – and later trade – shares in privatized state enterprises has not been a viable policy option for Laos' state sector divestment program."[179]

Prices

Market-based price system is in place for most products. Prices on all but strategic commodities are determined by the market forces of demand and supply.[180] Average inflation, which reached a staggering 128% in 1999, was reduced to single figures by 2002. Likes its neighbor Cambodia, Laos is dependent upon foreign aid, grants and forgiveness, which has been a contributing factor that affects market prices.[181]

Factor Markets

Land is already transferable and an active real estate market already exists. However, the turnover figures as measured in recorded land transactions are not high and transactions are hampered by the problem of establishing ownership as long as the legislation (Land Law) is not yet amended or existing Decrees (Land Decree) are not fully implemented in land titling process. Most residential land is sold on a cash basis, while the lending which is occurring with respect to commercial or agricultural properties is made with cash flow in mind rather than the security of the title. There are inadequacies in existing mortgage laws and therefore inevitably a prevalence of illegal possession, sale and use of land and a large number of court cases relating to land: all these are symptoms of existing, vivid but still inefficient land markets.[182] The Land Law allows the state intervention in land allocation and allow for different interpretation depending on the local social relationships, which has a negative impact on rural development and environmental conservation.[183] The labor market is largely free while the capital market is still dominated by state banks in Laos.

Control of Resources

Laos PDR simply does not have many industrial enterprises (both state and private). Even so, Vientiane has been slow to liberalize and restructure those state enterprises, particularly large corporations.[184] Vientiane has decentralized some decisions on investment to its provincial governments, but transportation, health, education and energy are controlled by Vientiane.[185] The government controls land, energy, and natural resources as "strategic" for the "national security."[186]

Financial Institutions

There are eight banks in Laos PDR, including joint ventures and foreign banks, such as Thai-Lao or Vietnam-Lao. However, Laos PDR' financial institutions are largely dominated by three state-owned commercial banks and the Agricultural Promotion Bank. A single state bank, *Banque pour le Commerce Exterieur Lao (BCEL)*, has 50 percent of the country's total banking assets. The state bank controls entry of other banks and non-bank financial institutions. Foreign banks are allowed to open branches since 1992, but they are limited to the Vientiane municipality. Vientiane has pledged to reduce overstaffing in the banking sector as well as commissioning international accountants to audit the state-owned Bank for Agricultural Promotion, which provides credit for farmers. Despite actual changes and pledges, there is often a significant chasm between rhetoric and reality in Laos. There are still major problems in the banking sector, in which politically motivated lending remains the norm. According to the IMF, the next stage of banking and enterprise reform is to be particularly difficult and will require substantial political will.[187] Although the restructuring and recapitalization program has attempted to get the other two state banks – Lane Xang Bank and Lao May Bank – merged into a new single entity, there is no plan to wholly or partially divest any of these banks and introduce any private equity.[188]

Monetary Policy

Though Vientiane has been slow to liberalize its financial institutions, it has, nonetheless, achieved a modicum of success with monetary policy reform. Its monetary policy was galvanized by recent calls for fiscal decentralization as a means to increase revenue collection and foster provincial development and growth. Moreover, Laos has ceded some autonomy to its provincial governments by permitting them to approve all investment projects below two million U.S. dollars. The managed floating exchange rate has been in place since 1998. The kip's exchange rate remains stable, with the spread between the official and market exchange rates remained at 2.0%. [189]

Trade Policy

Laos has opened itself up to foreign trade and FDI. Aside from activities that may affect national security, strategic areas, and health, the entire economy is open to foreign investment. Laotian law permits 100 percent foreign ownership in all sectors except hydropower and mining. However, new investment in telecommunications, travel and tour services and import-export businesses is typically and frequently closed to foreigners. Furthermore, investment in wood processing is open only to joint ventures with the government.[190] As part of its obligations to ASEAN and the IMF, Laos is expected to reduce some taxes and boost interest on bonds and treasury bills so as to increase market attractiveness and foster increased domestic and international trade.[191] Laos is continuing to lower import tariffs in line with its commitments to the AFTA by 2006. It has until 2008 to lower tariffs below 5%; reductions are being implemented each year toward this end.[192] Other notable reforms introduced by Vientiane include streamlining the investment approval process for both domestic and foreign investors in 2003 and at the same time introducing the first "special economic zone" in Savannakhet province, permitting provincial authorities to license foreign investment projects valued at US$ 2 million or less while foreign investment projects of US$ 2-10 million still require an approval from Committees for Investment and Cooperation at the central level and projects above US$ 10 will need the approval of the government.[193] Like its neighbor Cambodia, however, trade policy is likely to be overshadowed by the inherent need to promote and stimulate domestic markets, development, infrastructure and economic culture. Vientiane is currently working on membership to the WTO. Most of Laos' foreign trade is conducted with its neighbors Thailand and Vietnam, although investment has increased dramatically in the past few years with China.[194]

Laos has made the departure from the centrally planned economy and transitioned towards a market socialist economy. What has emerged is a "dual structure" or "hybrid economic system" combining state and market roles and blending market and socialist principles. Such reform efforts are comparable to those measures introduced in China and Vietnam. Table 5.11 is a summary of the key indicators along the two dimensions.

Summary Remarks

Property rights is one of the most important dimensions of economic systems. Land as the most important resource is still a state property, but individual peasants have use rights that are transferable and heritable. In the mid-1980s, the state sector accounts for some 80 percent of Laos' industrial production while the remaining 20 percent, mostly small workshops and handicraft shops, were for the most part in private hands. During the 1990s, the reform of SOEs was launched. However, only small SOEs were transferred partly or wholly to the private sector, mostly through leasing, not sell-off. In strictly legal terms, the property ownership does not change under a leasing agreement. This "raises the question of whether ownership of these firms was really transferred from the state – and therefore can be regarded as genuine privatization."[195] Private ownership has gained ground rapidly in the service sector, particularly in wholesale and retail sales, transport, restaurants, hotels, and other service activities, and in the form of joint ventures in the banking and insurance sectors. However, private ownership is still a minor property rights form in the industrial sector.[196]

Table 5.11   Key indicators along the two dimensions (Lao PDR)

Public vs. Private ownership	
Public/private share of GDP	The public sector accounts for 20 percent of GDP, but the state, non-state, and private sector statistics are murky.
Public/private share of national assets	Public sector is dominant. No specific data is available
Public/private share of industrial output	Public sector share of industrial output is dominant. The private sector consists mainly of small family trading and food-related businesses. No reliable data is found.
Privatization	Most of SOEs are leased rather than "privatized." There are growing joint-ventures and private businesses in non-strategic sectors. Private property right and its legal status are formally recognized.

Market vs. State Control	
Prices	Prices on all but strategic commodities are determined by the market forces of demand and supply.
Factor markets	Insufficient land market, restricted capital market, but relatively free labor market
Control of resources	Government control of land, energy, and natural resources and the "commanding heights" of the economy.
Financial institutions	State banks dominate, with some foreign bank branches and joint-ventures
Monetary policy	Managed floating exchange rate, with a loose monetary policy subject to political influence of the party policy
Trade Policy	Largely liberal – reduced tariff and quantitative control, but informal barriers are employed, such as priority list, SEZs, restrictive licensing for foreign investment projects, prohibited import goods.

Although NEM and the Laotian constitution have been largely successful in mapping out changes, the actual implementation of reforms has moved gradually. This would be most apparent in the banking and financial sectors. Despite promises and expectations to the contrary, Laos' financial institutions continue to be largely state-centric. These state commercial banks account for about 65 percent of total banking assets in Laos while the remaining 35 percent are held by the state-owned Agricultural Promotion Bank (5 percent), three joint venture banks (10 percent), and a handful of foreign bank branches (20 percent).[197]

Although some non-strategic SOEs were reportedly to be privatized, most of them were divested through leasing agreements, which do not change the ownership in legal terms. The decision was made in 1997 to "commercialize" strategic SOEs, as its neighboring China and Vietnam did, which involved converting them into public joint-stock companies, appointing board of directors, financial restructuring, and establishing performance criteria and objectives. But they continue to report to individual ministries or provincial authorities.[198]

Efforts were also made in the 1990s to develop private sector in Laos. Nevertheless, the private sector continues to be stunted by a weak legal system, poor infrastructure and unfavorable business environment, overly bureaucratic and porous financial system, and lack of skilled labor. Like Cambodia, growth often occurs at slow pace due to inadequate access to most kinds of financing from state banks, foreign concerns about credibility, corruption and rule of law, and the inability of domestic entrepreneurs and enterprises to procure credit and capital.[199] The process is largely influenced by the government policy that remains socialist in its approach to economic development and reform, and sensitive to the ideological ramifications of state enterprise divestment and private sector development. The recent decentralization measures have returned some of former SOEs to public ownership as the existing leasing arrangements come to an end and also allow whole new SOEs to be established by provincial governments. The playing field for state and private enterprises is favorable to the former as the "strategic" enterprises continue to "soak up" a large proportion of available financial resources.[200]

However, the Lao leadership has continued the NEM-inspired economic reforms, and "Laos has been undergoing an economic transition process similar to those of neighboring China and Vietnam since the mid-1980s,"[201] which is oriented toward market socialism rather than market capitalism.

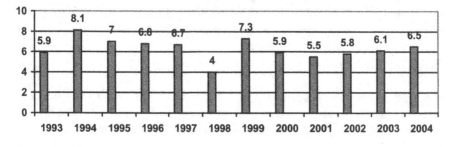

Figure 5.6 Real GDP growth by year in Lao PDR (%)

Sources: CIA World Factbook; Asian Development Outlook; National Statistical Centre of Lao PDR (various issues).

CAMBODIA

Public Sector Share of GDP

According to World Bank, the public sector share of GDP fixed investment is at 23.7% in 2001.[202] Some other sources reported that public sector share of Cambodian GDP was 17 percent in 2001.[203]

Private Sector Share of GDP

World Bank put private sector share of GDP fixed investment at 76.3 percent in 2001.[204] According to the other source, the Cambodian private sector makes up roughly 60% of GDP in 2002. However, this figure is somewhat misleading, because Cambodia's private sector is mostly comprised of rural family farming units rather than corporations and enterprises. As such, the actual GDP share of Cambodia's private sector – as represented by private businesses – is likely to be smaller and still underdeveloped.[205]

Privatization Policy

Phnom Penh has encouraged foreign and private investment in Cambodia. State enterprises have been substantially reduced through long term leases to private citizens. Though it has indeed made significant strides in textiles, agriculture and general services, it still lags behind many of its neighbors in privatization, technology, education, infrastructure, market creation, and market accessibility. As a member of APEC and ASEAN, Phnom Penh has received and will continue to receive assistance for development and greater economic liberalization.[206] Cambodia was the largest Southeast Asian recipient of foreign aid in 2003 (US $635 million).[207] However, political instability may slow down reform and even derail current reforms. Like neighboring Laos, Cambodia needs the help of the international community to build its foreign reserves and promote wider privatization and development. However, one of the main concerns is that foreign aid might be used to refinance its debt and deficit in perpetuity and the economy would become too dependent on foreign succor.[208]

Stock/Shareholding Companies

Currently, Cambodia does not have a stock market, and its companies – both state-run and private – are not listed on other national markets.[209] Mature stock enterprises of any substance and scope are typically foreign-owned.[210]

Prices

In Cambodia, the role of prices in the economic allocation system has fundamentally changed and all prices have been brought closer to international prices. The two-tier price system for rice, introduced in 1984, under which farmers were taxed indirectly by being compelled to sell a portion of their output to the state at below market prices, was abolished in 1989. Market prices were formally decontrolled and official procurement came to an end, although the state continued to purchase rice, but at considerably higher prices. Commodity prices are now essentially market determined, although sometimes under monopoly control, and are open to the influence of international prices. Direct subsidies for commodity purchases have been virtually eliminated.[211]

Factor Markets

There exist labor, capital, commercial, industrial, and real estate markets in Cambodia. Land is still mainly owned by the state, but land leasing is given to individual households. Only 10 percent of rural households hold legal land titles.[212] Land reform is slow, and further reforms are called for in the areas of land, forestry, and fisheries concessions, as well as land ownership. Much good land is tied up in public land concessions, which are not fully utilized and, as a result, farmers do not have access to enough farmland.[213]

Control of Resources

Like Laos, Cambodia's most vital resources and sectors – health, education, environment, transportation, electric power, energy, mining, fishing, forestry, beer, and alcoholic beverages – are controlled by the government.[214] But, Phnom Penh has tolerated and even solicited greater degrees of assistance and proprietorship from the private sector, and not surprisingly, much of this succor has come from donor nations and organizations. Recently, Phnom Penh has ceded much autonomy on agricultural resources to provinces, villages and farmers.[215]

Financial Institutions

The National Bank of Cambodia (the central bank) previously fulfilled central and commercial banking functions. Banking reforms in 1993, however, defined it as solely the central bank, with oversight on commercial bank regulation, printing money, and controlling foreign exchange. Therefore, two-tier banking system was established. More reforms were made following the adoption of the Banking and Financial Institutions Law in 1999. In 1999, there were 31 registered commercial banks in Cambodia; foreign banks have been permitted to operate since the early 1990s, specifically, Thai banks. Under the amended Law on Banking and Financial Institutions, all of Cambodia's commercial banks had to reapply for licenses from the NBC, and meet new, stricter capital and prudential requirements. As a result, there was a significant amount of shakeout and consolidation within the banking sector and the number of commercial banks was reduced from 31 to 14 by December 2003.[216]

Significantly, Phnom Penh privatized the Foreign Trade Bank in 2001. Despite substantial banking reforms, there is a widespread distrust of the banking system among Cambodians. Banks still cannot fully perform their role as financial intermediaries and the banking system remains underdeveloped. The economy is highly dollarized, with the ratio of foreign currency deposits to broad money amounting to nearly 70 percent. Therefore, the scope of the central bank to pursue monetary policy is limited. The high proportion of foreign-currency deposits in the money supply indicates a continued preference for dollars and distrust of Cambodian banks. Moreover, the sector is further weakened by the lack of a well-developed rural banking network.[217]

Monetary Policy

Cambodia's market reform has improved public finances and made monetary policy more effective, but progress has been slow. Central control over revenue is fairly weak, and Phnom Penh relies on foreign aid for over 80% of capital expenditure. The ability of the National Bank of Cambodia to fine-tune and correct the economy – by using monetary instruments – is weak. Phnom Penh has tied its monetary policy and its economic fortunes to the structures and guidelines of regional and international organizations, institutions and obligations. In line with IMF and World Bank protocols from which it has recently accepted assistance, Phnom Penh attempts to keep inflation stable (2%-3.5% per annum) and build its domestic and foreign reserves so as to secure some degree of autonomy and assuage currency and investment shock.[218] "In the context of low inflation, the nominal exchange rate remained sable. The spread between the official and market exchange rates remained with 1.0%."[219] All domestic interest rates have been totally liberalized, and reserve requirements are in place in the banking system.[220]

Trade Policy

Phnom Penh has begun in recent years to build a liberal trade regime. Despite a lack of development, weak infrastructure, illiteracy and unskilled labor (like Laos) and political uncertainty, Cambodia has managed an open trade regime: private sector trading is permitted; licensing requirements are removed for most of goods; import tariff system is streamlined; export restrictions are reduced; and foreign companies are allowed in import and export activities. Phnom Penh reduced tariffs further in line with its obligations under the ASEAN Free Trade Agreement CEPT protocol.[221] Cambodia is currently negotiating to accede to the WTO. In preparation for this, it has signed tariff- and quota-reducing agreements with Australia, United States, Canada, Japan and the EU.[222] The U.S. represents its largest export market, followed by Vietnam. Thailand represented the largest importing nation, followed by Hong Kong.[223] Table 5. 12 is a summary of the key indicators along the two dimensions.

Table 5.12 Key indicators along the two dimensions (Cambodia)

Public vs. Private ownership

Public/private share of GDP	The public sector accounts for 17 percent of GDP and 23.7 percent of GDP fixed investment, while the private sector accounts for 60 percent of GDP and 76.3 percent of GDP fixed investment. The actual GDP share of domestic private sector is small and underdeveloped.
Public/private share of national assets	The total assets of Cambodia's banking system as of August 2004 were approximately 4,106 billion Riel ($1030 million). No specific data on public/private share of national assets is found.
Public/private share of industrial output	Public sector share of industrial output is dominant. The private sector consists mainly of small family trading and food-related businesses. No data on public/private share of industrial output is found.
Privatization	Most of SOEs are leased rather than "privatized." Private property right and its legal status are formally recognized.

Market vs. State Control

Prices	Prices are determined by the market forces of demand and supply.
Factor markets	Weak land market, insufficient capital market, but free labor market
Control of resources	Government control of land, energy, and natural resources and the "commanding heights" of the economy or the most vital resources and sectors.
Financial institutions	Two-tier banking system with one central State bank and registered commercial banks. Foreign banks are permitted.
Monetary policy	Managed floating exchange rate, with a loose monetary policy. The ability of state bank to fine-tune and correct the economy is weak as the economy is highly dollarized and relied upon foreign aid.
Trade Policy	Largely liberal – reduced tariff and quantitative control, but informal barriers are employed, such as priority list, SEZs, restrictive licensing for foreign investment projects, prohibited import goods.

Summary Remarks

In the early stage of economic transition, the new Cambodian government proposed a much moderate form of socialization – a collective economy that incorporated a three-tiered structure of collectivized groups (*rom samaki*).[224] However, it was the party officials that broke down the system – they failed to adhere to the principles of collectivization, sold land, allowed peasants to work on the land in the manner in which they chose, and ultimately led to economic reform of the collectives. By February of 1989, the Party had gone as far as stating "Citizens have full rights to hold (kan kap) and use (bra braoe bras) land and have the right to inheritance of land that the state has granted them to live on and to conduct business on."[225] Agricultural land was divided into private holdings in 1989. However, the legal framework to grant land titles was never fully implemented, and only 10 percent of rural households have full legal rights to their land.[226]

Cambodia has made significant strides in market reforms. Cambodia has directed many of its reform efforts toward its notoriously corrupt and creaky financial sector. Despite substantive liberalization, there is still widespread distrust of the banking system among Cambodians. Moreover, the sector is further weakened by the lack of a well-developed rural banking network.[227]

Cambodia appears to be committed to the gradual privatization of the state sector. However, it encourages its development as a means to promote national economic growth. Private enterprises, particularly joint ventures and foreign owned enterprises, have often proven to be more productive and efficient than their state-run counterparts. As of 2002, the Cambodian private sector made up roughly 60% of GDP. Though there are approximately 190 large garment manufacturing companies in Cambodia, however, a vast majority of these, at least 95%, are foreign-owned entities.[228] As such, the actual share of Cambodia's private sector, as represented by home-grown private businesses, is still largely small, nominal and underdeveloped.[229]

As previously noted, in order to attract both foreign aid and FDI, Phnom Penh has gone to great lengths to liberalize its investment and trade regime. Specifically, foreign investors are permitted to lease land for a period of up to 70 years, with the possibility of renewal thereafter. Moreover, Phnom Penh provides investors with a guarantee to neither nationalize foreign-owned assets nor establish price controls on goods and services produced in Cambodia. Investors are entitled to repatriate capital, interest and other financial obligations, and investors are allowed to set up 100% foreign-owned investment projects and employ skilled workers from overseas when such workers cannot be found in the domestic labor pool.[230]

However, Cambodia's nascent private sector and weak infrastructure have proven to be a hindrance for MNCs. Specifically, the economy is plagued by high incidences of land ownership disputes, insufficient legal and judicial framework and inconsistent tax structures.[231] Cambodia has made little progress in the way of political stability, development of credible and sustainable banking and judicial institutions, and the application of transparent and equitable guidelines and laws.

However, economic reform since 1993 has substantially reduced state sector through privatization and long term leases to private sector. As of 2001, there were 38 SOEs privatized and 219 leased out.[232] Most of prices are liberalized. Two-tier banking system has been established and open to entry by foreign and domestic commercial banks. The commercial bank re-licensing program was completed, and reforms in civil administration, customs and tax administration have also made progress. In the area of foreign trade, private sector trading is permitted and foreign companies are allowed in import-export activities. Liberal Foreign Investment Law has contributed to substantial increases in FDI inflow. Licensing requirements are eliminated for most goods. Import tariff system is streamlined, with limited export restrictions. Market-based exchange rate system has been set up, with the riel's official exchange rate kept within 1% band of parallel market rate.[233] All this has contributed an optimistic economic growth except the period of Asian financial crisis.

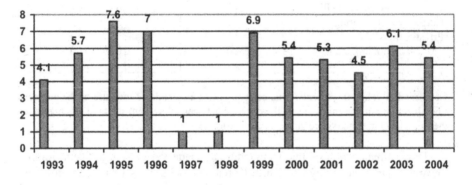

Figure 5.7 Real GDP growth by year in Cambodia (%)

Sources: CIA World Factbook; Cambodia Statistical Yearbooks of National Institute of Statistics (various issues).

Conclusion

Asian transition from the model of centrally planned economy has been under way for more than two decades, and all the countries have made a progress toward a market-based economy although the sequencing of reform and the achievements vary from one country to another. Even North Korea, in some respects, has begun to address those typical problems existing in its economy and made a considerable progress since 2002. Using the measurement scheme that includes 10 indicators along the two major dimensions, which are derived from the basic definition and requirement of a market economy, we can estimate how far each of these Asian transitional economies has traveled down the road to market economy. Table 5.13 assesses the status of market reforms by providing an estimated measure of economic liberalization in these countries.

Table 5.13 Transition toward market economy in East and Southeast Asia

Key indicators	China	DPRK	Vietnam	Laos	Cambodia
Market vs. State Control					
Prices	3	4	4	5	5
Factor markets	3	2	3	4	5
Control of resources	2	1	2	3	4
Financial institutions	1	1	1	2	4
Monetary policy	2	1	2	3	4
Trade Policy	3	2	3	4	5
Public vs. Private Ownership					
Public/private share of GDP	2	1	3	4	4
Corporate restructuring	3	1	3	3	3
Privatization policy	1	1	2	3	4
Stock/shareholding reform	3	0	2	0	0

Note: market value: 0 – 5 scale. This scale provides an estimated measure of the degree of liberalization, but does not indicate the distance between the current status of this region and the fully developed market economy of the world.

This estimate suggests that Cambodia has made the most significant progress toward a market economy and North Korea has made the least progress toward a market economy while others can be situated somewhere in between on the left-right spectrum. This estimate can be partially validated by a different but more rigorously designed measurement scheme, *Index of Economic Freedom* (IEF), though IEF estimate on North Korea does not match the reality in this country as the assignment of score "5" simply means no change, but it is evident that significant changes have indeed taken place in North Korea. IEF measures the degree of economic freedom in a vast array of countries around the globe based on a rigorous statistical evaluation of several aspects of their measurement scheme – trade policy, fiscal burden, government intervention, monetary policy, foreign investment, banking and finance, wages and prices, property rights, regulation, and informal market. According to IEF estimate, formerly communist countries in Eastern bloc are now among the most economically free, while communist states in East and Southeast Asia are still among the mostly unfree with only one exception, Cambodia, although most of these countries have achieved remarkable economic growth in the past years.

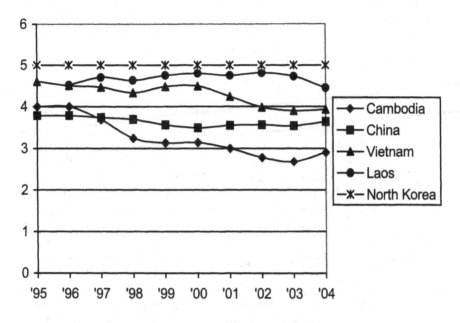

Figure 5.8   Economic freedom ranking of five countries under study

Sources: 2004 Index of Economic Freedom (The Heritage Foundation and *The Wall Street Journal*) http://www.heritage.org/research/features/index/countries.html.

Note: 1= Best   5=Worst

Index of Economic Freedom confirms that these Asian transitional economies, except Cambodia, are nowhere a true market economy of capitalism. What has emerged in these countries is a "dual structure" or "hybrid economic system" combining state and market roles and blending market and socialist principles, which is the defining feature of market socialism. Compared to the pre-reform model discussed in Chapter 2, a number of new characteristics can be identified although the situations in different countries may vary to a certain degree.

Macroeconomic means, such as monetary and fiscal policies, have been increasingly used by the governments to manage the economies. Prices are no longer determined by the state but increasingly in line with world-market prices. Investment decisions have been decentralized to enterprises and individual farmers. Agriculture is household based, and user rights have been incorporated into the constitutions. SOEs have been reformed through shareholding, leasing, joint ventures, or a certain degree of privatization. Light industry, like consumer-goods manufacture, gets priority. A labor market is developing rapidly. The banking systems are being reformed through separation of central and commercial banking. Foreign currency is still allocated administratively, but the banks and non-bank foreign exchange dealers have begun to sell foreign currency. A land market is emerging through the right to use and transfer the usufruct rights of land. An export-oriented and market-oriented economy is emerging to replace the old, closed economy and foreign trade earnings are contributing an important share of GDP. State monopoly of foreign trade has ceased and individual enterprises can enter into contracts with foreign companies. The private sector is playing an important role in the economies, contributing considerably to GDP through agriculture, manufacture, construction, trade, and other services. All countries have adopted liberal foreign-investment legislation which aims at attracting foreign capital and technology. The tax systems are being adjusted to the requirements of a market economy through the introduction of profit taxes, sales taxes, and income taxes. A legal framework in the form of company law, bankruptcy law, and so forth, has come into being. New ways have been sought to finance social services, such as fees and privatization. Social security network has become important on the agenda.[234]

However, in Asian transition economies, although many elements of a market economy has come into being, the economy cannot be characterized as a free market economy because the distortions of market are still severe due to the absence of adequate factor markets, the extensive government intervention in economic activities, and the continued domination of public ownership in the economy. State-owned enterprises still enjoy advantages over nonstate enterprises, particularly the private sector, in the form of government subsidies, bank loan and credit, preferential allocation of resources, and foreign aid and international loan.[235] The banking systems are controlled by the state and banks do not play an independent role. Real interest rates are still often negative. The exchange rate regime is still under the state control.[236] Asian transition model is different from neo-classical model in transition economies of East Europe and Western market economies. It is a third way that attempts to combine elements of both socialism and capitalism to avoid ideological and practical difficulties of wholesale privatization and marketization. It is a form of market socialism that blends state control and market forces in economic decision of resource allocation and maintains ideological commitment and practical need in pursuit of modernization.

Overall, except Cambodia, we have witnessed an emergence of some hybrid economy or mixed economy in Asian communist states, in which the socialist public sector co-exists and competes with a rising capitalist private sector in the political-economic-cultural context defined and controlled by the communist party-state. This is the most important and basic understanding in our observation and assessment of the Asian transition from communism. It is important to understand the fact that until a true free market has become established it is not the market alone that determines resource allocation, and the party-state has a dominant role to play in the process of resource allocation and transition direction. "The very nature of transition dictates that there has to be some hybrid between the old and the new."[237] In other words, what happens after the transition begins does not necessarily move toward a "free market economy" but can go in a number of different directions: free market economy of capitalism, state capitalism, or market socialism. These countries, except Cambodia, are evidently moving toward market socialism, which will be the major issue to be studied in Chapter 6.

This study also suggests some important lessons from Asian transitions, and their success can be largely attributed to the right choice of economic policy and sequencing of reforms rather than the initial conditions for transition. First, developing non-state sectors and improving corporate governance of state enterprises can be successful without a wholesale privatization of state sectors. That is to say, privatization of SOEs is not a necessary precondition for market reform, competition, and efficiency. These developments are achieved through a mixed ownership structure of state, collective, joint-ventured, foreign owned, individual, private owned enterprises and businesses, the merger and/or liquidation of nonviable small and medium scale SOEs, the conversion of SOEs into joint-stock and shareholding companies, and the restructuring of corporate governance.[238]

Second, gradualism characterized by the dual-track system, such as coexistence of state and nonstate sectors, state and market prices, soft-budget and hard-budget constraints, works well for the economic transition from state socialism. State, collective, private, individual, joint-ventured, foreign owned enterprises compete with each other, promoting economic growth without upsetting the social and economic stability.[239] Most of the five transitional economies of East and Southeast Asia have maintained strong growth throughout the transition period whereas in the transitional economies of Central and Eastern Europe, the Baltics, Russia, and the other countries of the former Soviet Union that adopted a "Big Bang" shock therapist approach, the transition have been accompanied by the decline of output, severe dislocation, large redistribution of income, and severe income losses by many people. Only a handful have seen output recover to pre-transition levels.[240]

Third, the sequencing of reforms in which microeconomic reforms are implemented prior to macroeconomic reforms has encouraged the development of institutional arrangements capable of responding to market signals and reducing social costs of adjustment.[241] Reforms usually start where possible and where there will be a quick payoff. The initial success would then strengthen the political support for more difficult reform. Therefore, the timing and priorities of reforms are often dictated by economic feasibility and political sustainability perceived by the leadership.[242]

Finally, careful sequencing of reforms requires a high degree of political control over the transition process that was not available in many of the transition economies of Eastern Europe, especially in the CIS countries. State capacity is the most important contributing factor to the success of such a regime-led, state-sanctioned, and carefully managed transition. "Reforms have been gradual but far reaching. They have remained on track in part because they were initiated and implemented in a stable political climate, a luxury not on offer elsewhere."[243]

While the experience of Asian economic transitions has been successful, the reforms are not flawless. For example, the gradualist approach usually creates "dual track systems" in all major areas, which induces rent seeking behavior and activities and corrupts the government officials. SOE reforms have not been very successful, contributing to a worsening financial situation, which in term has resulted in a substantial accumulation of nonperforming bad loans in state-owned banks.[244] It appears that blending of markets and socialist principles creates more problems than they can be resolved, particularly the structural problems that hinders the reform from proceeding and deepening further. However, the problem is not the gradualist approach per se, but something else. Identifying the major problems in the socialist market reform and finding viable solutions to them will become the major task in the next chapter.

Notes

[1]　　Thomas G. Rawski, "Chinese Industrial Reform: Accomplishments, Prospects, and Implications," *American Economic Review*, vol. 84, no. 2, 1994, pp. 271-275.

[2]　　Eduardo R. Borensztein and Manmohan Kumar, "Proposals for Privatization in Eastern Europe," *IMF Staff Papers*, vol. 38, no. 2, 1991, p. 302.

[3]　　János Kornai, *The Road to a Free Economy: Shifting from a Socialist System, the Example of Hungary* (New York: W.W. Norton and Company, 1990) p. 57.

[4]　　Dic Lo, *Market and Institutional Regulation in Chinese Industrialization, 1978-1994* (London: Maclillan Press, 1997), p. 47, 49.

[5]　　Stephanie Fahey, "Vietnam and the Third Way: the Nature of Socio-economic Transition," *Journal of Economic and Social Geography*, vol. 88, no. 5, 1997, p. 476.

[6]　　Mark N. Hagopian, *Regimes, Movements, and Ideologies* (New York and London: Longman, 1978), pp. 436-437. According to Hagopian, the means of production include such things as energy resources, land, raw materials, tools, machines, and factories. The means of exchange include transportation and communication facilities, whole sale and retail outlets, banking and credit institutions, etc.

[7]　　Thomas M. Magstadt and Peter M. Schotten, *Understanding Politics: Ideas, Institutions, and Issues* (New York: St. Martin's Press, 1996), p. 367; Robert J. Jackson and Doreen Jackson, *A Comparative Introduction to Political Science* (New Jersey: Prentice Hall, 1997), p. 160; Jack C. Plato and Roy Olton, *The International Relations Dictionary* (Santa Barbara, CA: ABC, 1982), p. 81.

[8]　　Leon P. Baradat, *Political Ideologies: Their Origins and Impact* (New Jersey: Prentice Hall, 1979), p. 186.

[9]　　For a detailed discussion, see Yu-Shan Wu, *Comparative Economic Transformations: Mainland China, Hungary, the Soviet Union, and Taiwan* (Stanford, CA: Stanford University Press, 1994), pp. 7-9.

[10]　Eduardo R. Borensztein and Manmohan Kumar, p. 302.

[11]　http://www.amosweb.com/cgi-bin/wpd.pl?fcd=dsp&key=ownership+and+control

[12]　Ibid.

[13]　Ibid.

[14]　Stanley Fischer and Alan Gelb, "The Process of Socialist Economic Transformation," *Journal of Economic Perspectives*, vol. 5, no 4, Fall 1991, pp. 91-105; Martha De Melo, Cevdet Denizer, and Alan Gelb, "Pattern of Transition from Plan to Market," *The World Bank Economic Review*, vol. 10, no. 3, 1996, pp. 397-424; European Bank for Reconstruction and Development (EBRD), *Transition Report 1999*. London:

EBRD, 1999; IMF, "Transition-Experience and Policy Issues," *World Economic Outlook*, Washington: International Monetary Fund, autumn 2000, Chapter 3.

[15] Chen Jia-gui and Huang Qun-hui, "Comparison of Governance Structures of Chinese Enterprises with Different Types of Ownership," *China & World Economy*, vol. 9, no. 6, 2001, p. 5, http://www.iwep.org.cn/ wec/english/articles/2001_06/6chenjiagui.htm

[16] Xinhua News Agency, http://www.china.org.cn/english/BAT/28846.htm

[17] http://www.pwcglobal.com/extweb/newcolth.nsf/ docid/3D15C57A6D220BB985256 CF6007B9607#1

[18] Xinhua News Agency, http://www.us.tom.com/english/4490.html

[19] Economist Intelligence Unit, Country Report China > Product sample (2003) > "Further Liberalization in 2004," http://store.eiu.com/index.asp?layout=country_ home_page&ref=country_jump_home&country_id=CN

[20] Ibid.

[21] Xinhua News Agency, http://www.china.org.cn/english/BAT/28846.htm

[22] Allan Zhang, "China's New Leadership Rolls out Its Reform Agenda," in PricewaterhouseCoopers,http://www.pwc.com/extweb/newcolth.nsf/docid/CE98119E 9205D7D985256E2800760ABE

[23] Zhang Chunlin, "Financing the SOE Sector: Institutional Evolution and Its Implications for SOE Reform," *China & World Economy*, vol. 10, no. 6, 2002, pp. 1-11 (China Academy of Social Sciences, China)

[24] Peter H. Sturm and Bennett Sutton, "The Transition Process in China: A Comparative View," *China & World Economy*, vol. 9, no. 5, 2001, pp. 2-3.

[25] Cyril Lin, "Corporatization and Corporate Governance in China's Economic Transition," *Economics of Planning*, vol. 34, no. 1-2, 2001, pp. 5-6, 8.

[26] Zhang Chunlin, pp. 1-11.

[27] Cyril Lin, p. 24.

[28] Zhang Chunlin, pp. 1-11.

[29] http://www.Tradewatch.dfat.gov.au/TradeWatch/TradeWatch.nsf/vChangesWeb/China

[30] Cyril Liu, pp. 7-8.

[31] Sujian Guo, "Ownership Reform in China," *Journal of Contemporary China*, vol. 12, no. 36, 2003, pp. 553-573.

[32] Economist Intelligence Unit, Country Profile China (Sample), "Economic Sectors," http://store.eiu.com/index.asp?layout=show_sample&product_id=30000203&country _id=CN

[33] Economist Intelligence Unit, Country Report China (Sample), "Financial Outlook," http://store.eiu.com/index.asp?layout=country_home_page&ref=country_jump_home &country_id=CN

[34] Economist Intelligence Unit, Country Profile China (Sample), "Tax Structure," http://store.eiu.com/index.asp?layout=show_sample&product_id=30000203&country _id=CN

[35] Economist Intelligence Unit, Country Report China (Sample), "2003-2004 Foreign Exchange (peg vs. float), Prices, Inflation & Interest Rates," http://store.eiu.com/ index.asp?layout=country_home_page&ref=country_jump_home&country_id=CN

[36] "WTO Obligations, Tariffs & Foreign Investment (JV/FDI)." http://www.Tradewatch. dfat.gov.au/TradeWatch/TradeWatch.nsf/vChangesWeb/China

[37] Allan Zhang, http://www.pwc.com/extweb/newcolth.nsf/docid/CE98119E9205D7D9 85256E2800760ABE

[38]   Australian Department of Foreign Affairs and Trade, "Chinese Imports/Exports." http://www.dfat.gov.au/geo/fs/chin.pdf

[39]   Paul Heytens, "State Enterprise Reform," in Wanda Tseng and Markus Rodlauer, eds., *China: Competing in the Global Economy* (Washington: D.C.: International Monetary Fund, 2003), p. 125.

[40]   Lixin Colin Xu, Tian Zhu and Yi-min Lin, "Politician Control, Agency Problems and Ownership Reform: Evidence from China," *Economics of Transition*, vol. 13, no. 1, 2005, p. 2; Mary M. Shirley, "Bureaucrats in Business: the Roles of Privatization versus Corporatization in State-Owned Enterprise Reform," *World Development*, vol. 27, no. 1, 1999, pp. 115; World Bank, *Bureaucrats in Business* (New York: Oxford University Press, 1995).

[41]   Lixin Colin Xu, Tian Zhu and Yi-min Lin, p. 3.

[42]   Ibid., pp. 126-128.

[43]   *People's Daily*, May 27, 1997, p. 2.

[44]   Greg Mastel, *The Rise of the Chinese Economy: The Middle Kingdom Emerges* (NY: M.E. Sharpe, 1997), p. 71.

[45]   *People's Daily*, August 19, 1997, p. 1.

[46]   Dic Lo, *Market and Institutional Regulation in Chinese Industrialization, 1979-1994* (London: Macmillan Press, 1997), pp. 6, 89.

[47]   *Ibid.*, p. 90.

[48]   Economist Intelligence Unit, "Economic structure" *Country Profile China*, Sep 5th, 2001.

[49]   See *Xinhua Wenzhai*, no. 7, 1998, pp. 48-49.

[50]   Jinglian Wu, "China's Economic Reform: Past, Present and Future," *Perspectives*, vol. 1, no. 5, April, 2000.

[51]   Hu Jiayong, "An Empirical Analysis of the Amount of Resources Controlled by the Government," *Gaige* (Reform), no. 3, 1999.

[52]   Michael W. Bell et al., *China at the Threshold of a Market Economy* (Washington, DC: International Monetary Fund, 1993), p. 2.

[53]   *People's Daily*, October 21, 1993; Zhang, p. 215.

[54]   *People's Daily*, May 1, 1998, p. 1.

[55]   *China Daily,* April 4, 1998, p. 4.

[56]   Chen Xiaolong, "Where does Prosperity come from?" *China Spring*, vol. 165, 1997, pp. 12-13.

[57]   *Ibid.*, p. 12.

[58]   *People's Daily*, October 13, 97, p. 2.

[59]   *Ibid.*

[60]   *China Daily – Business Weekly*, March 30, 1998, p. 3.

[61]   Cem Karacadag, "Financial System Soundness and Reform," in Wanda Tseng and Markus Rodlauer, eds., *China: Competing in the Global Economy* (Washington: D.C.: International Monetary Fund, 2003), p. 149.

[62]   Ibid., pp. 152-155.

[63]   Ibid., p. 164.

[64]   Paul Heytens, p. 145.

[65]   Li Rongrong, Chairman of SETC, answered questions raised by journalists at the press conference for the Fourth Session of the Ninth National People's Congress on March 10, 2001, http://www.setc.gov.cn/english/setc_tpxw_main.htm

66 Guy S. Liu and Gaia Garino, "China's Two Decades of Economic Reform," *Economics of Planning*, vol. 34, no. 1-2, 2001, p. 4.

67 Digital Kotra NK, North Korean Economy, Public sector activity – conglomerates, cooperatives, enterprises – can be viewed at the link, "Company List," while investment & foreign trade can be viewed at their respective links. http://crm.kotra.or.kr/main/info/nk/eng/main.php3

68 "Korea Now," *Politics & Policy*, http://kn.koreaherald.co.kr/SITE/data/html_dir /2002/05/08/200205080007.asp; Economist Intelligence Unit, *Country Profile 2004: North Korea* (London: Patersons Dartford, 2004); Economist Intelligence Unit, *Country Report: North Korea February 2004* (London: Patersons Dartford, 2004), http://korea.co.kr/korealink/kn.html

69 David S. Kelleher and Hak-Min Kim, "Post-Unification Privatization of North Korean Enterprises," *Korea Observer*, vol. 36, no. 1 (2005), p. 75.

70 Jung-chul Lee, "The Implications of North Korea's Reform Program and Its Effects on State Capacity," *Korea and World Affairs*, vol. 26, no. 3, 2003, pp. 357-364; Economist Intelligence Unit, *Country Report: North Korea February 2004* (London: Patterns Dartford, 2004).

71 Economist Intelligence Unit, *Country Profile 2004: North Korea* (London: Patersons Dartford, 2004); Economist Intelligence Unit, *Country Report: North Korea February 2004* (London: Patersons Dartford, 2004), http://korea.co.kr/korealink/kn.html

72 Economist Intelligence Unit, Country Report North Korea: "State-directed Liberalization, Sunshine Policy & the Specter of Nukes." http://store.eiu.com/index.asp?layout=show_sample&product_id=50000205&country_id=KP

73 Australian Department of Foreign Affairs and Trade, "Economic Overview: Farming Reform," *Country Brief: Democratic People's Republic of Korea*, http://www.dfat.gov.au/geo/dprk/dprk_brief.html.

74 Yukie Yoshikawa, "The Prospect of Economic Reform in North Korea," 2004. http://www.nautilus.org/DPRKBriefingBook/transition/200312NKecon.html

75 Yukie Yoshikawa; Ruediger Frank, "A Socialist Market Economy in North Korea? Systemic Restrictions and a Quantitative Analysis," 2003, p. 8, http://www.nautilus.org/DPRKBriefingBook/economy/R_FrankonMarketEconomyinNorthKorea_08_May2003.pdf

76 Jung-chul Lee, pp. 357-364; Economist Intelligence Unit, *Country Report: North Korea February 2004* (London: Patterns Dartford, 2004); The Nautilus, *DPRK Briefing Book*, http://www.nautilus.org/DPRKBriefingBook.html; Australian Department of Foreign Affairs and Trade, Country Brief: Democratic People's Republic of Korea, "Economic Overview," http://www.dfat.gov.au/geo/dprk/dprk_brief.html

77 James Brooke, "Quietly, North Korea Opens Markets," *New York Times*, November 19, 2003.

78 Economist Intelligence Unit, *Country Profile 2004: North Korea* (London: Patersons Dartford, 2004); Michael Shuman, "The Hermit Kingdom's Bizarre SAR," *Time Asia Magazine*, October 7, 2002.

79 James Brooke, November 19, 2003.

80 Moon Ihlwan and Ira Sager, "Reforms are Starting to Bear Fruit," *Business Week*, July 26, 2004.

[81]   Economist Intelligence Unit, Country Report North Korea: "Market Sectors and Yield,"http://store.eiu.com/index.asp?layout=show_sample&product_id=50000205& country_id=KP

[82]   Digital Kotra NK, North Korean Economy. Click on "Laws and Regulations," and then "Economy." The economic section indicates a lack of privatization in banking and financial institutions, http://crm.kotra.or.kr/main/info/nk/eng/main.php3

[83]   *North Korea Banking*, http://www.vyapaarasia.com/n.korea/banks.asp

[84]   Marc A. Miles, Edwin J. Faulkner, Jr., and Mary Anastasia O'Grady, *2004 Index of Economic Freedom: Establishing the Link between Economic Freedom and Prosperity* (Washington, DC: The Heritage Foundation), pp. 251-252.

[85]   James Brooke, November 19, 2003.

[86]   Kongdan Oh and Ralph Hassig, "North Korea between Reform and Collapse," *Asian Survey*, vol. 39, no. 2, 1999, pp. 287-309.

[87]   "Guidelines on Economic Policies," http://www.asiatradehub.com/n.korea/eco.asp

[88]   Victor D. Cha, "North Korea's Economic Reforms and Security Intentions," Testimony before US Senate Committee on Foreign Relations, http://foreign.senate. gov/ testimony/2004/ChaTestimony040302.pdf

[89]   Marcus Noland, "West-Bound Train Leaving the Station: Pyongyang on the Reform Track" October 14-15, 2002, http://www.iie.com/publications/papers/noland1002.htm

[90]   "NK Embarks on Initial Phase of Market Economy," *Korea Update* vol. 14, no. 10, September 30, 2003.

[91]   Editorial Comment, *Rodong Shinmun*, November 21, 2001, cited from Victor D. Cha.

[92]   Yukie Yoshikawa, "The Prospect of Economic Reform in North Korea" http://www.nautilus.org/DPRKBriefingBook/transition/200312NKecon.html

[93]   Ibid.

[94]   Chung Young Chul, "North Korean Reform and Opening: Dual Strategy and 'Silli (Practical) Socialism," *Pacific Affairs,* vol. 77, no. 2 (2004), 300-302.

[95]   Kim Jong-il, "The 21st Century is a Century of Great Change and Creation," *Rodong Sinmun*, January 4, 2001, p. 2.

[96]   *People's Korea*, "Kim Jong-il's Plan to Build a Powerful Nation," January 31, 2002.

[97]   Jong-Heon Lee, "Analysis: North Korean Economy in Better Shape," *The Washington Times*, May, 31, 2005, http://washingtontimes.com/upi-breaking/20050531-032755-9016r.htm; Young-Hoon Lee, "An Analysis of the Effect of North Korea's International and Inter-Korean Trade on its Economic Growth," *Economic Papers*, vol. 8, no. 1, 2005, Bank of Korea, http://www.bok.or.kr/contents_admin/ info_admin/eng/home/public/public03/info/081.pdf

[98]   Ibid.

[99]   *People's Korea*, "New Economic Policy Enforced in DPRK: Seeking Maximum Profits while Maintaining Principles," August 17, 2002; *Rodong Sinmun*, "Let us Fully Demonstrate Dignity and Power of DPRK under Great Banner of Army-Based Policy" (New Year Joint Editorial), January 11, 2003, p. 2.

[100] Figures provided by Industry Minister Hoang Trung Hai to Vietnam News, 01/07/04, posted to Vietnam Economy Archives (News Online – Vietnam Economic Times) http://www.vneconomy.com.vn/en_index.php?action=preview&cat=02&id=0401071 02020; homepage: http://www.vneconomy.com.vn/eng/

101 Adam McCarty and Carl Kalapesi, "The Economics of the 'Non-Market Economy' Issue: Vietnam Catfish Case Study," Mekong Economics Ltd., January 29, 2003, http://www.eldis.org/fulltext/vietnam.pdf

102 Mekong Capital, "Vietnam Investment," http://www.mekongcapital.com/html/mr_vietnam_ps.htm

103 Economist Intelligence Unit, "Country Briefings: Vietnam Economic Structure," April 14, 2004, http://www.economist.com/countries/Vietnam/profile.cfm? folder= Profile%2DEconomic%20Structure

104 Asian Development Bank, *Asian Development Outlook 2003*, www.ADB.org

105 Figures provided by Industry Minister Hoang Trung Hai to Vietnam News, 01/07/04, posted on Vietnam Economy Archives (News Online – Vietnam Economic Times) http://www.vneconomy.com.vn/en_index.php?action=preview&cat=02&id=040107102020; homepage: http://www.vneconomy.com.vn/eng/

106 Mekong Capital, "Vietnam Investment," http://www.mekongcapital.com/html/mr_vietnam_ps.htm

107 Ibid.

108 Vietnam Net Bridge, "Enterprise Law Energizes Economic Changes," October 30, 2003, http://english.vietnamnet.vn/reports/2003/10/17/17602

109 Takeshi Machida, "Vietnam Stock Market's Real Recovery Awaits Listing of Giant State-Run Firms," *The Nikkei Weekly* (Japan), April 26, 2004.

110 BBC International Monitoring Reports, "Vietnam Government's Report on 2003 Socioeconomic Achievements and Tasks for 2004," November 8, 2003.

111 China-ASEAN Business Net, ASEAN Business information Vietnam. Link = Vietnam, Country Economy, "Vietnam's Economy Overview," http://www.china-asean.net/asean_biz/vietnam/country_econ/asean_vi_econ_basic.html

112 Adam McCarthy and Carl Kalapesi, http://www.eldis.org/fulltext/vietnam.pdf

113 *Nhan Dan*, Hanoi (in Vietnamese), March 16, 20004, p. 2., cited from "Vietnam: Party Daily on Equitization of State Enterprises," *BBC World Monitoring*, March 19, 2004 (accessed at Lexis-Nexis)

114 Asia Africa Intelligence Wire, "Banking & Finance: Vietnam to Issue Regulations for Bank Listing in May," April 23, 2004 (accessed at Lexis-Nexis)

115 Mekong Capital, "Vietnam Stock Market," http://www.mekongcapital.com/html/mr_vietnam_se_htm

116 Asia Africa Intelligence Wire, "Banking & Finance: Vietnam to Mobilize $3.2 Bln Via Bond this Year," January 30, 2004 (accessed at Lexis-Nexis)

117 Dragon Capital, "Vietnam Stock Market Overview," http://www.dragoncapital.com/sm_index.htm

118 "Legal Updates on Investment, Infrastructure and Finance," *Indochina Notes*, Freshfields Bruckhaus Deringer, September 2003.

119 Asian Development Bank, *Asian Development Outlook 2003*, ADB.org.

120 *Europa World Year Book 2003*, vol. II, 44th ed., New York: Europa Publications, 2003, p. 4587.

121 The Heritage Foundation, "2004 Index of Economic Freedom," http://heritage.org/research/features/index/countryFiles/English/individual_pdfs/Vietnam.pdf

122 BBS International Monitoring Reports.

123 "Government Acts to Steady Fluctuating Prices," *Vietnam News*, March 15, 2004, p. 1. http://vietnamnews.vnagency.com.vn/2004-03/13/Stories/22.html

[124]   Asia Africa Intelligence Wire, "Vietnam's Economy Grows over 7 Percent in 2003," December, 16, 2003 (accessed at Lexis-Nexis)

[125]   Europa, p. 4587.

[126]   "Buyers Wait for Vietnam's Land Policy," *Asia Pulse*, February 25, 2004, p. 1. (accessed at Lexis-Nexis)

[127]   Adam McCarty and Carl Kalapesi.

[128]   "Legal Updates on Investment, Infrastructure and Finance," *Indochina Notes*, Freshfields Bruckhaus Deringer, September 2003.

[129]   Vietnam Net Bridge.

[130]   Martin Painter, "The Politics of Economic Restructuring in Vietnam: The Case of State-Owned Enterprise Reform," *Contemporary Southeast Asia*, vol. 25, no. 1, 2003, p. 29; Decision 202/1992/CT, Circular 84/1993/TTg.

[131]   Adam McCarty and Carl Kalapesi.

[132]   APEC, "Economy Report: Improving the Climate for Enterprises," http://www.apec. org/apec/member_economies/economy_reports/vietnam.html#top

[133]   Le Phu Cuong, "Monopoly Situation in Vietnam," http://www2.jftc.go.jp/eacpf/ 02/monopoly_vn_cuong_030825.pdf

[134]   Ibid.

[135]   Ibid.

[136]   Ibid.

[137]   *Statistical Yearbook 2002* (Hanoi, Vietnam: The General Statistical Office, 2002)

[138]   China-ASEAN Business Net, "Country Economy: Vietnam's Economy Overview," http://www.china-asean.net/asean_biz/vietnam/country_econ/asean_vi_econ_basic. html

[139]   APEC, "Economy Report: Strengthening the banking System." http://www.apec.org/ apec/member_economies/economy_reports/vietnam.html#top

[140]   The Heritage Foundation.

[141]   "Bankers Cheer Third Fund Injection," *The Vietnam Investment Review*, January 12, 2004, p. 1 (accessed at Lexis-Nexis)

[142]   Ibid.

[143]   The Vietnam Investment Review, "Foreign Banks Banking on Reforms," January 12, 2004 (accessed at Lexis-Nexis)

[144]   APEC, "Economy Report: Exchange Rate." http://www.apec.org/apec/member_ economies/economy_reports/vietnam.html#top

[145]   Asian Development Bank, *Asian Development Outlook 2003*, www.ADB.org; The Heritage Foundation.

[146]   Vietnam Chamber of Commerce and Industry, "The State Bank will Intervene when Necessary to Maintain a Reasonable Exchange Rate," November 6, 2001, http://www.vcci.com.vn/English/BusinessNews/Banking/StateBankWillIntervene.asp

[147]   APEC, "Economy Report: Integrating into the World Economy." http://www.apec.org/apec/member_economies/economy_reports/vietnam.html#top

[148]   China-ASEAN Business Net, "Country Economy: Vietnam's Economy Overview," http://www.china-asean.net/asean_biz/vietnam/country_econ/asean_vi_econ_basic. html; Embassy of the Socialist Republic of Vietnam in the United States of America, "Business Advisor: Export and Import." http://www.vietnamembassy-usa.org/ business/exim.php3

[149]   Asian Development Bank, *Asian Development Outlook 2003*, www.ADB.org.

150   China-ASEAN Business Net, "Country Economy: Vietnam's Economy Overview,"
       http://www.china-asean.net/asean_biz/vietnam/country_econ/asean_vi_econ_basic. html
151   Australian Department of Foreign Affairs and Trade, Vietnam Country Brief,
       December 2003, "Economic Performance and Reform," http://www.dfat.gov.au/
       geo/vietnam/vietnam_brief.html#eco
152   http://www.us-asean.org/vietnam.asp
153   Stephanie Fahey, "Vietnam and the Third Way," p. 475
154   Constitution of Socialist Republic of Vietnam, 1992, p. 7
155   Allen Jennings and Michael Karadjis, "Vietnam: Communist Party Resolves to Stay
       on Socialist Path," Green Left Weekly (online edition), http://www.greenleft.org.au/
       back/2001/447/447p21.htm
156   Martin Ravallion and Dominique van de Walle, "Breaking up the Collective Farms,"
       Economics of Transition, vol. 12, no. 2, 2004, pp. 203-206.
157   Carolyn L. Gates. "Vietnam's Integration into AFTA: Theoretical and Empirical
       Perspectives," in Mya Than and Carolyn Gates, eds., ASEAN Enlargement: Impacts
       and Implications (Singapore: Institute of Southeast Asian Studies, 2001), pp. 345-351.
158   James Riedel and William S. Turley, "The Politics and Economics of Transition to an
       Open Market Economy in Viet Nam," Technical Papers, no. 152, OECD
       Development Centre, 1999, p. 32.
159   Keith Griffin, "The Role of the State in the New Economy," in Keith Griffin, ed.,
       Economic Reform in Vietnam (London, UK: Macmillan Press, 1998), pp. 43-45.
160   Martin Painter, "The Politics of Economic Restructuring in Vietnam: The Case of
       State-Owned Enterprise Reform," Contemporary Southeast Asia, vol. 25, no. 1, 2003,
       p. 27.
161   http://www.utoronto.ca/env/ies/ap/chapter4.htm
162   Nguyen Thanh and Nguyen Vo Hung, "Background Paper: Institutional Development
       and FDI in Vietnam," Project Working Papers, No. 10, February 2003, Centre for
       New and Emerging Markets, London Business School, p. 12.
163   Gregory N. Leidner, "Entrepreneurial Environment in Vietnam," March 20, 2001, in
       http://www.mit.edu/afs/athena/course/15/15.395/attach/Vietnam.doc
164   Le Khuong Ninh, "Investment of Rice Mills in Vietnam: the Role of Financial Market
       Imperfections and Uncertainty," Chapter 1, http://www.ub.rug.nl/eldoc/dis/eco/
       1.khuong.ninh/
165   Melanie Beresford, "The Vietnamese Transition from Plan to Market: Transformation
       of the Planning Mechanism," Macquarie Economics Research Papers, Macquarie
       University, 1999, pp. 18-24.
166   Stephanie Fahey, "Vietnam and the 'Third Way': The Nature of Socio-Economic
       Transition," Journal of Economic and Social Geography, vol. 88, no. 5, 1997, pp.
       469-468.
167   Ibid., p. 471; Adam Fforde and Stefan de Vylder, From Plan to Market: The
       Economic Transition in Vietnam (Boulder, CO: Westview Press, 1996), p. 155.
168   Pamela L. Polevoy, "Privatization in Vietnam: The Next Step in Vietnam's Economic
       Transition from a Nonmarket to a Market Economy," Brooklyn Journal of
       International Law, vol. 23, no. 3, 1998, pp. 912-919.
169   "Vietnam - An Asian developing country in transition," http://www.globaleducation.
       edna.edu.au/archives/secondary/casestud/economics/5/viet-eco.html

170   China-ASEAN Business Net, "Country Economy: Vietnam's Economy Overview," http://www.china-asean.net/asean_biz/vietnam/country_econ/asean_vi_econ_basic.html

171   China-ASEAN Business Net, "Country Economy: Vietnam's Economy Overview," http://www.china-asean.net/asean_biz/vietnam/country_econ/asean_vi_econ_basic.html

172   Kenji Suzuki, "Economic and Social Data Ranking: Laos – Public Sector," http://www.dataranking.com/default.htm

173   Mekong Capital Group, Mekong Region: Laos Private Sector (Profile of Laos' Private Sector) http://www.mekongcapital.com/html/mr_laos_ps.htm

174   Clay G. Wescott, ed., *Key Governance Issues in Cambodia, Lao PDR, Thailand, and Viet Nam* (Manila, Philippines: Asian Development Bank, 2001), Chapter 3, http://www.adb.org/Documents/Books/Key_Governance_Issues/

175   Australian Department of Foreign Affairs and Trade, Laos Country Brief: "Political Overview." http://www.dfat.gov.au/geo/laos/laos_brief.html

176   Frederico Bonaglia and Andrea Goldstein, "Private Sector Development and Trade Capacity Building" OECD Development Centre, Paris, December 2003, www.oecd.org; Pradumna B. Rana and Naved Hamid, *From Centrally Planned to Market Economies: The Asian Approach* (Oxford University Press, 1995), pp. 169-170; Asian Development Bank, *Asian Development Outlook 2003*, www.ADB.org.

177   Nick J. Freeman, "Laos: Exiguous Evidence of Economic Reform and Development," *Southeast Asian Affairs*, 2004, pp. 128.

178   Mekong Capital, Mekong Region: Laos Private Sector. "Small Size of Private Sector in Laos," "Taxation in Laos" and "Access to Credit for private Companies," http://www.mekongcapital.com/html/mr_laos_ps.htm

179   Nick J. Freeman, "Pragmatism in the Face of Adversity: Enterprise Reform in Laos," *Journal of Communist Studies and Transitional Politics*, vol. 19, no. 1, 2003, p. 37.

180   "Laos Country Report," *Economist Intelligence Unit*, www.economist.com/countries/laos

181   Australian Department of Foreign Affairs and Trade, Laos Country Brief: "Economic Overview." http://www.dfat.gov.au/geo/laos/laos_brief.html

182   Michael Kirk, "Land Tenure Development and Divestiture in Lao P.D.R.," http://www.gtz.de/orboden/kirk/kil3_1.htm

183   Olivier Ducourtieux, Jean-Richard Laffort and Silinthone Sacklokham, "Land Policy and Farming Practices in Laos," *Development and Change*, vol. 36, no. 3, 2005, pp. 499-526.

184   Economist Intelligence Unit, Country Report Laos: "Outlook for 2003-2004, Policy Trends,"http://store.eiu.com/index.asp?layout=show_sample&product_id=50000205&country_id=LA

185   Economist Intelligence Unit, Country Report Laos: "Economic Policy: National Assembly Delegates Call for Fiscal Decentralization" http://store.eiu.com/index.asp?layout=show_sample&product_id=50000205&country_id=LA

186   Frederico Bonaglia and Andrea Goldstein, "Private Sector Development and Trade Capacity Building" OECD Development Centre, Paris, December 2003 www.oecd.org

187   Asian Development Bank, *Asian Development Outlook 2003*, www.ADB.org; Economist Intelligence Unit, Country Report Laos: "Outlook for 2003-04: Policy Trends." http://store.eiu.com/index.asp?layout=show_sample&product_id=50000205&country_id=LA

[188] Nick J. Freeman, "Pragmatism in the Face of Adversity: Enterprise Reform in Laos," *Journal of Communist Studies and Transitional Politics*, vol. 19, no. 1, 2003, pp. 40-42.

[189] Asian Development Bank, *Asian Development Outlook 2003*, www.ADB.org; The Economist, www.economist.com/countries/laos

[190] China-ASEAN Business Net, ASEAN Business Information: Laos. "Laws and Regulations: Openness to Foreign Investment," http://www.china-asean.net/asean_biz/laos/laws_regulations/asean_la_law_basic.html#

[191] Australian Department of Foreign Affairs and Trade, Laos Country Brief: "Economic Overview." http://www.dfat.gov.au/geo/laos/laos_brief.html

[192] Economist Intelligence Unit, Country Report Laos: "Economic policy: national assembly delegates call for fiscal decentralization," "Economic policy: provinces can approve investments up to US$2m," "Economic policy: development of the first SEZ proceeds slowly" and "The domestic economy: inflation picks up in early 2003."http://store.eiu.com/index.asp?layout=show_sample&product_id=50000205&country_id=LA

[193] Nick J. Freeman, "Laos: Exiguous Evidence of Economic Reform and Development," *Southeast Asian Affairs*, 2004, pp. 126 and 134 endnote 5.

[194] Economist Intelligence Unit, Country Report Laos: "Economic Structure: Annual indicators," "The domestic economy: China leads the way on investment," "Economic policy: Russia writes off 70% of Laos's Soviet-era debt" and "Foreign trade and payments: The granting of NTR status could be delayed." http://store.eiu.com/index.asp?layout=show_sample&product_id=50000205&country_id=LA

[195] Nick J. Freeman, "Pragmatism in the Face of Adversity: Enterprise Reform in Laos," *Journal of Communist Studies and Transition Politics,* vol. 19, issue 1, 2003, p. 39.

[196] Yves Bourdet, *The Economics of Transition in Laos*: *From Socialism to ASEAN Integration* (Cheltenham, UK: Edward Elgar, 2000), pp. 13-15.

[197] Nick J. Freeman, 2003, pp. 40-42.

[198] Ibid., pp. 42-43.

[199] Mekong Capital Group; Mekong Region, Laos. Laos Overview: "Economic Growth." http://www.mekongcapital.com/html/laos.htm

[200] Nick J. Freeman, 2003, pp. 45-46.

[201] Ibid., p. 35.

[202] *World Development Indicators*, World Bank, 2001, p. 270.

[203] Kenji Suzuki, "Economic and Social Data Ranking: Cambodia – "Public Sector." http://www.dataranking.com/default.htm

[204] *World Development Indicators*, World Bank, 2001, p. 270.

[205] James Brooke, "Cambodia is Working to Escape its Past," *New York Times*, Wednesday, February 25, 2004.

[206] Australian Department of Foreign Affairs and Trade, Cambodia Country Brief, September 2003: "Economy," http://www.dfat.gov.au/geo/cambodia/cambodia_brief.html#econ

[207] James Brooke, "Cambodia is Working to Escape its Past."

[208] Economist Intelligence Unit, Country Profile: Cambodia (Sample), "Political background: international relations and defense," "Economy: economic policy," "External sector: capital flows and foreign debt" and "External sector: foreign reserves and the exchange rate," http://store.eiu.com/index.asp?layout= show_sample &product_id=30000203&country_id=KH

[209]   James Brooke, "Cambodia is Working to Escape its Past."

[210]   Mekong Capital, Mekong Region: Cambodia; Cambodia Private Sector: "Profile of Cambodia's Private Sector." http://www.mekongcapital.com/html/mr_cambodia_ps. htm

[211]   http://www.ocm.gov.kh/c_med2.htm

[212]   Ronald Bruce St. John, *Asian Affairs: An American Review*, vol. 21, no. 4, 1995.

[213]   Asian Development Bank, *Asian Development Outlook 2003*, ADB.org

[214]   *World Almanac & Book of Facts*, 2004, p. 767; James Brooke, "Cambodia is Working to Escape its Past," *New York Times*, Wednesday, February 25, 2004.

[215]   Economist Intelligence Unit, Country Profile: Cambodia (Sample), "Resources and infrastructure: natural resources and the environment," "Economy: economic structure," "Economic sectors: agriculture, fishing and forestry," http://store.eiu.com/ index.asp?layout=show_sample&product_id=30000203&country_id=KH

[216]   U.S. Department of State, "2005 Investment Climate Statement – Cambodia," http://www.state.gov/e/eb/ifd/2005/41991.htm

[217]   Asian Development Bank, *Asian Development Outlook 2003*, www.ADB.org; Economist Intelligence Unit, Country Profile: Cambodia (Sample), "Economic sectors: financial services," http://store.eiu.com/index.asp?layout=show_sample& product_id=30000203&country_id=KH

[218]   Economist Intelligence Unit, Country Profile: Cambodia (Sample), "Economic Profile," "Foreign Investment," "Prices," http://store.eiu.com/index.asp?layout= show_sample&product_id=30000203&country_id=KH

[219]   Asian Development Bank, "Asian Development Outlook 2003: Economic Trends and Prospects in Developing Asia," http://www.ABD.org

[220]   Economist Intelligence Unit, Country Profile: Cambodia (Sample), "Economy: economic policy," "External sector: capital flows and foreign debt," http://store.eiu.com/index.asp?layout=show_sample&product_id=30000203&country _id=KH

[221]   Australian Department of Foreign Affairs and Trade, Cambodia Country Brief, September 2003: "Economy," http://www.dfat.gov.au/geo/cambodia/cambodia_brief. html#econ

[222]   China-ASEAN Business Net, ASEAN Business Information, Cambodia, "Business Guide: Summary of Foreign Invest Policy," http://www.china-asean.net/asean_biz/ cambodia/business_guide/asean_ca_bguide_basic.html

[223]   Asia Development Bank, Key Economic Indicators: Cambodia, http://www.adb.org/ Documents/Books/Key_Indicators/2003/pdf/CAM.pdf

[224]   Vichery, 1986, p. 139; Ljunggrean, pp. 74-75.

[225]   Kimmo Kiljunen, *Kampuchea: Decade of the Genocide* (London: Zed Books Ltd., 1984), p. 276.

[226]   Cambodian Development Resource Institute (CDRI), *Land Ownership, Sales, and Concentration in Cambodia* (Phnom Penh: CDRI, March 2001), p. 1.

[227]   Economist Intelligence Unit, Country Profile: Cambodia (Sample), "Economic sectors: financial services." http://store.eiu.com/index.asp?layout=show_sample &product_id=30000203&country_id=KH

[228]   Mekong Capital Group, The Mekong Region, the Cambodia Private Sector, "Profile of Cambodia's Private Sector." http://www.mekongcapital.com/html/mr_cambodia _ps.htm

[229] James Brooke, "Cambodia is Working to Escape its Past."

[230] China-ASEAN Business Net, ASEAN Business information, Cambodia: "Summary of Foreign investment Policy," http://www.china-asean.net/asean_biz/cambodia/business_guide/asean_ca_bguide_basic.html

[231] Mekong Capital Group, The Mekong Region, the Cambodia Private Sector, "Enabling Environment for Private Sector Companies."

[232] Toshinori Doi, Philippe Marciniak, Kotaro Ishi, Alejandro Lopez-Mehia, and Mitsutoshi Adachi, "Cambodia: Statistical Appendix," International Monetary Fund, January 23, 2002, pp. 31-32.

[233] IMF, "Cambodia – Recent Developments," July 2002, http://www.imf.org/external/country/KHM/rr/2002/eng/wn073102.hmt

[234] Börje Ljunggren, "Market Economies under Communist Regimes: Reform in Vietnam, Laos, and Cambodia," in Börje Ljunggren, ed., *The Challenge of Reform in Indochina* (Cambridge, MA: Harvard University Press, 1993), pp. 107-109.

[235] Ibid., p. 92.

[236] http://www.iie.com/publications/papers/goldstein1003.htm

[237] Adam Fforde and Stefan de Vylder, *From Plan to Market: The Economic Transition in Vietnam* (Boulder, CO: Westview, 1996), p. 35.

[238] Pradumna B. Rana, "Reforms in the Transitional Economies of Asia," *Asian Development Bank Occasional Papers*, no. 5, 1993, pp. 14-15.

[239] Ibid.

[240] Stanley Fischer, "Ten Years of Transition: Looking Back and Looking Forward," *IMF Staff Papers*, vol. 48, Special Issue, May 2002.

[241] Pradumna B. Rana, 1993.

[242] John McMillan and Barry Naughton, eds., *Reforming Asian Socialism: The Growth of Market Institutions* (Ann Arbor, MI: The University of Michigan Press, 1996), p. 14.

[243] Stanley Fischer, 2002.

[244] Ibid.

Chapter 6

Redesigning Market Socialism: A Future for Socialism

Michael Mandelbaum declared in his book *The Ideas that Conquered the World*, "In the Cold War economic contest between East and West, as in the two World Wars, the tide eventually turned. In the last three decades of the century communist economic principles were in retreat. By the century's end they were as thoroughly defeated as Germany had been in 1919 and 1945. The command system was all but extinct.[1] However, some others demurred. "To some thinkers, the collapse of communism, far from presaging the downfall of socialism, could be the source or is renewal."[2] The debate over the winner or loser of capitalism and communism came right after the October Revolution in Russia. Lenin saw the competition between capitalism and communism and addressed this issue that could arise as a result of his market-oriented NEP in his report to the Second All-Russia Congress of Political Education Departments on October 17th, 1921:

> We must face this issue squarely – who will come out on top? Either the capitalists succeed in organizing first – in which case they will drive out the communists and that will be the end of it. Or the proletarian state power, with the support of the peasantry, will prove capable of keeping a proper rein on those gentlemen, the capitalists, so as to direct capitalism along state channels and to create a capitalism that will be subordinate to the state and serve the state. The question must be put soberly.[3] (V. I. Lenin, *Collected Works*, Moscow: Progress, 1966, p. 66.)

With the collapse of communism and state socialism in Eastern Europe and the Soviet Union, is it only the capitalist economic model that remains? Is there another way that is neither capitalist nor state socialism? Or is there a third way for economic development? Asian communist and post-communist states have provided an answer to these questions and attempted a third way which can be called "market socialism" – "a species of economic system which is, in a number of ways, a cross between capitalism and socialism as it has been practiced."[4] Market reform or market socialist practice in East and Southeast Asian communist states has renewed worldwide academic interest in the study of market socialism in the past two decades. The final chapter attempts to address such a question: Can market socialism, a market-based form of socialism within the political context of one-party communist rule become a competitive and efficient economy like market capitalism? A rethinking of socialism based on our empirical observation of the development of market socialism in China and other Asian countries will not only help to address these questions but also provide a better understanding of the practical and theoretical implications of market socialism for the future of these East and Southeast Asian countries.

What is Market Socialism?

The general literature on market socialism has provided sufficient knowledge about this historical phenomenon. Market socialism is a type of economy, or economic system that would combine the basic socialist principle of public ownership with the basic principle of market economy, with the predominant public ownership in those areas that are deemed critical to the implementation of socialist principles and social policy. Market socialism is a market-based form of socialism that attempts to blend private ownership and market exchanges with public ownership and government control. It was developed during the late 1960s and early 1970s, primarily by socialist economies in Eastern Europe, in an attempt to address the inefficiencies of socialism.

Market socialism resides in the middle of the spectrum of economic systems, bounded by a pure market economy on one end and a pure command economy on the other. It is, perhaps more so than other economic systems, a prime example of a mixed economy. Allocation decisions are undertaken by both governments and markets.[5] Therefore, market socialism does incorporate some methods that are kindred to market capitalism. For example, enterprises may be independently run by appointed managers who would be instructed to manage the entity in a manner that maximizes profits (at market price). Furthermore, said enterprises would adjust their production to an equilibrium of supply and demand as previously noted. Like capitalism, the allocation and diffusion of resources would be efficient.[6]

Market socialism, being a theory, is inherently malleable and thus subject to change and interpretation. Over the course of time, in the theoretical economic literature, we have observed four versions of market socialism although these are just several of many versions in the literature.

- Langian market socialism: central planning agency simulates market forces and sets and adjusts prices according to changes in demand and supply. Enterprises respond to the state-determined prices and seek "profit maximization" under perfect market competition.[7] It is a father theory of market socialism by which other successive hybrid theories derive.
- Service market socialism: enterprises seek to maximize output and revenue instead of using "profit maximization" as the basic economic incentive. The advancement of an individual enterprise manager should be tied to the revenue or output of that enterprise, and therefore it is "output-oriented" production.[8]
- Cooperative market socialism: enterprises are governed by employees for the benefit of their employees, and enterprises are presumably autonomous in decision making. However, the state is the de facto proprietor, since

employees are controlled by it in market socialism.[9]

- Pragmatic market socialism: seek to establish a market socialist economy that would operate exactly like market capitalism that preceded it. Executives and managers are motivated by profit incentive in a competitive climate, but all are subject to outside control by owners, which presumably the state.[10]

In the history of communist practice, the real word cases would be the Yugoslavian model of workers' self-management and the cooperative farm (*kolkhoz*) under Soviet communism.[11] However, no success was found in these forms of market socialism. However, market reform or market socialist practice in Asian communist or post-communist states has shown a great success in economic growth and renewed a worldwide academic interest in the study of market socialism in the past two decades. The viability of market socialism as an effective alternative to capitalism has become the most interesting debate in the theoretical economic literature on market socialism and the literature on transitional economies in communist and post-communist states.[12]

James A. Yunker, one of the well-known market socialist economists, identifies three market socialist approaches that have been proposed to improve upon Lange's earlier position, including his own version of "pragmatic market socialism," in which some form of government ownership agency, which he refers to as the Bureau of Public Ownership (BPO), would become the repository for the ownership rights "once vested in the stocks, bonds, and deeds of the capitalist class. The question is how the BPO is to handle these ownership rights. The fundamental idea of pragmatic socialism is that these rights should be handled exactly as they are handled under capitalism, which is to say that the same pattern of incentives and motivations that had inspired the enterprise managers under capitalism would apply equally under socialism."[13] This is a breakthrough idea as it focuses on the property rights which is the fundamental problem under market socialism while most of debaters have focused on the distribution, the production, the consumption, desirable goals of socialism, or the morality in human society. This idea is based on an important assumption that "the market characteristics of the modern U.S. economy may be duplicated almost exactly within a socialist economy, and that it is these market characteristics, rather than the capitalist characteristics, which are responsible for the current level of efficiency in the U.S. economy."[14] John Roemer, another well-known market socialist economist, also assumes that the mechanisms that have evolved and designed under capitalism can be transported into a socialist framework and be accommodated in the political context of a socialist party-state system.[15] This assumption, rather than "the end of history," would become the starting point of my critical analysis of the fundamental problems in market socialism and investigation of a feasible solution to these problems in this concluding chapter. This chapter attempts to find a feasible solution to the problems by investigating these problems, providing a blueprint of a feasible reform plan in the political context of a socialist state, and designing an effective mechanisms to carry out this reform plan in China and other market socialist countries.

Does Market Socialism Work?

For many critics of market socialism, market socialism is not considered as a viable alternative to capitalism not only because market socialism cannot resolve the problems of alienation, inequality, investment irrationality, and lack of economic democracy under capitalism but also because market relations and socialism are mutually incompatible and therefore infeasible in practice. Some of the major critiques include the inability of market socialism to compete against market capitalism because it does not take into full consideration the individual's constant need for incentive.[16] Others contended that market socialism suffers from its inability to diffuse capital to entities and actors who possess unique abilities and skills.[17] Still others argued that the theory of market socialism purports that it can achieve and sustain employment, but it is unlikely that all employable persons could and would be employed. Furthermore, if a worker is virtually guaranteed a job in such a system, it is more inclined to be unproductive, inefficient and even lazy. After all, there are no underlying incentives to change his or her behavior.[18] Many others have mainly focused on the critique of market socialism, political morality of market socialism, or the merits of socialism based on Marxian theories.[19]

However, the key issue to be addressed is not whether market socialism is theoretically possible but whether it can be realized in practice and capable of competing with market capitalism in the globalization of the world economy. Oskar Lange demonstrated to most economists' satisfaction that a well-functioning market is possible with state ownership of enterprises, provided that those enterprises follow the profit maximization rule.[20] However, some economists disagree. Neoclassical economics and researchers from the World Bank denounce market socialism or the third way as theoretically unacceptable and impossible. Janos Kornai contends that market socialism is not capable of becoming a robust economic system.[21] In market socialism, the communist party's political monopoly is in direct conflict with the market economic law, because each precludes the realization of the other. In market socialism, owners or shareholders seek to maximize their financial gain and the value of their property in the short and long term, whereas the communist party-state in market socialism combines political, economic, social functions and has complex motives that are ultimately subordinate to political goals. This is the context in which the syndrome of soft budget constraint emerges. In market capitalism, with a hard budget constraint, a loss-making firm cannot survive. But in market socialism, a loss-making firm has to survive for political and social reasons. The bureaucratic redistribution of profits are taken away from profit-making firms and given as assistance to loss-making firms. Firms do not have freedom of exit and entry into all business areas. Exist or entry into markets is largely decided by the government or influenced by the principal that has an administrative jurisdiction over its area. The state cannot let down an insolent firm and has to bail it out, because the state bears ultimate responsibility for the fate of firm. Moreover, the principal-agent problem that has been resolved in market socialism cannot be resolved in market socialism. A manager of a business firm is a bureaucrat. The motivation of the subordinate agent is loyalty to superiors to retain his or her career prospects, not business success or concern for customers. Therefore, the quest for a truly competitive and efficient economy is hopeless in market socialism.[22]

Janos Kornai's major contribution to the study of market socialism is his critical analysis of the fundamental problems in market socialism, such as the soft budget constraint, the principal-agent problem, and the lack of free entry and exit for firms. However, can these problems be resolved in market socialism or can it become a competitive and efficient economy? The market socialist practice has so far not provided a conclusive answer to this question, but instead, in many respects, it has cast more doubt on the feasibility of transforming it into a truly competitive and efficient market economy. A retrospect of the market socialist practice and its fundamental problems may provide a new way of thinking about a feasible solution to the fundamental problems.

The root to those fundamental problems lies in the property rights relations, which, in market socialism, is the ambiguity of property rights relations. In market capitalism, private property rights provide hard budget constraint, freedom of entry into and exist from the market, and natural selection of principal-agent relations. Responsibility, power, profit, and risk are symmetrical, integrated, and interconnected in the principal-agent relationship, therefore, there is an essential requirement for a hard budget constraint on both the principal and the agent. In state socialism, responsibility and power are asymmetrical, disintegrated, or disconnected in the principal-agent relationship: the government (the principal) has power in decision making, but bears no responsibility for money losing; it gains profit, but bears no risk for investment, whereas the manager or executive director (the agent) has responsibility for business operation, but has limited power in decision making; it bears no risk and gain limited profit for investment. Market reforms in market socialism have improved the property rights relationship by implementing the separation of ownership and control, particularly defining the principal-agent relationship more clearly. The separation of ownership and control reflected an effort in dealing with this fundamental problem, but it is still far from being successful in coping with agency problems, political control in business, corruption, plight of state assets, etc. Managers enjoy managerial autonomy in business decisions, but as agents of the state, they also have a strong incentive to use or abuse their power in their own self-interest, resulting in the short-run impact on performance, the plight of state assets, etc. Politician control over the selection and replacement of mechanism of management also increases political costs and often results in rent-seeking behavior and corruption. "Consequently, both political control and managerial moral hazard continue to pose problems in reformed enterprises."[23]

Socialism is a theory upon which various economic models have been formed and tested. Theories are constantly evolving and changing over time as new data and evidence are gathered. When a theory no longer seems valid, the choice can be made to either discard it or amend it. When one economic model failed, it will be subject to critique, remodeling, or redefining to meet the needs of a modern economy rather than simply be replaced by its opponent theories. The large majority of socialist economies that have failed were based upon Stalinist model and his interpretation of socialism. However, the Stalinist economic model had serious flaws that eventually led to the radical rejection of socialism in the former Soviet Union and its satellite communist states and a gradual incorporation of markets into the socialist systems of East and Southeast Asia. The successful blending socialist principles and market mechanisms in these Asian countries suggest that the failure of experiments based upon one of the economic models does not approve that the entire socialist theory should be dismissed or other economic models and approaches are impossible. Market socialism has emerged as an important development in post-communist transition in many developing countries, such as China, Vietnam, Laos, and some other East, Southeast, Central Asian countries. Market socialist practice has a significant impact on the success or failure of economic development in those countries where these practices are adopted by the party-state communist governments. Therefore, market reform or market socialist practice in communist or post-communist states has a renewed worldwide academic interest in the study of market socialism in the past two decades. There are many aspects of socialism, such as markets, were totally neglected by socialist practitioners, or they were misunderstood and misapplied in the pursuit of political goals of socialism. Market socialism is a practice that embraces both socialist principles and market rules in the operation of the economy. Market socialism is not an economic model or system that is immune to flaws as market capitalism is not a perfect system. For example, the same soft budget constraints under socialism exist in a comparable form under market capitalism. Political favoritism, tax incentives, tax write-offs, government contracts, subsidies, bailout of bankrupted companies, and lobbyists always disrupt the invisible hand of market capitalism. Therefore, the question is how to reform the economy and resolve the problems in market socialism, such as the soft budget constraint, the principal-agent problem, and the lack of free entry and exit for firms. Can these problems be resolved in market socialism or can socialist market economy become a competitive and efficient economy? This is the major task of this chapter.

Redesigning Market Socialism

As we discuss above, the root to those fundamental problems lies in the property rights relations, which, in market socialism, is the ambiguity of property rights relations. Market reforms have improved the property rights relationship by implementing the separation of ownership and control. There are many practices that have emerged in market reforms, such as reorganization, association, merger, administrative delegation, leasing, contract, shareholding cooperatives, and sell-off. Shareholding has become one of the most promising practices for the separation of ownership and control.

However, the current shareholding system is seriously flawed: who is the shareholder? In practice, there are different types of shares: state share, enterprise share, external share, and individual share. For example, Article 4 of the Company Law in China requires the state to hold controlling stocks of pillar industries and subscribe at least 35 percent of total shares in shareholding companies, which enables the state to be the largest shareholder since the other shareholders are often highly dispersed in China.[24] In most cases, however, the state share is greater than 50 percent. If corporate shares of enterprises (*qiye faren gu* in the Chinese case) are also taken into account, the state actually holds controlling stakes of shareholding companies since the holders of corporate share are state agents and such shares are indirectly owned by the state.[25] Therefore, the administrative subordinate-superior relationship remains intact in the principal-agent relations where the state constitutes the principal and the executives of enterprises the agent. In such a relationship each enterprise continues to have its own information channel and superior, and tends to monopolize its own markets and industrial sectors, and therefore it does not encourage competition. Moreover, state share is impersonal with no direct personal interests, incentives, responsibilities, and disciplines. Therefore, the separation of ownership and control in market reform has not fundamentally changed the impersonal property rights under state socialism nor achieved the goal of efficient allocation of resources and free market competition. The problems in existing market socialism can be clearly demonstrated if we examine more carefully the evolution of property rights reforms in socialist states in the context of China. The history of property rights reforms in China can be divided into several major stages.

The Centralized and Unified System (da yi tong)

In state socialism, the state exercises all three powers simultaneously: administration, ownership, and control. The enterprises have no power. This can be illustrated in Figure 6.1.

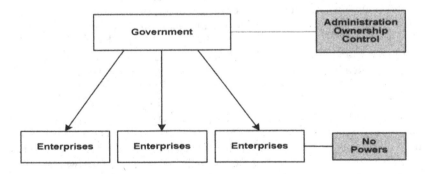

Figure 6.1 The centralized and unified system (*da yi tong*)

The Decentralized and Unified System (tiao kuai feng ge)

In the early stage of socialist reforms, three powers were combined and decentralized to regional/local governments as shown in Figure 6.2. This is also true in almost all countries of state socialism.

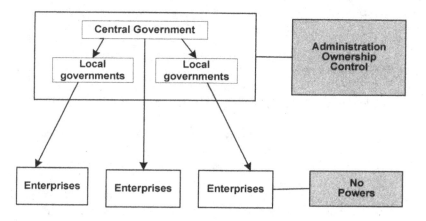

Figure 6.2   The decentralized and unified system (*tiao kuai feng ge*)

The Reform in Separation of Two Powers

Decentralization provides more incentives to local governments, but nothing else changed at the micro level. Such a decentralization, however, increased *"tiao kuai feng ge"* – different enterprises belong to different *"tiaotaio"* (central industrial ministries) and *"kuaikuai"* (local governments). There is no horizontal flow of factors of production and efficient allocation of resources. Departmentalism and regionalism of various industrial ministries (*"xitong"*) and various local governments further undermined the efficient allocation of resources and cause serious disequilibria and shortage. The systemic flaws made socialist reformers of many communist states in 1980s realize that powers must be decentralized to enterprises or economic units, rather than to provincial and local governments, which was marked by the practice of separation of ownership and control as shown in Figure 6.3.

Ownership has been separated from control in modern market economy of capitalism. A joint stock company is owned by shareholders while control rests with the chief executives and managers. Shareholders can exercise only limited control over the executives of firms and this has actually strengthened the power of the executives and weakened that of the owners. This separation of ownership and control has worked so well in a free market economy of capitalism. This fact

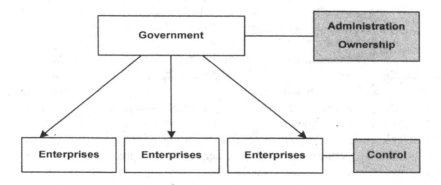

Figure 6.3 Separation of ownership and control

enlightened socialist reformers who wanted to maintain public ownership while improving economic efficiency and productivity. More than two decades of market reforms have developed all kinds of property rights relations and diversified ownership structure in China. In the state sector, enterprises not only have control rights but also some portions of ownership rights while the state retains ownership rights and some portions of control rights to intervene when necessary. In the reform practice, State Property Administration Bureau (SPAB) was created to exercise ownership rights and ensure the increase of state property value while delegating control rights and some portions of ownership rights to the enterprises. In practice, ownership rights are further divided into ownership right, use right, control right, and benefit right, which are divided and shared between the principal and the agent as shown in Figure 6.4.

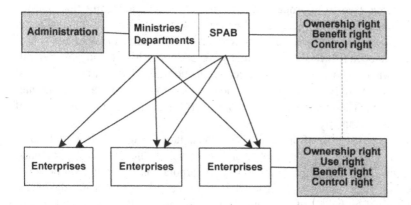

Figure 6.4   Divided and shared rights between the principal and the agent

In the practice of sharing property rights between the government and enterprises, "a clear, plain assignment of property rights is lacking."[26] The ambiguity and impersonal character of property rights have maintained the principal-agent relationship as "mother-in-law and daughter-in-law" relationship (*poxi guangxi*), or administrative jurisdiction of subordinates and superiors. Therefore, this relationship allowed the government to intervene at its pleasure. The subordinate continued to be loyal to superiors and the decision was made on the basis of "ad hoc negotiations between the upper level of the bureaucracy and the managers of the firm. The relative bargaining position is uncertain... This is the context in which the syndrome of *soft budget constraint* emerges."[27]

This has suggested that, although a substantial part of property rights have shifted from the government to the management of the enterprise, the rights are not clearly defined and separated, and therefore ownership and control are not completely separated. As a department of the government, SAAB is a bureaucracy, not a natural person, and therefore has no real incentive and discipline to ensure the increase of state property value and bears no responsibility for loss and no risk for investment. Therefore, an officially imposed division of ownership rights or separation of ownership and control between the state and the enterprises does not resolve the fundamental problems of soft budget constraint, motivation of bureaucratic and corporate behavior, and inefficient allocation of resources in market socialism. Socialist reformers have come to the realization that administration must stay with the government, control right must be given to the enterprises, but the key is where to place ownership right. If we continue to think about the two levels between the government and the enterprises, we will never get out of the vicious cycle, because both the government and the enterprises are not natural persons.

The very foundation of market capitalism is the private ownership or the "impersonalization" of property rights. According to Kornai, the state-owned enterprises in socialist countries are characterized by the "soft-budget constraint" – as an economic theorist of property rights put it: "the residual income that emerges as the difference between receipts and expenses does not pass into the pockets of natural persons, and the losses are not covered by the same natural party."[28] This embraces the central thesis of the property rights approach: it is only the natural-personal owners who control and direct production and distribution of residual income, and it is only based on this condition that modern capitalist economies have developed. The impersonalization of property rights is the very foundation of the free market economy.[29]

From the perspective of property rights, the solution is to insert a middle level between the state and the enterprises, and this level should not be governmental organizations nor administrative monopolistic corporations, but a natural person – a trustee of state property (TSP), who should be delegated with the entire ownership right on behalf of the state. This will constitute the very foundation or starting point of our new thinking.

The Trustee of State Property

A TSP is a natural person, who should not only be entrusted with power and responsibility but also be bestowed with benefit and risk to exercise ownership right on behalf of the state. A TSP acts like a member of Board of Directors under market capitalism and the agent of government under market socialism. This system of "Trustee of State Property" can be illustrated as in Figure 6.5.

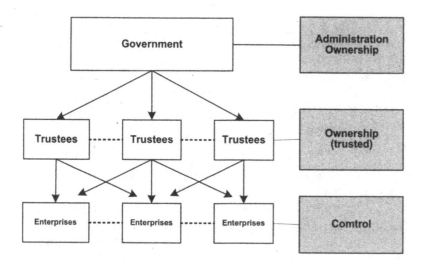

Figure 6.5   The trustee of state property

The Model: the Trustee of State Property under Market Socialism

The crux of the feasibility of schedules of market socialism lies in the mechanism design of the TSP. The TSP system is designed to resolve the fundamental problems of the ambiguity of property rights, soft budget constraint, lack of free entry into and exit from the market, and state intervention in the operation of enterprises, and fundamentally transform market socialism into an efficient and competitive economy. It emulates all key functional features of a free market economy of capitalism within the political economic context of communist political leadership and public ownership. A more detailed framework of property rights relations is constructed and presented in Figure 6.6.

In this model, property rights relationships include the following most important variables: 1 = ownership trusted, 1' = tax and profit (deduct a percentage from local governments), 2 =ownership trusted, 2' = tax and profit (deduct a percentage from firms), 3 = investment and influence on firm management, 3' = profit and dividends earned by firm management, 4 = labor, 4' = wages and bonus,

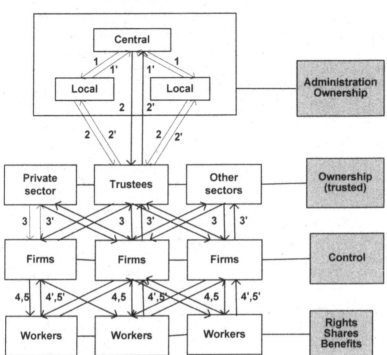

Figure 6.6 The framework of property rights relations

5 =sale of shares, 5' = profits and dividends. There are four major actors: the government, the trustees, the enterprises, and the workers, who are entitled to different rights, objectives, and roles, which are clearly defined by the law. The government has the authority to perform multiple functions: set rules, enforce laws, arbitrate conflicts, redistribute national revenue and income, dispense social security, and administer taxation and other administrative responsibilities, and legally entitled to ownership of state property. The trustees are entrusted with full responsibility, power, benefit, and risk to exercise ownership rights on behalf of the state to enhance the value of the state property. The enterprise managers are entrusted with control right to manage the enterprises and maximize profit. The workers have free choice of occupation, democratic rights in the economic units, and dividends of shares.

In this model, the assignment of property rights is clear and separated, property rights and resources are transferable horizontally and allowed to move freely cross departments, industries, and sectors, the trustees have freedom of entry into all areas, and a hard budget constraint becomes an essential requirement for the functional TSP system. As a result, the principal-agent problems are resolved as has been in market capitalism, even though the owner is still the socialist state, and market socialism can be transformed into a competitive and efficient market economy that can compete with a capitalist market economy. In what follows, we will lay out in more detail the blueprint of the TSP system under market socialism.

1. State Property Administration Bureaus (SPAB) are established at all levels of government to exercise the legal rights of ownership, perform the functions of administration, protect the rights and benefits of state property, evaluate the value of state property, set principles, rules, and criteria for selection of TSPs, draw experts from related areas to form special committees to evaluate and recruit the trustees of state property through public bidding, and delegate TSPs with legal authority to exercise ownership rights on behalf of the state. TSPs are entrusted with the major responsibility to enhance the economic return and the value of state property, and with full responsibility for and full authority in major decisions of investment and its directions and consequences. However, TSPs must also bear risk for their decision and operation using their personal property as a pledge and attain comparable benefit. Their benefit should be proportional or symmetrical with their risk, and their benefit should also be proportional or symmetrical with increase and decrease in the value of state property and profit and loss of enterprises. Therefore, the incentive and discipline problem of TSPs can be resolved and their potential short sighted and short-term behavior can be prevented. The major instruments used by the government to adjust or influence the behavior of TSPs and the enterprises are mainly tax rates, interest rates, exchange rates, profit retention rates, intentional investment rates of annual budget, and other macro-level industrial policies.

2. All state owned enterprises (SOEs) are shareholding companies or cooperatives. Shareholders may be a number of TSPs, individual shareholders, and other non-state economic sectors, but TSPs maintain a controlling share and one of the TSPs who has the largest share should be the Chairman of the Board of Trustees. TSPs as a whole act as the owner of state property on behalf of the state and constitute the operational main body of the state property ownership while Chairman should have the final say in major decisions, including the appointment of the executives or managers of SOEs. The current managers or directors of SOEs can become TSPs through competitive public bidding. The executives or managers are accountable to the Board of Trustees dominated by TSPs and their objectives are maximization of profit, increase in the value of state property, and efficiency of investment. This will fundamentally transformed the basic structure of the state sector – SOEs "belong" to the government, through its industrial departments and bureaus in one way or another, and the government exercises its property rights over the enterprises through these industrial departments and bureaus, which in turn interfere with the activities of their subordinate enterprises.

However, in the TSP system, TSPs bear full responsibility and full risk for the investment and profit, and therefore they have the power in decision-making without being interfered with by the government and have all the freedoms of entry into and exit from the market without having to get approval from the government. The state in the TSP system only exercises its property rights through its trustees and collects tax and income revenue from the profit of SOEs. A part of state revenue can be reinvested through TSPs with intentional investment package or program to carry out its industrial policy, meet social demands, and achieve national goals, while the other part can be trusted to TSPs without intentional investment orientation with a primary goal to increase the state property value and the economic return of investment.

3. A pluralistic ownership structure is one of the key features of market socialism, which encourages horizontal capital flow, optimizes grouping of factors of production, and increases the efficient allocation of resources. Shareholding enterprises in market socialism should be multiple forms, cooperative shareholding or joint stock between SOEs, between SOEs and collectives, between collectives, between public sectors and private sectors, etc. Private and foreign owned enterprises should be treated equally with SOEs. TSPs of SOEs have to compete with all different economic sectors for survival and growth. When enterprises profit, all share holders gain dividends; when enterprises loss, all shareholders loss. When all parties involved share benefits and costs according to their shares, hard budget constraint becomes an essential requirement for the TSP system. Because the interaction between ownership and control occurs between TSPs and enterprises, not between the governments and the enterprises, the state will no longer intervene in the activities of enterprises and all levels of governments will concentrate their attention on other important functions, such as rule-making, law-enforcement, conflict resolution, redistribution of national revenue and income, delivery of social security, and administration of taxation and other administrative responsibilities. If the mechanisms between the state and the TSPs is well designed, particularly the TSP benefit and cost mechanisms, this system will begin to kick off and function well. "The mechanisms that have evolved (or been designed) under capitalism that enable owners to control management can be transported to a socialist framework."[30] By what mechanism the principal-agent problems under market socialism can be resolved in the new TSP system is a central problem or a main task in the next section.

A Formal Modeling of the TSP Mechanisms

The key of the TSP system lies in the mechanism design of the relationships between the state and the TSPs, which must be able to guarantee the autonomy and freedom of TSPs from the state intervention, make the TSP's goal functions as profit maximization and capital appreciation of state property analogous to that of owners or stockholders under capitalism, and the efficiency of investment in competitive markets, keep the personal interest of TSPs in line with the interest of enterprises, make their gains and losses mutually interconnected, inhibit the short-term economic behavior of TSPs and enterprises, and prevent the excessive differential income of TSPs. This mechanism design must be able to address the central economic issues of any model of market socialism: "how to monitor the managers of public firms to maximize profits, to get them involved in competitive races for innovation, to discipline laxity, and how to separate political from economic criteria in decision-making."[31] However, this requires an effective mechanism of the "separation of ownership and control" (management) analogous to that in the modern capitalist economy in which the owners are self-interestedly concerned with profits and capital appreciation and able to retain as part of their own income some percentage of the property return and structure remuneration of firm managers to duplicate this concern.[32] The fundamental principles of the mechanism design are symmetrical or proportioned relationships between power, responsibility, benefit, and risk (cost), which not only guarantee the full autonomy and freedom of TSPs in the exercise of trusted ownership rights, but also overcome incentive and discipline problems under market socialism and ensure the validity and efficiency of the state macroeconomic policy and guidance. To be specific, this mechanism includes the following 18 major points, which are subject to modification and addition:

1. TSPs are selected through a competitive public bidding mechanism based on examination and evaluation. TSPs should have term limit with predicted goals within their tenure for 3-5 years and can be renewable at the end of the term depending on the assessment of their achievements of predicted goals.

2. Potential TSPs should contest each other to bid on the value of state property, which will be taken as comparables to the property appraisal of an independent appraiser or company, which would be then calculated into the arithmetic mean as the original value of state property, represented as C_o.

3. Bidders must put down a certain amount of personal property as down payment or personal risk fund, represented as **a,** which should be a certain percentage of the state property to be trusted, and which should constitute a real risk for the bidders.

4. Bidders must also offer a quote for the part of the profits turned over to the state each year during their tenures and the highest bidding wins if everything being equal. The total sum of profits within tenure is represented as **p**. The winner signs a contract with the State Property Administration Bureau (SPAB). The contract has legal binding for both parties after public notarization.

5. The winner becomes the TSP, and should be entrusted with the power and responsibility to exercise the ownership rights on behalf of the state within his/her term of tenure. However, since all enterprises are shareholding firms in practice, multiple TSPs should emerge and become members of Board of Trustees, and the one who has the largest share would become the Chairman of Board of Trustees.

6. TSPs constitute Board of Trsutees and behave as owners seeking to enhance the value of their property, that is, capital appreciation, exercise control over the management of enterprises, and have the power in decision making regarding the investment orientation, goal functions of enterprises, and major appointments, such as managers or directors of firms, who can be appointed or selected through a competitive mechanism of public bidding. The retention or dismissal of firm executives is the decision of the Board of Trustees rather than the state administration. However, Board of Trustees Chairman or other TSPs on Board could become the chief executives in the enterprises.

7. CEOs or Managers act as the chief executives of enterprises under market capitalism, and have the power to appoint or dismiss staff on the management, recruit or layoff workers by law and due process, decide on salary and bonus, sub-contract or sub-lease within or outside the enterprises, decide on sale prices according the changes of demand and supply in the market, borrow bank loans, and so forth. All decisions are only constrained by law and legal contract without being subject to the government intervention.

8. Gross profit is the total sum after deducting total costs from total revenue of sales. Net profit is the total sum after deducting total wages and bonus from gross profit. Post-tax profit is the total sum after deducting tax from net profit. Post-tax profit includes a percentage of profit turned over to the state, a percentage of profit retained at enterprises, and extra profit after all these deductions. Extra profit is the sum after deducting profits for the state and the enterprise from post-tax profit. The point to be made here is that extra profit should be at the discretion of TSPs who use it for technological renovation, job training, or reinvest in other products or areas of business as long as making profit out of this investment. But, this extra profit cannot be used for increasing their personal income. TSPs can also put it in the bank, but the amount of deposit and its interest should be added to the value of property at the end of their term. The components of gross profit are shown in Figure 6.7.

9. At the end of the term, another public bidding for TSPs should be conducted and incumbents should be allowed to seek renewal of their term based on external assessment and evaluation. The final value of state property, represented as C_1, which is based on the arithmetic mean of the new highest bid price on the total property value and the property appraisal of an independent appraiser or company, is the net increase in property value (value

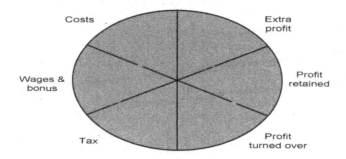

Figure 6.7 The components of gross profit

added), represented as $\Delta C = C_1 - C_o$, which should deduct retained profits and interest. If the net value in property increases, i.e. $\Delta C > 0$, reward for TSPs should be rendered; if the net value in property decreases, i.e. $\Delta C < 0$, penalties should be warranted.

10. TSPs are entrepreneurs and, during their tenure, should be paid at a special, higher level of salary, but they should not receive any form of bonus, because they will receive reward or penalty based on the evaluation of their performance and the assessment of property value at the end of their term. The salary scale of TSPs should be determined by the government and approved by the legislature. If a TSP's annual salary is designated as **b**, years of tenure as **n**, a certain percentage of the total salary (**nb**), $x = \frac{nb}{2}$, should constitute the TSP's personal risk fund, represented as $a + \frac{nb}{2}$.

11. Benefits and losses should be shared between the TSP and the state and be proportional to the risk each bears. The risk mechanism formula for the TSP reward and penalty is essential for the functional TSP system: suppose the TSP's part of shared risk is Y_1, the part of shared risk for the state would be $\Delta C - Y_1$, which would be $|\Delta C|$.

$$\frac{Y_1}{\Delta C - Y_1} = \frac{a + \frac{nb}{2}}{|\Delta C|}$$

$$Y_1 |\Delta C| = (a + \tfrac{nb}{2})\Delta C - (a + \tfrac{nb}{2})Y_1$$

$$Y_1 |\Delta C| + (a + \tfrac{nb}{2}) = (a + \tfrac{nb}{2})\Delta C$$

$$Y_1 = \frac{(a + \frac{nb}{2})\Delta C}{|\Delta C| + (a + \frac{nb}{2})}$$

If $\Delta C > 0$, i.e. property value added, $Y_1 > 0$, reward is rendered;

If $\Delta C < 0$, i.e. property value reduced, $Y_1 < 0$, penalty is warranted.

12. The above risk benefit equation can be further illustrated in Figure 6.8 and Figure 6.9.

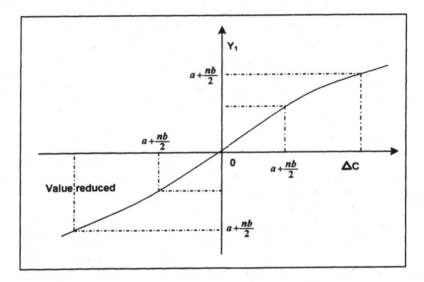

Figure 6.8   Changes in TSP reward and property value

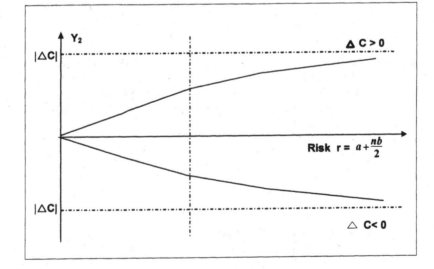

Figure 6.9   Changes in TSP reward and personal risk fund

In the light of TSP's reward curve line that changes along with changes in value added (Figure 8), TSP's reward and risk are symmetrical and proportional, depending on the changes in value added. The more state property value increases, the more TSP's reward increases, and vice versa. Suppose that when value added is zero, reward is zero; when value added is equal to personal risk fund $a + \frac{nb}{2}$, reward is equal to a half of personal risk fund, etc. For example, if a = ¥100,000, b = ¥100,000, n = 3 years, then, $a + \frac{nb}{2} = ¥250,000$.

In the light of TSP's reward curve line that changes along with changes in personal risk fund (Figure 9), although personal risk fund $a + \frac{nb}{2}$ may increase at the time when the TSP is "re-elected" in the next public bidding, the only way to secure personal reward is to increase the trusted state property value, because the precondition for increasing personal reward is the increase in state property value though registered personal risk fund can be increased when entering the contract. If TSPs choose to increase their personal risk fund, it means that TSPs would bear more risk for themselves, which would provide more incentives for working hard to increase the trusted property value, because their penalty also increases if the property value decreases at the end of their term. Both incentive and discipline are real.

13. Suppose that the difference between annual average profit value accomplished by the current TSPs and expected profit bided in the next public bidding is Δp. If $\Delta p > 0$, it indicates that the average profit value has increased as a result of the good performance of the current TSPs, and therefore they should receive reward, and vice versa. The relationship between reward and profit should be treated in the same way as the relationship between reward and property value added was formulated. Suppose that personal reward is Y_2,

$$Y_2 = \frac{\Delta p(a + \frac{nb}{2})}{|\Delta p| + (a + \frac{nb}{2})}$$

14. To avoid penalty and receive reward, TSPs must ensure efficient allocation of resources and move capital from location where marginal rate of economic return is lower to location where marginal rate is higher. TSPs would also seek a longer term of tenure to increase n in order to increase b and ultimately the amount of income and benefit. The total income of TSPs during their tenure is comprised of two parts: one is salary (nb) and the other is risk benefit ($Y_1 + Y_2$).

15. TSPs should buy "TSP Bankrupt Insurance" from China's People Insurance Company, because in the worse scenario TSPs may end up with $Y_1 + Y_2 \approx -2$

$(a + \frac{nb}{2})$, i.e. the amount of penalty exceeds the total amount of personal risk fund. However, if a TSP fails to buy insurance or gets a full coverage from the insurance company, the SPAB would auction his or her personal property through legal process to compensate losses. If it is not enough to cover losses, the TSP could be sentenced to debt prison. Term of imprisonment would depend on the amount of debt, which should be determined by a supplementary clause of Criminal Law, but it should be lower than term of imprisonment for graft and embezzlement.

16. TSP's salary, reward, and penalty should be disbursed from profit of the trusted state property, and added to the balance of account of the current TSPs. That is to say, TSP's salary, reward or penalty should be added onto the average value between the bidding of the next TSPs and the appraisal of an independent appraiser or company in the next public bidding, which would become the new property value to be trusted for the next TSPs.

17. TSPs have freedom to move the state property they are entrusted to any sector of Chinese industry where the marginal rate of economic return is higher, which would enhance the mobility of productive factors and state property across localities, industries, or ministerial affiliations, and promote productivity growth through a dynamic and competitive market. TSPs would create a socialist market economy in which the market is the invisible hand that ensures resources being allocated to their most productive uses in line with the principle of consumer choice and utility maximization.[33]

18. Breach of contract would be subject to legal penalty. All parties involved should have legal rights to seek compensation for losses incurred by breach of contract, and all parties are equal before the law. If the SPAB breaches the contract, the state agency should bear responsibility and the person who is in charge should also bear economic responsibility to indemnify for the damages or losses to the state property. If a TSP breaks the contract, he or she also pays the losses or damages incurred by their actions. If a TSP terminates the contract by force of circumstances that is beyond his or her own control, such as death or disabilities caused by accidents or serious injuries, another public bidding should be conducted by the SPAB. If a contract is terminated because of TSP's self-inflicted injury or imprisonment, the TSP must bear all the consequences. If an enterprises that is entrusted bankrupts, the enterprises will be auctioned under the SPAB, the penalty should be calculated by risk and benefit formula. The amount of penalty could be twice as much as the amount calculated by the formula, because personal reward Y_2 no longer exists and therefore, $Y' = 2Y_1$. The above 18 clauses would constitute the basic framework of TSP Law.

This study is an attempt to examine the fundamental problems of market socialism based on the property rights theory and the principal-agent theory, seek feasible solutions to those problems by developing a TSP system with the risk and benefit mechanism design, and demonstrate that TSP's goal functions and behavior can satisfy the conditions for the functioning of a healthy and competitive microeconomic mechanism and can be subject to the state's macroeconomic adjustment and guidance.

The driving force of the TSP system is market competition and self-interest, which ensure that TSPs are not political appointees but those entrepreneurs who have courage, management skill and know-how, and experience and who can win in a competitive public bidding based an examination and evaluation system. Therefore it offers a feasible solution to the problem of discipline in management of state properties through the competitive labor market for trustees and managers. The TSP risk and benefit mechanism is based a rigorous and scientific design of personal benefit and risk fund, which is interconnected with property value increase and profit maximization. The TSP risk and benefit mechanism ensures a symmetrical or proportioned relationships between power, responsibility, benefit, and risk (cost), which not only guarantee the full autonomy and freedom of TSPs in the exercise of trusted ownership rights, but also overcome incentive and discipline problems under market socialism, because reward and penalty in this system is not fictitious but real and serious, and it is therefore possible to motivate TSPs to fulfill their goals with all their hearts and all their might and to avoid or minimize penalty as much as they can.

The TSP goal functions in the mechanism design are clearly defined. Results and benefits are proportional. For their own interests, TSPs must seek to enhance entrusted property value, ensure efficiency of investment, and maximize profit, in order to expand their final reward or benefits. The property rights are impersonalized, and this provides TSPs with hard budget constraint, freedom of entry into and exist from the market, and natural selection of principal-agent relations. Responsibility, power, profit, and risk are symmetrical, integrated, and interconnected in principal-agent relations, therefore, there is an essential requirement for a hard budget constraint on both the principal and the agent. The residual income passes into the pockets of natural persons, and the losses are covered by the same natural party. This supports the central thesis of the property rights theory: it is only the natural-personal owners who control and direct production and distribution of residual income, and it is only based on this condition that a dynamic and competitive economy can function well under market socialism.[34]

In the TSP system, the horizontal flow and optimization of capital and production factors, as well as the compensated transfer of state property, become an essential requirement for the functioning of TSPs, because TSPs have full autonomy and freedom of entry into or exit from the market and their goal functions are to maximize profit, property value, and efficiency of investment. The horizontal flow and optimization of capital and production factors would promote rational and efficient allocation of the entire socioeconomic resources and transform a market socialist economy into to dynamic, competitive, and efficient economy.

To achieve their goals, TSPs have to rely on the talents and appoint financial experts, technological and managerial experts as managers, directors, and various managerial staff through the labor market based on a competitive and natural selection mechanism. In the long term, a technological and managerial entrepreneur class would come into being, which promotes the separation of two kinds of entrepreneurs: TSPs may come and go, but technological and managerial entrepreneurs would stay. To provide incentives for employees, TSPs have to design a wage system which corresponds to the increase and decrease of profit, i.e. the total amount of wages constitute a percentage of gross profit, which can be negotiated between Board of Trustees and employee unions, and it varies according to increase and decrease of profit. When profits increase, wages increase, and when profits decrease, wages decrease. But, the state legislature should make a law providing a total amount of wages to protect the interests of employees.

To maximize profits, TSPs should recognize the advantages of scale economy and specialization and try to promote optimal combination of specialized production. An incorporated enterprise or joint venture is naturally a shareholding or joint stock company. The state can guide the directions and activities of these enterprises by regulating stock markets and law making, and providing a legal framework within which a shareholding or joint stock company should operate and develop.

TSPs have a tendency of engaging large-scale economics or excessive investment in fixed assets, and sometimes, they may even seek to borrow loans to expand the investment in fixed assets. Borrowing loans to invest in fixed assets is beneficial to TSPs as long as reduced value caused by interest is lower than increased value generated by investment. Therefore, the TSP demand for loans is very sensitive to changes of interest rate. When interest rate increases, demand for loans tends to decrease, and vice versa. The state can use adjustment of interest rate as an effective means of macroeconomic control. The state can also use intentional or unintentional investment as an effective means to guide and control the investment orientation of TSPs. The state can manipulate the ratio between intentional and unintentional investment to manage a proper ratio between key industries and ordinary industries and between key projects and ordinary projects, which would set the parameters within which TSPs can invest and re-invest.

The TSP system is the new pathway to be created for state owned enterprises in market socialist reforms and it is the key chessman in a chessboard game. It requires an establishment of a set of legal system to facilitate its implementation. The objective of the TSP system is to combine the merits of markets with public ownership which would contribute to the achievement of goals associated with the socialist tradition. The TSP system could become a promising experiment for transforming market socialism in Asian reforming countries into a truly competitive and efficient economy, which shall simulate the same pattern of incentive and motivation that has inspired the owners and managers under capitalism and duplicate the market characteristics of a modern market economy and achieve the same level of efficiency and productivity in the U.S. economy. Moreover, the TSP system can apply equally to all market socialist economies and the TSP can be used as a concept of broad comparative scope in the comparative study of communism and post-communism. Based on the insights yielded by this model, researchers could modify the model by dropping some features while retaining others of the model. As the TSP system is an attempt to resolve the principal-agent problems under market socialism from the perspective of property rights theory, in what follows, we will discuss the property rights issue and its important implications for the success of market socialism, and thus a future for socialism.

Property Rights and a Future for Socialism

The successful experience in China and other Asian reforming countries has suggested that the resolution of property rights problem in market socialism is important because property rights are not only related to incentive structures for decision making but also to the efficient allocation of resources. In the transition from state socialism to market-based socialism, restructuring property rights has become the most difficult and central task in these countries, and the fundamental cornerstone for restructuring market socialism.

Under state socialism, as the state sector was dominant in the economy, which was centrally planned, there was no efficient and clear property rights regime. Although the means of production were publicly owned or people owned, the state acted as an amorphous owner of "people's property" and property rights were blurred, which led to the lack of effort-reward incentives, mismanagement of state property, principal-agent problems, soft-budget constraints, inefficient use and allocation of resources by political authority and administrative agents.

Transition economies of Eastern Europe and Russia have shown that full-scale privatization itself does not necessarily guarantee the efficient use and allocation of resources, and it fails to achieve the economic efficiency and productivity as expected by neoclassical economists. "Even privatized assets, except those in which FDI has taken a considerable stake, are not necessarily being utilized more efficiently than they were under state socialism."[35] Most of these transition economies fell into protracted economic recession, hyperinflation, and slow recovery.

Under market socialism, administrative decentralization and economic liberalization have allowed a multi-level structure of ownership to emerge and a dynamic market environment to develop in most of those Asian reforming countries. However, in restructuring property rights of state and collective owned enterprises, the usufruct rights, separated from the ownership rights, have been entrusted to enterprise managers with the management responsibility transferred to these individuals. As a result, those entrusted with the usufruct rights began to take advantage of their positions and powers to make fortunes on the state assets which they use for free, which leads to informal "privatization" of state assets into their private pockets, irresponsible and abusive use of state assets and resources for personal capital gains, and massive corruption through the power-money exchange in Asian reforming countries. This experience has suggested that free use of usufruct rights without carefully designed risk-reward mechanism and lack of effective monitoring and supervision over assets use and management has not solved the typical problems under state socialism, but also created some new problems in a new market environment. The TSP system provides a promising experiment for solving those problems and transforming market socialism into a competitive and efficient economy with almost all characteristics of a modern market economy. The TSP system and its core mechanism design are well grounded in the basic theories of property rights economics and the market socialist practice of transition economies in East and Southeast Asia in the past two decades.

It might be reasonable to question the efficacy to replicate the mechanisms under market capitalism. If a reforming economy attempts to replicate a private property system, it may still have moral hazard and corporate theft, particularly the problem of how to prevent corrupt bureaucrats, board directors, and managers from looting even more state assets. This might be true in our empirical observation of massive corruption in reforming China and other Asian reforming economies, because the state property is still under the management of bureaucrats or short of feasible risk and reward mechanism design in the corporate governance that would place systemic constraints on their economic behavior while preventing bureaucrats and administrative units from intervention. The proposed TPS system with risk and reward mechanism design is an attempt to fix this problem. The risk and reward mechanism design based on the competitive selection process would be the only way to prevent corrupt bureaucrats and corporate theft from looting the state property as the TSPs are no longer bureaucrats but entrepreneurs who are willing to take risk by putting down their personal assets on the public bidding and they are clients bound by legal contracts with the principal – legally, the state is the owner of state property – to maximize profits and increase the value of state assets, or they will face economic and legal punishments for failing to do so. Moreover, the duplication of those mechanisms from market economy of capitalism takes place not in the context of capitalist private property but in the context within which the state property is owned and controlled by the state and directed by the state policy. Socialism could replicate not only the invisible hand, as China and other Asian reforming economies has done successfully, but also the other useful methods and mechanisms created in human history, particularly the mechanisms of the corporate governance under private ownership. Socialism can only be improved and advanced if it can skillfully incorporate useful mechanisms of modern production and exchange organizations. This is one of the serious lessons we have learned from the failure of socialist practice in the former Soviet Union and Eastern Europe.

The essence of the market economy is the separation of political intervention and economic transactions or distinction between the state and economic actors, regardless of whether private, cooperative, or state, who enjoy a great degree of sovereignty within a set of "rules of the game" which are predictable, reliable, and transparent and based on an unambiguous property rights regime protected by the rule of law.[36] Those who take the risk of penalty in case of failure should be able to anticipate a reasonable return in the case of success, and their power to use and manage state assets should be accompanied by responsibility for protecting and increasing the value of the assets. Therefore, those who control and use state assets and resources must be strictly monitored by the state agency (the legal owner) using an effective mechanism of rights, responsibilities, reward and risk or placed under a symmetrical or proportioned relationships between power, responsibility, benefit, and risk (cost), which would not only guarantee the full autonomy and freedom of TSPs in the exercise of trusted ownership rights, but also induce economic agents to act in the interest of their principals in a competitive environment and ultimately overcome incentive and discipline problems under market socialism. Only through such a mechanism design can the efficient use and allocation of resources be guaranteed when property rights are unbundled under market socialism. The purported "superiority" of the capitalist market economy is more an argument for the superiority of market competition and efficiency in the allocation of resources than for private ownership *per se*.[37] If market socialism can improve the efficiency in the allocation of resources, a future for socialism – an efficient and competitive socialist market economy on a par with the most advanced market economy of modern capitalism – can be foreseen.

Notes

1   Michael Mandelbaum, *The Ideas that Conquered the World: Peace, Democracy and Free Markets in the Twenty-first Century,* Public Affairs Publishing, 2002, p. 279.
2   Joshua Muravchik, *Heaven on Earth: The Rise and Fall of Socialism,* (San Francisco, CA: Encounter Books, 2002), p. 301.
3   Vladimir I. Lenin, *Collected Works* (Moscow: Progress, 1966), p. 66.
4   Pranab K. Bardhan and John E. Roemer, eds., *Market Socialism: The Current Debate* (New York: Oxford University Press, 1993), p. 3.
5   http://www.amosweb.com/cgi-bin/wpd.pl?fcd=dsp&key=market+socialism
6   Drexel university (William-King), Market Socialism, http://william-king.www.drexel. edu/top/prin/txt/comsysf/cs9.html
7   James A. Yunker, *On the Political Economy of Market Socialism* (Burlington: Ashgate, 2001), pp. 5-7.
8   Ibid., pp. 13-14.
9   Ibid., pp. 15-18.
10   Ibid., pp. 18-19.
11   Ibid., p. 16.
12   Julian Le Grand and Saul Estrin, ed., *Market Socialism* (Oxford: Clarendon Press, 1989); Pranab K. Bardhan and John E. Roemer, ed., *Market Socialism: The Current Debate* (Oxford: Oxford University Press, 1993); John E. Roemer, *A Future for Socialism* (Cambridge: Harvard University Press, 1994); Christopher Pierson, *Socialism after Communism: the New Market Socialism* (PA: Penn State University Press, 1995);

Lance L. P. Gore, *Market Communism: the Institutional Foundation of China's Post-Mao Hyper-Growth* (Oxford: Oxford University Press, 1998);   Bertell Ollman, ed., *Market Socialism: The Debate among Socialists* (New York: Routledge, 1998); James A. Yunker, *On the Political Economy of Market Socialism: Essays and Analyses* (Aldershot: Ashgate, 2001).

[13]   James A. Yunker, p. 18.

[14]   Ibid., p. 37.

[15]   John E. Roemer, "A Future for Socialism," *Politics & Society*, vol. 22, no. 4, December 1994, p. 454.

[16]   Stiglitz, Joseph, *Market Socialism and Neoclassical Economics*, http://econc10.bu.edu/economic_systems/theory/nonmarx_socialism/market%20socialism/Stiglitz_marksoc_n eoclass.htm

[17]   Anders   Aslund,   "Market   Socialism   or   the   Restoration   of   Capitalism" http://econc10.bu.edu/economic_systems/theory/nonmarx_socialism/market%20socialis m/market_socialism_frame.htm

[18]   Ibid.

[19]   Ibid.; Janos Kornai, *The Socialist System: The Political Economy of Communism* (Princeton, Princeton University Press, 1992); John E. Roemer, "A Future for Socialism," *Politics and Society*, vol. 22, no. 4, 1994, pp. 451-478; Harry Brighouse, "Transitional and Utopian Market Socialism," *Politics and Society*, vol. 22, no. 4, 1994, pp. 569-584; Frank Roosevelt and David Belkin, *Why Market Socialism?* (Armonk, NY: M.E. Sharpe, 1994); David Schweichart, et al., *Market Socialism: The Debate Among Socialists* (New York and London: Routledge, 1998).

[20]   Dwight H. Perkins, "Reforming the Economic Systems of Vietnam and Laos," in Börje Ljunggren, ed., *The Challenge of Reform in Indochina* (Cambridge, MA: Harvard University Press, 1993), p. 8.

[21]   Janos Kornai, "Market Socialism Revisited," in Pranab K. Bardhan and John E. Roemer, eds., *Market Socialism: the Current Debate* (New York: Oxford University Press, 1993), p. 47.

[22]   Ibid. pp. 48-55.

[23]   Lixin Colin Xu, Tian Zhu and Yi-min Lin, "Politician Control, Agency Problems and Ownership Reform: Evidence from China," *Economics of Transition*, vol. 13, no. 1, 2005, pp.5-6.

[24]   Shu Y. Ma, "The Chinese Route to Privatization," *Asian Survey*, vol. 38, no. 4, April 1998, p. 382.

[25]   Ibid. p. 388.

[26]   Janos Kornai, p. 52.

[27]   Ibid.

[28]   Janos Kornai, *The Road to a Free Economy: Shifting from a Socialist System, the Example of Hungary* (New York: W.W. Norton and Company, 1990) p. 57.

[29]   Dic Lo, *Market and Institutional Regulation in Chinese Industrialization, 1978-1994* (London: Maclillan Press, 1997), pp. 47, 49.

[30]   John E. Roemer, "A Future for Socialism," *Politics & Society*, vol. 22, no. 4, 1994, p. 454.

[31]   Pranab K. Bardhan and John E. Roemer, p. 11.

[32]   James A. Yunker, p. 19.

[33] Thomas Rawski, "Chinese Industrial Reform: Accomplishments, Prospects, and Implications," *American Economic Review*, vol. 84, no. 2, 1994, pp. 271-275.

[34] Janos Kornai, 1990, p. 57; Dic Lo, 1997, pp. 47, 49.

[35] Jozef M. van Brabant, *The Political Economy of Transition: Coming to Grips with History and Methodology* (London and New York: Routledge, 1998), p. 247.

[36] Ibid., pp. 252-253.

[37] Ibid., p. 255.

Selected Bibliography

Abuza, Zachary, "The Lessons of Le Kha Phieu: Changing Rules in Vietnamese Politics," *Contemporary Southeast Asia*, vol. 24, no. 1, April 2002.

Aghion, Philippe and Blanchard, Oliver Jean, "On the Speed of Transition in Eastern Europe," Mimeo, MIT, 1993.

Ahn, Yinhay, "North Korea in 2001: At a Crossroads," *Asian Survey*, vol. 42, no. 1, 2002.

Almond, Gabriel A. and Roselle, Laura, "Model Fitting in Communism Studies," in Frederic J. Fleron, Jr. and Erik P. Hoffmann, eds., *Post-Communist Studies and Political Science: Methodology and Empirical Theory in Sovietology* (Boulder, CO: Westview Press, 1993).

Almond, Gabriel and Verba, Sidney, *The Civic Culture* (Princeton: Princeton University Press, 1963).

Aslund, Anders, "Principles of Privatization," in Laszlo Csaba, ed., *Systemic Change and Stabilization in Eastern Europe* (Dartmouth, UK: Aldershot, 1991).

———, *How Russia Became a Market Economy* (Washington, DC: Brookings Institution, 1995).

Bardhan, Pranab K. and Roemer, John E., eds., *Market Socialism: The Current Debate* (New York: Oxford University Press, 1993).

Bell, Michael W. et al., *China at the Threshold of a Market Economy* (Washington, DC: International Monetary Fund, 1993).

Beresford, Malanie, *National Unification and Economic Development in Vietnam* (London: Macmillan, 1989).

———, "The Vietnamese Transition from Plan to Market: Transformation of the Planning Mechanism," *Macquarie Economics Research Papers*, Macquarie University, 1999.

Berg, Andrew and Sachs, Jeffrey, "Structural Adjustment and International Trade in Eastern Europe: The Case of Poland," *Economic Policy*, April 1992.

Borensztein, Eduardo R. and Kumar, Manmohan, "Proposals for Privatization in Eastern Europe," *IMF Staff Papers*, vol. 38, no. 2, 1991.

Bourdet, Yves, "Laos in 1995: Reform Policy, Out of Breadth?" *Asian Survey*, vol. 36, no. 1, 1996.

———, "Laos in 2000: The Economics of Political Immobilism," *Asian Survey*, vol. 41, no. 1, 2001.

———, Laos in 2001: Political Introversion and Economic Respite," *Asian Survey*, vol. 42, no.1, 2002.

————, "Rural Reforms and Agricultural Productivity in Laos," *Journal of Developing Areas*, no. 29, January 1995.

————, *The Economics of Transition in Laos: From Socialism to ASEAN Integration* (Cheltenham, UK: Edward Elgar, 2000).

Bova, Russell, "Political Dynamics of the Post-Communist Transition: A Comparative Perspective," in Frederic J. Fleron and Erick P. Hoffmann, eds., *Post-Communist Studies & Political Science* (Westview Press, Boulder, 1993).

Brighouse, Harry, "Transitional and Utopian Market Socialism," *Politics and Society*, vol. 22, no. 4, 1994.

Cao, Lan, "Chinese Privatization between Plan and Market," *Law and Contemporary Problems*, vol. 63, no. 4, 2000.

Chandler, David P., *A History of Cambodia* (Boulder, Colorado: Westview Press, 1993).

————, *Brother Number One: A political Biography of Pol Pot* (Boulder, CO: Westview Press, 1999).

————, *The Tragedy of Cambodian History* (New Haven: Yale University Press, 1991).

Chen, Jia-gui and Huang, Qun-hui, "Comparison of Governance Structures of Chinese Enterprises with Different Types of Ownership," *China & World Economy*, vol. 9, no. 6, 2001.

Chen, Xiaolong, "Where does Prosperity come from?" *China Spring*, vol. 165, 1997.

————, "North Korean Reform and Opening: Dual Strategy and 'Silli (Practical) Socialism," *Pacific Affairs*, vol. 77, no. 2, Summer 2004.

Cima, Ronald J., *Vietnam: A Country Study* (Washington, DC: U.S. Department of the Army, 1987).

Dabrowski, Marek, "Different Strategies of Transition to Market Economy: How Do They Work in Practice?" *World Bank, Policy Research Dept. Working Paper*, No. 1579, March 1996.

Dahl, Robert, *Who Governs? Democracy and Power in an American City* (New Haven, CT: Yale University Press, 1961).

De Melo, Martha et al., "Circumstances and Choice: The Role of Initial Conditions and Polices in Transition Economies," *World Bank Mimeo*, 1997.

————, "Patterns of Transition from Plan to Market," *World Bank Economic Review*, vol. 10, no. 3, 1996.

De Zamaroczy, Mario and Sa, Sopanha, "Macroeconomic Adjustment in a Highly Dollarized Economy: The Case of Cambodia," International Monetary Fund, May 2002.

Dewatripont, Mathias and Roland, Gerard, "Economic Reform and Dynamic Political Constraints," *The Review of Economic Studies*, vol. 59, no. 4, 1992.

Dewatripont, Mathias and Roland, Gerard, "The Design of Reform Packages under Uncertainty," *The American Economic Review,* vol. 85, no. 5, 1995.

Dewatripont, Mathias and Roland, Gerard, "The Virtues of Gradualism and Legitimacy in the Transition to a Market Economy," *Economic Journal*, March 1992b.

Di Palma, Giuseppe, *To Craft Democracies: An essay on Democratic Transitions* (Berkeley: University of California Press, 1990).

Dinh, Quan Xuan, "The Political Economy of Vietnam's Transformation Process," *Contemporary Southeast Asia*, vol. 22, no. 2, August 2000.

Doi, Toshinori et al., "Cambodia: Statistical Appendix," International Monetary Fund, January 23, 2002.

Ducourtieux, Olivier, Laffort, Jean-Richard and Sacklokham, Silinthone, "Land Policy and Farming Practices in Laos," *Development and Change*, vol. 36, no. 3, 2005.

Elliott, David W. P., "Dilemma of Reform in Vietnam," in William S. Turley and Mark Selden, eds., *Reinventing Vietnamese Socialism: Doi Moi in Comparative Perspective* (Boulder, CO: Westview, 1993).

Fahey, Stephanie, "Vietnam and the 'Third Way': The Nature of Socio-Economic Transition," *Journal of Economic and Social Geography*, vol. 88, no. 5, 1997.

Fang, Xinghai, "Government Commitment and Gradualism," in John McMillan and Barry Naughton, eds., *Reforming Asian Socialism* (Ann Arbor, MI: The University of Michigan Press, 1996).

Feltenstein, Andrew and Nsouli, Saleh M., "Big Bang Versus Gradualism in Economic Reforms: An Intertemporal Analysis with an Application to China," *IMF Working Paper*, August 2001.

Fernandez, Raquel and Rodrik, Dani, "Resistance to Reform: Status Quo Bias in the Presence of Individual-Specific Uncertainty," *The American Economic Review*, vol. 81, no. 5, 1991.

Fforde, Adam and De Vylder, Stefan, *From Plan to Market: The Economic Transition in Vietnam* (Boulder: Westview Press, 1996).

Fischer, Stanley and Gelb, Alan, "The Process of Socialist Economic Transformation," *Journal of Economic Perspectives*, vol. 5, no. 4, 1991.

Frank, Ruediger, "Economic Reforms in North Korea (1998-2003): Systemic Restrictions, Quantitative Analysis, Ideological Background," *Journal of the Asia Pacific Economy*, vol. 10, no. 3, 2005.

Freeman, Nick J., "Laos: Exiguous Evidence of Economic Reform and Development," *Southeast Asian Affairs*, 2004.

Frydman, Roman and Rapaczynski, Andrzej, *Privatization in Eastern Europe: Is the State Withering Away?* (London: Central European University Press, 1994).

Funck, Bernard, "Laos: Decentralization and Economic Control," in Borje Ljunggren, ed., *The Challenge of Reform in Indochina* (Cambridge, MA: Harvard University Press, 1993).

Gainsborough, Martin, "Beneath the Veneer of Reform: the Politics of Economic Liberalization in Vietnam," *Communist and Post-Communist Studies*, vol. 35, no. 3, September 2002.

Gang, Fan, "Incremental Changes and Dual-Track Transition: Understanding the Case of China," *Economic Policy*, vol. 19, December 1994.

Gao, Shangquan, *China's Economic Reform* (New York: St. Martin Press, 1996).

————, *Two Decades of Reform in China* (Singapore: World Scientific,1999).

Gates, Carolyn L., "Vietnam's Integration into AFTA: Theoretical and Empirical Perspectives," in Mya Than and Carolyn Gates, eds., ASEAN Enlargement: Impacts and Implications (Singapore: Institute of Southeast Asian Studies, 2001).

Gilboy, George and Heginbotham, Eric, "China's Coming Transformation," *Foreign Affairs*, vol. 80, no. 4, 2001.

Gilley, Bruce, "Communist Party Grapples with Reform," *Far Eastern Economic Review*, vol. 164, no. 19, May 17, 2001.

Gore, Lance L. P., *Market Communism: the Institutional Foundation of China's Post-Mao Hyper-Growth* (Oxford: Oxford University Press, 1998).

Gottesman, Evan, *Cambodia After the Khmer Rouge: Inside the Politics of Nation Building* (New Haven: Yale University Press, 2003).

Griffin, Keith, ed., *Economic Reform in Vietnam* (London, UK: Macmillan Press, 1998).

Guo, Sujian, "Ownership Reform in China," *Journal of Contemporary China*, vol. 12, no. 36, 2003.

————, "Designing Market Socialism: Trustees of State Property," *Journal of Policy Reform*, Vol. 8, No. 3, September 2005.

————, "Economic Transition in China and Vietnam: A Comparative Perspective," *Asian Profile,* vol. 32, no. 5, October 2004.

————, "Political Economy of FDI and Economic Growth in China: A Longitudinal Test at Provincial Level" (with Han Gyu Lheem), *Journal of Chinese Political Science*, vol. 9, no. 1, Spring 2004.

————, "Enigma of All Enigmas: Capitalist Takeover? Assessment of the Post-Mao Economic Transformation," *Chinese Journal of Political Science*, vol. 4, no. 1, Spring 1998.

————, *Post-Mao China: from Totalitarianism to Authoritarianism?* (Westport, CT: Praeger Publishers, 2000).

Harding, Harry, *China's Second Revolution: Reform after Mao* (Washington, DC: The Brookings Institute, 1987).

Hendrickson, Dylan, "Globalization, Insecurity and Post-War Reconstruction: Cambodia's Precarious Transition," *IDS Bulletin*, vol. 32, no. 2, 2001.

Heytens, Paul, "State Enterprise Reform," in Wanda Tseng and Markus Rodlauer, eds., *China: Competing in the Global Economy* (Washington: D.C.: International Monetary Fund, 2003).

Hu, Jiayong, "An Empirical Analysis of the Amount of Resources Controlled by the Government," *Gaige* (Reform), no. 3, 1999.

Hughes, Caroline, *The Political Economy of Cambodia's Transition, 1991-2001* (London and New York: RoutledgeCurzon, 2003).

Jennar, Raoul M., *The Cambodian Constitutions: 1953-1993* (Bangkok: White Lotus, 1995).

Jeon, Jei Guk, "North Korean Leadership: Kim Jong Il's Balancing Act in the Ruling Circle," *Third World Quarterly*, vol. 21, no. 5, 2000.

Kelleher, David S. and Kim, Hak-Min, "Post-Unification Privatization of North Korean Enterprises," *Korea Observer*, vol. 36, no. 1 (2005).

Kheang, Un, "Patronage Politics and Hybrid Democracy: Political Change in Cambodia, 1993-2003," *Asian Perspective*, vol. 29, no. 2, 2005.

Khng, Russell Heng Hiang, "Leadership in Vietnam: Pressures for Reform and Their Limits," *Contemporary Southeast Asia*, vol. 15, no. 1, 1998.

Kiljunen, Kimmo, *Kampuchea: Decade of the Genocide* (London: Zed Books Ltd., 1984).

Kim, Ilpyong J. and Zacek, Jane Shapiro, *Reform and Transformation in Communist Systems* (New York: Paragon House, 1991).

Kitschelt, Herbert, "Political Regime Change: Structure and Process-Driven Explanations?" *American Political Science Review*, vol. 86, no. 4, December 1992.

Koh, David, "The Politics of a Divided Party and Parkinson's State in Vietnam," *Contemporary Southeast Asia*, vol. 23, no. 3, 2001.

Koh, David, "The Politics of a Divided Party and Parkinson's State in Vietnam," *Contemporary Southeast Asia*, vol. 23, no. 3, December 2001.

Kornai, János, "Market Socialism Revisited," in Pranab K. Bardhan and John E. Roemer, eds., *Market Socialism: the Current Debate* (New York: Oxford University Press, 1993).

Kornai, János, *The Road to a Free Economy: Shifting from a Socialist System, the Example of Hungary* (New York: W.W. Norton and Company, 1990).

Kornai, János, *The Socialist System: The Political Economy of Communism* (Princeton, Princeton University Press, 1992).

Kurlantzick, Joshua, "Laos: Still Communist after All These Years," *Current History*, vol. 104, issue 680, March 2005.

Kyvelidis, Ioannis, "State Isomorphism in the Post-Socialist Transition," *European Integration online Papers* (EIoP), vol. 4, no. 2, February 2000.

Laffont, Jean-Jacques and Qian, Yingyi, "The Dynamics of Reform and Development in China: A Political Economy Perspective," *European Economic Review*, vol. 43, no. 4-6, 1999.

Lay, Prohas, "Transition from Centrally Planned Economy to a Market Economy in Cambodia," in Mathews G. Chunakara, ed., *Indochina: From Socialism to Market Economy* (Hong Kong, China: Indochina Concerns Conference, 1996).

Le Grand, Julian and Estrin, Saul, eds., *Market Socialism* (Oxford: Clarendon Press, 1989).

Lee, Doowon, "North Korean Economic Reform: Past Efforts and Future Prospects," in John McMillan and Barry Naughton, eds., *Reforming Asian Socialism* (Ann Arbor: The University of Michigan Press, 1996).

Lee, Hy-Sang, "The Economic Reforms of North Korea: the Strategy of Hidden and Assimilable Reforms," *Korea Observer*, vol. 23, no. 1, Spring 1992.

Lee, Jong-Heon, "Analysis: North Korean Economy in Better Shape," *The Washington Times*, May, 31, 2005.

Lee, Jung-chul, "The Implications of North Korea's Reform Program and Its Effects on State Capacity," *Korea and World Affairs*, vol. 26, no. 3, 2003.

Lee, Young-Sun, "The Kim Jong-Il Regime and Economic Reform: Myth and Reality," in Chung-in Moon, ed., *Understanding Regime Dynamics in North Korea* (Seoul, Korea: Yonsei University Press, 1998).

Lenin, Vladimir I., *Collected Works* (Moscow: Progress, 1966).

Lijphart, Arend, *The Politics of Accommodation: Pluralism and Democracy in the Netherlands* (Berkeley: University of California Press, 1968).

Lim, Hyun-Chin and Chul, Chung Yong, "Is North Korea Moving toward a Market Economy?" *Korea Focus*, vol. 12, Issue 4, July-August 2004.

Lin, Cyril, "Corporatization and Corporate Governance in China's Economic Transition," *Economics of Planning*, vol. 34, no. 1-2, 2001.

Linz, Juan and Stepan, Alfred, eds., *The Breakdown of Democratic Regimes: Crisis, Breakdown and Reequilibration* (Baltimore: Johns Hopkins University Press, 1978).

Lipset, Seymour Martin, "Some Social Requisites of Democracy," *American Political Science Review*, 53, March 1959.

Lipton, David and Sachs, Jeffrey, "Creating a Market Economy in Eastern Europe: The Case of Poland," *Brookings Papers on Economic Activities*, 1, (1990a).

Lipton, David and Sachs, Jeffrey, "Privatization in East Europe: The Case of Poland," *Brookings Papers on Economic Activities*, 2, (1990b).

Litwack, John and Qian, Yingyi, "Economic Transition Strategies: Imperfect Fiscal Commitment Can Favor Unbalanced Investment," Mimeo, Stanford University, 1993.

Liu, Guy S. and Garino, Gaia, "China's Two Decades of Economic Reform," *Economics of Planning*, vol. 34, no. 1-2, 2001.

Ljunggren, Börje, "Market Economies under Communist Regimes: Reform in Vietnam, Laos, and Cambodia," in Börje Ljunggren, ed., *The Challenge of Reform in Indochina* (Cambridge, MA: Harvard University Press, 1993).

Ljunggren, Börje, ed., *The Challenge of Reform in Indochina* (Cambridge, MA: Harvard University Press, 1993).

Lo, Dic, *Market and Institutional Regulation in Chinese Industrialization, 1978-1994* (London: Maclillan Press, 1997).

Ma, Shu Y., "The Chinese Route to Privatization," *Asian Survey*, vol. 38, no. 4, April 1998.

Mandelbaum, Michael, *The Ideas that Conquered the World: Peace, Democracy and Free Markets in the Twenty-first Century*, Public Affairs Publishing, 2002.

Marsh, Christopher, "Learning from Your Comrade's Mistakes: the Impact of the Soviet Past on China's Future," *Communist and Post-Communist Studies*, vol. 36, 2003.

Mastel, Greg, *The Rise of the Chinese Economy: The Middle Kingdom Emerges* (NY: M.E. Sharpe, 1997).

McKinnon, Ronald I., *Gradual versus Rapid Liberalization in Socialist Countries* (San Francisco, CA: ICS Press, 1994).

——, *The Order of Economic Liberalization* (Baltimore, MD: Johns Hopkins University, 1991).

McMillan, John and Naughton, Barry, "How to Reform a Planned Economy: Lessons from China," *Oxford Review of Economic Policy*, vol. 8, no. 1, 1992.

McMillan, John and Naughton, Barry, eds., *Reforming Asian Socialism: The Growth of Market Institutions* (Ann Arbor, MI: The University of Michigan Press, 1996).

Miles, Marc A. et al., *2004 Index of Economic Freedom: Establishing the Link between Economic Freedom and Prosperity* (Washington, DC: The Heritage Foundation).

Miller, Richard W., *Fact and Method: Explanation, Explanation, Confirmation and Reality in the Natural and the Social Sciences*, (Princeton, NJ: Princeton University Press, 1988).

Misra, Kalpana, "Neo-Left and Neo-Right in Post-Tiananmen China," *Asian Survey*, vol. 43, no. 5, 2003.

Moon, Chung-in and Kim, Yongho, "The Future of the North Korean System," in Samuel S. Kim, ed., *The North Korean System in the Post-Cold War Era* (New York: Palgrave, 2001).

Muravchik, Joshua, *Heaven on Earth: The Rise and Fall of Socialism*, (San Francisco, CA: Encounter Books, 2002).

Murphy, Kevin, et al., "The Transition to a Market Economy: Pitfalls of Partial Reform," *Quarterly Journal of Economics*, vol. 107, no. 3, 1992.

Murrell, Peter, "Conservative Political Philosophy and the Strategy of Economic Transition," *East European Politics and Society*, vol. 6, no. 1, 1992.

Naughton, Barry, *Growing Out of the Plan: Chinese Economic Reform, 1978-1993* (Cambridge: Cambridge University Press, 1995)

Naughton, Barry, "Distinctive Features of Economic Reform in China and Vietnam," in John McMillan and Barry Naughton, eds., *Reforming Asian Socialism: The Growth of Market Institutions* (Ann Arbor, MI: The University of Michigan Press, 1996).

Noland, Marcus, "Famine and Reform in North Korea," *Working Paper*, Institute for International Economics, July 2003.

O'Donnell, Guillermo, and Schmitter, Philippe, eds., *Transitions from Authoritarian Rule: Tentative Conclusions about Uncertain Democracies* (Baltimore: Johns Hopkins University Press, 1986).

O'Donnell, Guillermo, *Modernization and Bureaucratic Authoritarianism: Studies in South American Politics* (Berkeley: Institute of International Studies, University of California, 1979).

Oh, Kongdan and Hassig, Ralph, "North Korea between Reform and Collapse," *Asian Survey*, vol. 39, no. 2, 1999.

Ollman, Bertell, ed., *Market Socialism: The Debate among Socialists* (New York: Routledge, 1998).

Otani, Ichiro and Pham, Chi Do, "The Lao People's Democratic Republic: Systemic Transformation and Adjustment" *Occasional Paper 137*, International Monetary Fund, May 1996.

Painter, Martin, "The Politics of Economic Restructuring in Vietnam: The Case of State-Owned Enterprise Reform," *Contemporary Southeast Asia*, vol. 25, no. 1, 2003.

Park, Han S., ed., *North Korea: Ideology, Politics, and Economy* (Englewood Cliffs, NJ: Prentice Hall, 1996).

Park, Young-Ho, "North Korea in Transition?" *Korea and World Affairs*, vol. 25, no. 1, 2001.

Peou, Sorpong, "Hun Sen's Pre-Emptive Coup: Causes and Consequences," *Southeast Asian Affairs*, 1998.

————, "The Cambodian Elections of 1998 and Beyond: Democracy in the Making?" *Contemporary Southeast Asia*, vol. 20, no. 3, 1998.

Perkins, Dwight H., "Reforming the Economic Systems of Vietnam and Laos," in Börje Ljunggren, ed., *The Challenge of Reform in Indochina* (Cambridge, MA: Harvard University Press, 1993).

Pierson, Christopher, *Socialism after Communism: the New Market Socialism* (PA: Penn State University Press, 1995).

Polevoy, Pamela L., "Privatization in Vietnam: The Next Step in Vietnam's Economic Transition from a Nonmarket to a Market Economy," *Brooklyn Journal of International Law*, vol. 23, no. 3, 1998.

Pomfret, Richard, *Asian Economics in Transition* (Cheltenham, UK: Edward Elgar, 1996).

Portes, Richard, "Introduction to Economic Transformation of Hungary and Poland," *European Economics*, March 1990.

Portes, Richard, "The Path of Reform in Central and Eastern Europe: An Introduction," *European Economics*, No. 2, 1991.

Raiser, Martin, "Lessons for Whom, from Whom? The Transition from Socialism in China and Central Eastern Europe Compared," *Communist Economies and Economic Transformation*, vol. 7, no. 2, 1995.

Rana, Pradumna B. and Hamid, Naved, *From Centrally Planned to Market Economies: The Asian Approach* (Oxford University Press, 1995).

Ravallion, Martin and De Walle, Dominique van, "Breaking up the Collective Farms," *Economics of Transition*, vol. 12, no. 2, 2004.

Rawski, Thomas, "Chinese Industrial Reform: Accomplishments, Prospects, and Implications," *American Economic Review*, vol. 84, no. 2, 1994.

Rhee, Sang-Woo, "North Korea in 1990" Lonesome Struggle to Keep Chuch'e," *Asian Survey*, vol. 31, no. 1, 1991.

Riedel, James and Turley, William S., "The Politics and Economics of Transition to an Open Market Economy in Viet Nam," *Technical Papers*, no. 152, OECD Development Centre, 1999.

Roberts, David, "From 'Communism' to 'Democracy' in Cambodia: a Decade of Transition and Beyond," *Communist and post-Communist Studies*, vol. 36, no. 2, 2003.

———, "Political Transition and Elite Discourse in Cambodia, 1991-99," *Journal of Communist Studies and Transition Politics*, vol. 18, no. 4, 2002.

Rodrik, Dani, "Understanding Economic Policy Reform," *Journal of Economic Literature*, vol. 34, no. 1, 1996.

Roemer, John E., *A Future for Socialism* (Cambridge: Harvard University Press, 1994).

Roh, Jeong-Ho, "Making Sense of the DPRK Legal System," in Samuel S. Kim, ed., *The North Korean System in the Post-Cold War Era* (New York: Palgrave, 2001).

Roland, Gerard, "Political Economy of Sequencing Tactics in the Transition Period," in Laszlo Csaba, ed., *Systemic Change and Stabilization in Eastern Europe* (Dartmouth, UK: Aldershot, 1991).

Roosevelt, Frank and Belkin, David, *Why Market Socialism?* (Armonk, NY: M.E. Sharpe, 1994).

Ross, Russell R., ed., *Cambodia: A Country Study* (Washingon, D.C.: U.S. Government Printing Office, 1990).

Rueschemeyer, Dietrich et al., *Capitalist Development and Democracy* (Chicago: University of Chicago Press, 1992).

Rustow, Dankwart A., "Transitions to Democracy: Toward a Dynamic Model," *Comparative Politics*, vol. 2, April 1970.

Sachs, Jeffrey and Woo, Wing Thye, "Structural Factors in the Economic Reforms of China, Eastern Europe, and the Former Soviet Union," *Economic Policy*, April, 1994.

Sachs, Jeffrey, *Poland's Jump to the Market Economy* (Cambridge, MA: MIT Press, 1993).

Sargis, Al L., "Ideological Tendencies and Reform Policy in China's Primary Stage of Socialism," *Nature, Society, and Thought*, vol. 11, no. 4, 1998.

Savada, Andrea Matles, *North Korea: A Country Study* (Washington, DC: U.S. Department of the Army, 1993).

Schweichart, David et al., *Market Socialism: The Debate Among Socialists* (New York and London: Routledge, 1998).

Shirk, Susan L., *The Political Logic of Economic Reform in China* (Berkeley, CA: University of California Press, 1993).

Shirley, Mary M., "Bureaucrats in Business: the Roles of Privatization versus Corporatization in State-Owned Enterprise Reform," *World Development*, vol. 27, no. 1, 1999.

St John, Ronald Bruce, "The\Political Economy of the Royal Government of Cambodia," *Contemporary Southeast Asia*, vol. 17, no. 3, December 1995.

Stuart-Fox, Martin, "Laos at the Crossroads," *Indochina Issues*, no. 92, March 1991.

———, *Laos: Politics, Economics, and Society* (Boulder, CO: Lynne Rienner, 1986).

Sturm, Peter H. and Sutton, Bennett, "The Transition Process in China: A Comparative View," *China & World Economy*, vol. 9, no. 5, 2001.

Thanh, Nguyen and Hung, Nguyen Vo, "Background Paper: Institutional Development and FDI in Vietnam," *Project Working Papers*, No. 10 (Centre for New and Emerging Markets, London Business School, February 2003).

Thayer, Carlyle A., "Vietnam in 2001: The Ninth Party Congress and After," *Asian Survey*, vol. 42, no. 1, 2002.

Tonkin, Derek, "Vietnam: Market Reform and Ideology," *Asian Affairs*, vol. 28, no. 2, 1997.

Tri, Vo Nhan, "Party Politics and Economic Performance: the Second and Third Five-Year Plans Examined," in David Marr and Christine P. White, eds., *Postwar Vietnam: Dilemmas in Socialist Development* (Ithaca: Southeast Asia Program, Cornell University, 1988).

Trigubenko, Marina Y., "Economic Characteristics and Prospect for Development," in Han S. Park, ed., *North Korea: Ideology, Politics, and Economy* (Englewood Cliffs, NJ: Prentice Hall, 1996).

Trung, Thai Quang, *Collective Leadership and Factionalism* (Institute of Southeast Asian Studies, Singapore, 1985).

Turley, William S. and Selden, Mark, eds., *Reinventing Vietnamese Socialism: Doi Moi in Comparative Perspective* (Boulder, CO: Westview, 1993).

Un, Kheang and Ledgerwood, Judy, "Cambodia in 2001: Toward Democratic Consolidation?" *Asian Survey*, vol. 42, no. 1, 2002.

Van Brabant, Jozef M., *The Political Economy of Transition: Coming to Grips with History and Methodology* (London and New York: Routledge, 1998).

Vickerman, Andrew, *The Fate of the Peasantry: Premature Transition to Socialism in the Democratic Republic of Vietnam* (New Haven: Yale Southeast Asian Studies Monograph Series 24, 1986).

Vickery, Michael, "Notes on the Political Economy of the People's Republic of Kampuchea (PRK)" *Journal of Contemporary Asia*, vol. 20, no. 4, 1990.

———, *Cambodia: 1975-1982* (Boston: South End Press, 1984).

———, *Kampuchea: Politics, Economics, and Society* (Boulder, CO: Lynne Rienner, 1986).

Walder, Andrew G., ed., *China's Transitional Economy* (New York: Oxford University Press, 1996).

Wei, Shang-Jin, "Gradualism versus Big Bang: Speed and Sustainability of Reforms," *Canadian Journal of Economics*, vol. 30, no. 4, 1997.

Wescott, Clay G., ed., *Key Governance Issues in Cambodia, Lao PDR, Thailand, and Viet Nam* (Manila, Philippines: Asian Development Bank, 2001).

Williams, Shaun, "Where Has All the Land Gone? Land Rights and Access in Cambodia, Volume 1," *Cambodia Land Study Project*, Oxfam, Phnom Penh, May 1999.

Winckler, Edwin A., ed., *Transition from Communism in China: Institutional and Comparative Analysis* (Boulder, CO: Lynne Rienner, 1999).

Wolff, Peter, *Vietnam – the Incomplete Transformation* (London and Portland: Frank Cass, 1999).

Woo, Wing Thye, "The Art of Reforming Centrally Planned Economies: Comparing China, Poland, and Russia," *Journal of Comparative Economics*, vol. 18, no. 3, 1994.

————, "The Economics and Politics of Transition to an Open Market Economy: China," *Technical Papers*, no. 153, OECD Development Centre, October 1999.

World Bank, *From Plan to Market: World Development Report* (Washington, DC: World Bank, 1996.

Wu, Jinglian, "China's Economic Reform: Past, Present and Future," *Perspectives*, vol. 1, no. 5, April, 2000.

Wu, Yu-Shan, *Comparative Economic Transformations: Mainland China, Hungary, the Soviet Union, and Taiwan* (Stanford, CA: Stanford University Press, 1994).

Xu, Lixin Colin et al., "Politician Control, Agency Problems and Ownership Reform: Evidence from China," *Economics of Transition*, vol. 13, no. 1, 2005.

Yunker, James A., *On the Political Economy of Market Socialism* (Burlington: Ashgate, 2001).

Zhang, Chunlin, "Financing the SOE Sector: Institutional Evolution and Its Implications for SOE Reform," *China & World Economy*, vol. 10, no. 6, 2002.

Zhebin, Alexander, "Russia and North Korea: An Emerging, Uneasy Partnership," *Asian Survey*, vol. 35, no. 8, 1995.

Index